TOURISM ENGLISH PROFICIENCY TEST

観光英検2級の精選過去問題

全国語学ビジネス観光教育協会
観光英検センター（編）
山口百々男（監修）

三修社

目　次

CD トラック対応表

第1回リスニング試験

Track	問題番号
01	試験アナウンス
02	**6** (51)
03	(52)
04	(53)
05	(54)
06	(55)
07	**7** (56)
08	(57)
09	(58)
10	(59)
11	(60)
12	**8** (61)
13	(62)
14	(63)
15	(64)
16	(65)
17	(66)
18	(67)
19	(68)
20	(69)
21	(70)
22	**9** (71)
23	(72)
24	(73)
25	(74)
26	(75)
27	(76)
28	(77)
29	(78)
30	(79)
31	(80)
32	**10** Part A (81) 〜 (85)
33	Part B (86) 〜 (90)

第2回リスニング試験

Track	問題番号
34	試験アナウンス
35	**6** (51)
36	(52)
37	(53)
38	(54)
39	(55)
40	**7** (56)
41	(57)
42	(58)
43	(59)
44	(60)
45	**8** (61)
46	(62)
47	(63)
48	(64)
49	(65)
50	(66)
51	(67)
52	(68)
53	(69)
54	(70)
55	**9** (71)
56	(72)
57	(73)
58	(74)
59	(75)
60	(76)
61	(77)
62	(78)
63	(79)
64	(80)
65	**10** Part A (81) 〜 (85)
66	Part B (86) 〜 (90)

第3回リスニング試験

Track	問題番号
01	試験アナウンス
02	**6** (51)
03	(52)
04	(53)
05	(54)
06	(55)
07	**7** (56)
08	(57)
09	(58)
10	(59)
11	(60)
12	**8** (61)
13	(62)
14	(63)
15	(64)
16	(65)
17	(66)
18	(67)
19	(68)
20	(69)
21	(70)
22	**9** (71)
23	(72)
24	(73)
25	(74)
26	(75)
27	(76)
28	(77)
29	(78)
30	(79)
31	(80)
32	**10** Part A (81) 〜 (85)
33	Part B (86) 〜 (90)

観光英語検定試験の概要

主催： 全国語学ビジネス観光教育協会
　　　観光英検センター

後援： 文部科学省
　　　一般社団法人　日本ホテル協会
　　　一般社団法人　日本旅行業協会
　　　株式会社 JTB 総合研究所

試験実施日

10 月下旬　1 級・2 級・3 級

願書受付期間：4 月初旬〜 9 月中旬

お問い合わせ　受験案内・願書等申込先

〒 101-0061 東京都千代田区神田三崎町 2-8-10　ケープビル 2F

観光英検センター（全国語学ビジネス観光教育協会内）

TEL 03-5275-7741　FAX 03-5275-7744

http://www.zgb.gr.jp　E-mail:info@zgb.gr.jp

（1）　観光英語検定試験

　観光英語検定試験（TEPT ＝ Tourism English Proficiency Test）は、グローバル化された世界の中での観光分野・旅行分野において、特定の資格を与えるために必要な「語学」（「読む・書く・話す・聞く」の総合的な英語コミュニケーション能力）と「文化」（海外または国内における「観光事情」や「日本事情」の総合的な基礎知識）に関する教養とその運用能力の有無をはかる試験である。
［注］以下、観光英語検定試験を「観光英検」と略す。

（2）　観光英検の認定基準と運用範囲

　観光英検には「1 級・2 級・3 級」の各レベルがあり、それぞれの到達レベルの目安は次のようなものである。

3級（初級レベル）

1. 英検（実用英語技能検定）3級程度／ TOEIC® L&R TESTスコア 220 − 470 程度
2. 海外における「団体旅行」に参加して、少人数での観光名所巡り、ホテル・レストラン、ショッピングなどにおいて必要とされる観光・旅行全般に関する基礎的な英語を運用することができる。
3. 国内において、外国人に対して「道案内」や「パンフレット類」などを英語で説明することができる。また日本の観光名所、さらには日本の伝統文化や現代文化をやさしい英語で紹介することができる。

2級（中級レベル）

1. 英検（実用英語技能検定）2級程度／ TOEIC® L&R TESTスコア 470 − 600 程度
2. 観光・旅行関係の業界において、海外業務に携わる時に必要とされる基礎的な英語を運用することができる。
3. 海外における「個人旅行」をするとき、個人で旅程を組み、乗り物やホテルの予約、また単独で観光や買い物などを英語で対処することができる。
4. 国内において、外国人に対して日本の観光名所や名所旧跡、また日本の伝統文化や現代文化など日本の観光事情や文化事情を英語で紹介することがきる。

1級（上級レベル）

1. 英検（実用英語技能検定）準1級・1級程度／ TOEIC® L&R TESTスコア 600 − 860 程度
2. 国内において、「外国人観光客」に対して日本各地の観光地や名所旧跡などを英語で紹介しながら「通訳ガイド」（Guide-Interpreter）ができる。
3. 海外において、日本から同行する「日本人観光客」などを接遇しながら英語で「添乗」（Tour Escort）することができる。
4. 国内または海外のエアライン関連の業務遂行にあたり、外国人に対して十分に接客できる「客室乗務員」（Flight Attendant）や「地上係員」（Ground Staff）として英語で対応することができる。
5. 国内または海外のホテル・レストラン関連の業務遂行において、外国人に対して十分に接客できる「ホテル主任」（Hotel Assistant Manager）として英語で対応することができる。
6. その他観光・旅行関連の広い教養と一般常識を保ちながら、海外また国内において英語で活躍できる。
7. 海外における風俗習慣や国際儀礼などの「異文化」を英語で理解することができる。

（3） 観光英検の試験方法

〈1〉 試験の所要時間

- ◆ 3 級　　筆記試験：60 分　　リスニング試験：約 30 分
- ◆ 2 級　　筆記試験：60 分　　リスニング試験：約 30 分
- ◆ 1 級　　筆記試験：10 分　　面接試験：約 10 分

〈2〉試験問題の出題数と番号

2 級・3 級

「筆記試験」は (1) 〜 (50)、「リスニング試験」は (51) 〜 (90)、合計 90 題となっている。

1 級

「筆記試験」は (1) 〜 (4) の 4 題、「面接試験」は (1) 〜 (4) の 4 題、合計 8 題となっている。

〈3〉 出題の方式

2 級・3 級

「筆記試験」と「リスニング試験」における全問は「客観問題」であり、4 つの選択肢のうちから正解を 1 つ選び、解答用紙のマーク欄を塗りつぶす「四肢択一・マークシート方式」となっている。

筆記試験

| 設問 1 | **「適語の選択」**：Part A では設問の下線部分の英語に対応する和訳を選ぶ。Part B では設問に「適語」を選択するように下線が施され、その空所に対して 4 つの選択肢の中から正解を 1 つ選ぶ。 |

設問 1　**「適語の選択」**：Part A では設問の下線部分の英語に対応する和訳を選ぶ。Part B では設問に「適語」を選択するように下線が施され、その空所に対して 4 つの選択肢の中から正解を 1 つ選ぶ。

設問 2　**「語句・適文の選択」**：設問には「語句・適文」を選択するように下線が施され、その空所に対して 4 つの選択肢の中から正解を 1 つ選ぶ。

設問 3　**「語句の整序」**：設問には「適切な文章」を構成するように下線が施され、その空所に対して 4 つの選択肢の中から正解を 1 つ選ぶ。

設問 4　**「正誤選択」**：英文資料を読み、その内容について正しいものを 4 つの選択肢の中から選ぶ。または内容と一致する「正しい文」、あるいは「正しくない文」を 4 つの選択肢の中から 1 つ選ぶ。

設問 5　**「空欄補充」**：設問を読み、その内容と一致するよう空所に「適切な語句」を 4 つの選択肢の中から 1 つ選ぶ。

設問 6 **「写真描写」**：設問の「写真」を説明しているものを4つの選択肢の中から1つ選ぶ。

設問 7 **「イラスト描写」**：設問の「イラスト」を説明しているものを4つの選択肢の中から1つ選ぶ。

設問 8 **「対話形式」**：設問の「対話文」においてコミュニケーションが成立するように、4つの選択肢の中から正解を1つ選ぶ。

設問 9 **「会話形式」**：設問の「会話文」においてコミュニケーションが成立するように、4つの選択肢の中から正解を1つ選ぶ。

設問 10 **「会話／説明文形式」**：「海外観光事情」または「国内観光事情」に関する会話／説明文形式の放送を聞き、4つの選択肢の中から正解を1つ選ぶ。

1 級

「筆記試験」は「英文和訳」「和文英訳」を記述方式で行う。

「面接試験」は特定課題について試験官と受験者とによる英問英答を行う。

（4）観光英検の問題の形式と内容

●「3級・2級」における問題の形式と内容

〈1〉問題の形式

筆記試験

[A] 語学面

設問 1 観光用語の問題 (Vocabulary)

適語の選択 (Fill-in-the-blank)

[Part A] 英－和形式：[1]〜[5]

[Part B] 和－英形式：[6]〜[10]

設問 2 英語コミュニケーションの問題 (Communication)

語句・適文の選択 (Fill-in-the-blank)

[Part A] 対話形式 :[11]〜[15]

[Part B] 会話形式 :[16]〜[20]

設問 3 英文構成の問題 (Composition)

語句の整序 (Word order/ Fill-in-the-underline)

「海外観光」・「国内観光」[21]〜[25]

設問 4 英文読解の問題 (Reading Comprehension)

正誤選択（Multiple-choice by filling-in-the-blank）

[Part A]『資料』「海外観光」[26] ～ [30]

[Part B]『資料』「国内観光」[31] ～ [35]

[Part C]『会話』「国内観光」[36] ～ [40]

[B] 知識面

設問 5 観光事情に関する内容把握の問題 (Overseas Tourism & Japanese Tourism)

空所補充 (Multiple-choice by filling-in-the-blank)

[Part A]「海外観光」[41] ～ [43]・「海外文化」[44] ～ [45]

[Part B]「国内観光」[46] ～ [48]・「国内文化」[49] ～ [50]

リスニング試験

[A] 語学面

設問 6 写真描写による状況把握の問題 (Picture Format)

「海外観光」[51] ～ [53]

「国内観光」[54] ～ [55]

設問 7 イラスト描写による状況把握の問題 (Illustration Format)

「海外観光」[56] ～ [58]

「国内観光」[59] ～ [60]

設問 8 対話に関する内容把握の問題 (Dialogue Format)

「海外観光」[61] ～ [65]

「国内観光」[66] ～ [70]

設問 9 会話に関する内容把握の問題 (Conversation Format)

「海外観光」[71] ～ [75]

「国内観光」[76] ～ [79]

[B] 知識面

設問 10 【3級】会話に関する内容把握の問題 (Conversation Format)

[Part A]「海外観光」[81] ～ [85]

[Part B]「国内観光」[86] ～ [90]

【2級】説明文に関する内容把握の問題 (Description Format)

[Part A]「海外観光」[81] ～ [85]

[Part B]「国内観光」[86] ～ [90]

〈2〉問題の内容

旅行関連

1. **エアライン**
   出発：自動搭乗手続き、検問、出入国手続き、顔認識機、搭乗、免税店など
   機内：設備、座席、化粧室、機内食、機内販売、離着陸など
   到着：通過乗客、乗り換え客、入国、荷物受取、税関申告など

2. **ホテル**
   フロント：自動チェックイン、チェックアウト、会計など
   宿泊：客室、客室設備、各種接客サービス、顔認識機など
   宴会：宴会、各種会議など

3. **レストラン**
   飲食：食堂、カフェショップ、バー、宴会など
   食堂：予約、注文、従業員など
   食事：朝食、昼食、夕食、バイキング、カフェテリアなど
   献立：飲み物、前菜、スープ、魚介類、肉類、果物など

4. **ショッピング**
   デパート：案内、売場（衣類、化粧品、靴、カメラ、バッグ）など
   専門店：装身具、宝石、美術品、工芸品、陶芸品など
   免税店：酒類、香水、菓子類など

5. **交通機関**
   陸運：鉄道（列車）、自動車（タクシー、バス等）、ホームドアなど
   航空：飛行機、航空会社、飛行場、飛行など
   海運：船舶、船舶会社、船着場、航海など

6. **観光・旅行**
   観光：見物、見学、観光地、観光名所、写真撮影など
   旅行：企画、手配、旅程、申込、予約、料金、運賃など
   案内：運送機関、切符の購入、掲示など

7. **通信・銀行**
   電話：携帯電話、Eメール、インターネット、ファックス、通信文など
   郵便：はがき、切手、郵便物、小包、配達など
   銀行：換金、クレジットカード、トラベラーズチェックなど

8. **娯楽・レジャー**
   観賞：美術館、博物館、演劇、音楽、コンサートなど
   娯楽：カラオケ、ディスコ、ナイトクラブ、カジノなど
   スポーツ：野球、テニス、ゴルフ、水泳、サーフィンなど

9. **病気・医薬**

   病院：病棟、施設、医者、患者、診察、医療器具など

   病気：内科、外科、婦人科、耳鼻咽喉科、歯科、精神科など

   医療：内服薬、薬剤、薬草、処方箋、服用など

10. **観光・旅行情報**

   世界の主要都市、空港コードなど

   国名、国民、国語、都市、通貨単位など

(**観光関連**)

★ 近年「全国通訳案内士試験」の受験者が「観光英検」を受験する傾向がある。前者は主
として「インバウンド」（海外からの外国人が訪日する旅行）を中心とするが、後者は「イ
ンバウンド」と「アウトバウンド」（日本から海外に向けての旅行）の両面を目標とする。
これは英語関連の検定試験の中で観光英検のみが有する特色である。

   観光英検は、海外と国内の「観光」と「旅行」を主たるテーマとし、英語で観光事情・
文化事情の「知識・教養」を検定するものとなっている。「設問5」と「設問10」がこれ
に相当する。特に「設問5」と「設問10」のPart B（国内観光）における「英語」と「知
識」については、「全国通訳案内士試験（第1次・第2次）」の出題と類似点がみられる。

【参考】

[設問 5] の既出例（海外観光と国内観光に関する問題）

[Part A] 海外観光

1. **世界遺産**：宗教施設（教会・寺院・モスク）、景勝地、遺跡と史跡、名所旧跡など

   【3級】 [1] Vatican City （バチカン市国：ローマにある世界最小の国家）

   [2] Machu Picchu （マチュ・ピチュ：インカ帝国の遺跡）

   [3] The Parthenon （パルテノン神殿の遺跡）

   【2級】 [1] Mont-Saint-Michel （モンサンミシェル：サン・マロ湾上に浮かぶ小島）

   [2] Borobudur （ボロブドゥール：古代寺院の遺跡）

   [3] The State Hermitage Museum （ロシアのエルミタージュ美術館）

2. **自然資源**：自然景観、国立公園、州立公園、半島、山岳、渓谷、湖沼など

   【3級】 [1] Iguazu Falls （ブラジルのイグアスの滝）

   [2] Ha Long Bay （ベトナムのハロン湾）

   [3] Easter Island （イースター島）

   【2級】 [1] The Yellowstone National Park （米国のイエローストーン国立公園）

   [2] The Jungfrau （スイスのユングフラウ山地の最高峰）

   [3] The Lake Baikal （ロシアのバイカル湖）

3. **文化資源**：歴史的建造物、教会、聖堂、寺院、宮殿、城郭、庭園など

   【3級】 [1] The British Museum （ロンドンの大英博物館）

   [2] The Taj Mahal Mausoleum （インドのタージ・マハル霊廟）

　　　　　　[3] Versailles Palace（フランスのヴェルサイユ宮殿）
　【2級】　[1] The Sistine Chapel（システィーナ礼拝堂）
　　　　　　[2] The Blue Mosque（ブルーモスク＝スルタンアフメト・モスク）
　　　　　　[3] The Ajanta Caves（アジャンター石窟群）

4. **伝統工芸・郷土芸能・衣食住**：郷土料理、工芸品、特産品、美術品、音楽など
　【3級】　[1] Continental breakfast（コンチネンタル朝食）
　　　　　　[2] Mushrooms（欧州で人気食品のキノコ）
　　　　　　[3] Manners（作法）
　【2級】　[1] Bone china（ボーンチャイナ：イギリスの磁器）
　　　　　　[2] Chador（チャドル：イスラム教の女性の衣装）
　　　　　　[3] Goulash（グーラッシュ：ハンガリー風シチュー）

5. **年中行事・祭事・風習**：国民の祝日、宗教行事、地域の例祭、慣習、娯楽など
　【3級】　[1] Holidays（祝日）
　　　　　　[2] Halal（イスラム法での合法食品）
　　　　　　[3] Doggy bag（持ち帰り袋）
　【2級】　[1] Carnival（謝肉祭）
　　　　　　[2] Fado（ポルトガル民謡）
　　　　　　[3] Dress code（服装規定）

[Part B] 国内観光

1. **世界遺産**：寺社、景勝地、遺跡と史跡、名所旧跡、城跡など
　【3級】　[1] Horyu-ji Temple（法隆寺）
　　　　　　[2] Himeji Castle（姫路城）
　　　　　　[3] (Lake) Motosu-ko（本栖湖：世界遺産「富士五湖」）
　【2級】　[1] Byodo-in（平等院）
　　　　　　[2] Kasuga-Taisha（春日大社）
　　　　　　[3] Oura Tenshu-do（大浦天主堂 [教会]）

2. **自然資源**：自然景観、国立 [国定] 公園、半島、山岳、渓谷、温泉、洞窟など
　【3級】　[1] Koya-san Mountain Range（高野山）
　　　　　　[2] Shima Peninsula（志摩半島）
　　　　　　[3] Amanohashidate（天橋立）
　【2級】　[1] Jodogahama Beach（浄土ヶ浜）
　　　　　　[2] Kusatsu-Onsen（草津温泉）
　　　　　　[3] Akiyoshido（Limestone Cave）（秋芳洞）

3. **文化資源**：歴史的建造物、神社仏閣、寺院、城郭、庭園など
　【3級】　[1] Senso-ji（浅草寺）
　　　　　　[2] Kenrokuen（兼六園）
　　　　　　[3] Adachi Museum of Art（足立美術館）
　【2級】　[1] Risshaku-ji（立石寺）
　　　　　　[2] Fushimi Turret（伏見櫓）

[3] National Museum of Western Art（国立西洋美術館）

4. **伝統工芸・郷土芸能・衣食住**：郷土料理、工芸品、特産品、美術品、音楽など

【3級】 [1] Bunraku（文楽）

[2] Matcha（抹茶）

[3] Tokonoma（床の間）

【2級】 [1] Noh（能楽）

[2] Arita-yaki（有田焼）

[3] Kaiseki-ryori（懐石料理）

5. **年中行事・祭事・風習**：国民の祝日、年中行事、地域の例祭、娯楽など

【3級】 [1] Aoi Matsuri（葵祭）

[2] O-Bon Event（お盆）

[3] Midori-no-hi（みどりの日）

【2級】 [1] Chichibu-Yo-matsuri（秩父夜祭り）

[2] Tsuno-kakushi（角隠し）

[3] Ukai（鵜飼）

設問 10 の既出例（海外観光と国内観光に関する問題）

[Part A] 海外観光の出題例	[Part B] 国内観光の出題例
【3級】	【3級】
[1] The Islandic Volcano	Matsuyama (Dogo Onsen)
[2] The Great Barrier Reef	Shonan Beach
[3] The Statue of David by Michelangelo	Fuji-Hakone-Shizuoka National Park
【2級】	【2級】
[1] Yosemite National Park	Mt.Fuji
[2] Amsterdam	Okinawa
[3] Tasmania	The Ogasawara Islands

●「1級」における問題（筆記試験・面接試験）の形式と内容

〈1〉筆記試験の形式と内容

◆ 試験時間は 10 分である。

◆ 会場では受験者 1 ～ 2 名が受験する。

◆ 試験内容は「英文和訳」と「和文英訳」で、それぞれ「海外観光」と「国内観光」が出題される。

1. 英文和訳

設問 1 海外観光：《出題例 1》イエローストーン国立公園（世界遺産）

設問 2 国内観光：《出題例 2》厳島神社（世界遺産）

2. 和文英訳

設問3　海外観光：《出題例3》バンコク（タイ王国の首都）

設問4　国内観光：《出題例4》中尊寺（世界遺産）

〈2〉面接試験の形式と内容

◆ 試験時間は約10分である。

◆ 受験者（1人）は試験官に「英問英答」と「英語による説明」が出題される。

◆ 面接内容は「海外観光事情」と「国内観光事情」に関する資料である。

1. 指定された資料に関する「英問英答」

各設問には5題の質問が設定されている。

設問1　英語で書かれた「海外観光事情」に関する資料について試験官から英語で質問される。受験者は資料を見ながら英語で答える。

《出題例1》ハワイ・ビッグアイランド「質問事項」：5題

設問2　日本語で書かれた「国内観光事情」に関する資料について試験官から英語で質問される。受験者は資料を見ながら英語で答える。

《出題例2》姫路城（世界遺産）「質問事項」：5題

2. 特定の課題（与えらえた題目）に関する「英語による説明」

受験者は試験官から特定の課題に関する設問が与えられ、英語で即答する。受験者が特定の課題について説明し終えると、試験官はその内容に関して質問をすることがある。

設問3　英語で問われた「海外観光」に関する課題について、受験者は試験官に英語で説明する。

《出題例3》ルーヴル美術館（世界最大の美の殿堂）「質疑応答」：1～3題

設問4　英語で問われた「国内観光」に関する課題について、受験者は試験官に英語で説明する。

《出題例4》有馬温泉（日本三古湯）「質疑応答」：1～3題

精選過去問題

筆記試験（60分）＋リスニング試験（約30分）

1. 最初に筆記試験（試験時間は60分）、引き続きリスニング試験（試験時間は約30分）が行われます。試験監督者の指示に従ってください。
2. 問題冊子は試験監督者から開始の合図があるまで開かないでください。
3. 解答用紙（マークシート）の記入欄に、氏名・生年月日・受験番号等を記入してください。
4. 試験開始の合図後、最初に問題冊子のページを確認してください。もし乱丁や落丁がある場合は、すみやかに申し出てください。
5. 解答は全て、解答用紙の該当するマーク欄を黒鉛筆で塗りつぶしてください。
   ・黒鉛筆またはシャープペンシル以外は使用できません。
   ・解答用紙には解答以外の記入をいっさいしないでください。
6. 辞書・参考書およびそれに類するものの使用はすべて禁止されています。
7. 筆記用具が使用不能になった場合は、係員にすみやかに申し出てください。
8. 問題の内容に関する質問には、一切応じられません。
9. 不正行為があった場合、解答はすべて無効になりますので注意してください。

【筆記試験について】

1. 試験監督者が筆記試験の開始を告げてから、始めてください。
2. 各設問は1から50までの通し番号になっています。
3. 試験開始後の中途退出はできません。（リスニング試験が受けられなくなります。）

【リスニング試験について】

1. 各設問は51から90までの通し番号になっています。
2. リスニング中に問題冊子にメモをとってもかまいませんが、解答用紙に解答を転記する時間はありませんので、注意してください。
3. 放送が終了を告げたら、筆記用具を置いて、係員が解答用紙を回収するまで席を立たないでください。

全国語学ビジネス観光教育協会

筆記試験 ┠─────────────────────────────

1 観光用語の問題

[**Part A**] Read the following English statements from (1) to (5) and choose the most appropriate Japanese translation for each underlined part from among the four alternatives: a), b), c) and d). Blacken the letter for your answer on the answer sheet.

(1) If you have a lot of <u>unaccompanied baggage</u>, you have to declare them to a customs official.

    a) 別送手荷物　　　b) 受託手荷物　　　c) 紛失手荷物　　　d) 超過手荷物

(2) If your journey is delayed by more than two hours, we will <u>compensate</u> the full cost of your ticket.

    a) 換金する　　　b) 交換する　　　c) 発行する　　　d) 補償する

(3) Many airlines in Europe have eliminated the <u>complimentary</u> beverage service on their short-haul flights.

    a) 追加の　　　b) 前払いの　　　c) 贈呈用の　　　d) 無料の

(4) The National Police Agency decided to revoke licenses of <u>tailgaters</u> in legal change.

    a) あおり運転手　　　b) 飲酒運転手　　　c) 無謀運転手　　　d) 無免許運転手

(5) Toyama Bay is famous for a rare phenomenon of <u>mirages</u> that can be observed on nearby beaches on clear days.

    a) 波の花　　　b) 流氷　　　c) 蜃気楼　　　d) 虹

[Part B] Read the following Japanese statements from (6) to (10) and choose the most appropriate English translation for each underlined part from among the four alternatives: a), b), c) and d). Blacken the letter of your answer on the answer sheet.

(6) 私は飛行中に乱気流の最悪な体験をした。

I had the worst experience with _____ during the flight.

a) air-conditioning　　　　b) oxygen shortage

c) sudden descent　　　　d) turbulence

(7) 旅程日程表では、夜行列車は朝早くアムステルダムに到着します。

According to my _____, the overnight train arrives in Amsterdam early in the morning.

a) e-ticket receipt　　　　b) flight information

c) travel account　　　　d) travel itinerary

(8) 私はローマの日本領事館を探しています。

I'm looking for the Japanese _____ General in Rome.

a) Ambassador　　b) Embassy　　c) Consul　　d) Consulate

(9) 黒部峡谷は起伏の多い山々の美観、そして黒部川の急流で有名である。

The Kurobe _____ is noted for the beauty of rugged mountains and the rushing waters of the river Kurobe.

a) Cliff　　　　b) Moat　　　　c) Rapids　　　　d) Ravine

(10) 鳥取砂丘は日本海に沿ってほぼ東西16キロ、南北2キロにも及んでいる。

Tottori Sand _____ stretch along the Japan Sea coast for 16 km from east to west and 2 km from north to south.

a) Cape　　　　b) Dunes　　　　c) Plateau　　　　d) Spit

2 英語コミュニケーションの問題

[Part A] Read the following English dialogs from (11) to (15) and choose the most appropriate utterance to complete each dialog from the four alternatives: a), b), c) and d). Blacken the letter of your answer on the answer sheet.

(11) A: I can't believe we were four hours late in arriving. Do you understand that I have missed my connecting flight? What am I supposed to do now?

　　 B: Yes, sir. ＿＿＿＿＿＿＿＿＿＿＿＿＿＿＿＿＿＿＿＿

　　　 We can provide you with a voucher for a hotel stay and a promise to get you on the next available flight.

　　 a) Let me apologize again for this inconvenience.

　　 b) I'd like your manager to say sorry when I talk to her.

　　 c) I'll call ahead to check that the flight is on schedule.

　　 d) Luckily you will be able to make it to the meeting on time.

(12) A: I'd like to make a reservation for the 13th and 14th of December. I'd like a twin or a double.

　　 B: I'm sorry, but we're filled to capacity on those dates. In the future, you could always visit our website to check availability and to make reservations. Sorry, and ＿＿＿＿＿＿＿＿＿＿＿＿.

　　 a) we have only a few tickets left

　　 b) our banquet rooms are all available

　　 c) payment can be made by credit card or cash

　　 d) we look forward to serving you some other time

(13) A: The half-day tour is 26 euros. And the full-day tour is 50 euros, with lunch included. It gets back at 6:00 pm. It's much more exciting.

    B: _____ Could I just get tickets for one adult and two kids for the morning tour?

    a) Oh, that sounds really great.

    b) There'll be four of us all together.

    c) I think we'll bring our own lunch if that's OK.

    d) I don't have enough time for the full-day tour.

(14) A: I hear Mt. Fuji is usually very beautiful at this time of year. It seems to be a very long way from Tokyo, though. And I can't figure out which train line to take.

    B: Actually it's not difficult to get there. _____

    a) Lines are short at this time of year, actually.

    b) You can save a lot by taking the cheapest way.

    c) The prettiest way to get to Tokyo is by train.

    d) The easiest way is to take an express bus from Shinjuku.

(15) A: Is this your first time to the Gion Festival?

    B: Yes. We're really looking forward to seeing _____.

    a) the latest animations

    b) the colorful carp streamers in the sky

    c) the festive floats proceeding along the main streets

    d) the lanterns floating in the river in the evening

[Part B] Read the following English conversations from (16) to (20) and choose the most appropriate utterance to complete each conversation from the four alternatives: a), b), c) and d). Blacken the letter of your answer on the answer sheet.

(16) A: One of our tour members will need to see a doctor tomorrow. She vomited again a few minutes ago. I think it might be a stomach infection.

　　 B: You mean, food poisoning? Don't you think it could be a flu?

　　 A: I doubt it. ＿＿＿＿＿＿＿＿＿＿＿＿＿＿＿＿ in the past few hours, and she doesn't have a fever.

　　 a) She's complained about the service

　　 b) She's missed her connection

　　 c) She's thrown up four times

　　 d) She's been eating a lot

(17) A: I'm planning to go to the city square today to do a little exploring and shopping downtown.

　　 B: Well, ＿＿＿＿＿＿＿＿＿＿＿＿＿＿＿＿＿＿＿. There have been many thefts recently—wallets and phones especially. Keep your hands on your bag.

　　 A: Thanks. I'll try.

　　 a) be careful of pickpockets in crowded places

　　 b) beware of restaurants overcharging customers

　　 c) watch out for sudden changes in the weather

　　 d) take care to avoid injuries that require medical attention

(18) A: Is there any place to get some bottled water around here? I don't want to drink the water in the restaurant.

B: Actually, _____ is pretty safe in this country. Everyone says it tastes pretty good, too. And it's free.

A: Really?

a) mineral water   b) tap water

c) carbonated water   d) canned water

(19) A: _____ during your stay.

B: That's great because we are really looking forward to trying everything.

A: I really recommend a *kaiseki*-style meal, especially at lunchtime. But if you want to eat like the locals, you should also try the *ramen*. There are lots of great little places around the station. Look for one with a long line.

a) You'll be able to visit all of the attractions you want

b) We've chosen the most gorgeous accommodations for you

c) There are many interesting cuisine options available for you

d) The highlight will certainly be a helicopter ride

(20) A: I would love to see that festival in Japan where they have a huge Chinese character burning on a mountain.

B: I think you mean the *Daimonji-yaki*. Actually there are several around Japan. The most famous is probably in Kyoto. But they _____.

A: Too bad. Next time I'll try to come in that season.

a) are now prohibited from using flammable materials

b) are held in the summer as part of the O-bon festival

c) take place every weekend throughout the year

d) can be purchased as souvenirs for friends and family

3 英文構成の問題

Read the following English paragraphs which contain incomplete sentences.
To complete the sentence, put each word into the best order. When you have finished, blacken letter on your answer sheet from among the four alternatives: a), b), c) and d) for the word in the position of the blank that has the question numbers from (21) to (25).

    Europe is the most _____ _____ (21) _____ the world. Six of the top ten destinations in the world—France, Spain, Italy, the United Kingdom of Great Britain, Turkey, and Germany—are located in Europe. Many of the tourists who visit European countries (22) _____ _____ _____ like North America, Japan, or increasingly, China. Europe is expensive and difficult to travel to. Why are European countries so popular? Well, many people visit European countries to see old things: old _____ _____ _____ (23) or castles, old museums with old paintings or artifacts, or old monuments. One writer, who recently wrote a book about travel and history, says that people don't visit these places because they are interested in old things especially. In their own countries, many of these people rarely go to museums or visit old buildings. He says it is very strange that people travel around the world and line up to visit museums, churches, or monuments.

    But why do they feel they should do this on their vacation? Westminster Abbey in London, the Louvre in Paris, or the Colosseum in Rome are among the most popular places in the world to visit. Why are they so popular? The answer lies partly in the history of travel. Many years ago, _____ (24) _____ _____ . Only very rich people could travel to another country just to experience going to another place. These people usually studied Roman and Greek history and literature, and Latin, the language of old Rome, as part of their education. So they were very interested in Roman history. That _____ _____ (25) _____ Italy, especially Rome became so popular and famous. The earliest travel guidebooks were written for these early travelers. As more and more people began to have the money and time to travel, they continued to use the same guidebooks. As they did, the culture of travel was developed.

(21) a) destination   b) in   c) popular   d) tourism

(22) a) faraway   b) places   c) from   d) come

(23) a) as   b) such   c) cathedrals   d) buildings

(24) a) people   b) could   c) travel   d) few

(25) a) why   b) reason   c) one   d) is

4

[Part A] Read the following information sheet and answer the questions from (26) to (30) by choosing the most appropriate answer for each question from among the four alternatives; a), b), c) and d). Blacken the letter of your

The Sound of Music Tour

Come and join us on a wonderful ride with breath-taking views of the landscape where the opening scenes of the movie "The Sound of Music" were filmed—not only in the city of Salzburg! Relax and listen to the Original Sound of Music soundtrack. You will not just see lots of highlights of the movie "The Sound of Music," but also get to know historical and architectural

[①] in the city as well as in the Lake District area.

- **Schedule:** 9:15 am, 2:00 pm
- **Duration:** 4.0 Hours
- **Price:** €40 Adult
  €20 Child (4-12)
- **Meeting spot:** Salzburg Panorama Tours GmbH Austria-5020 Salzburg-Mirabellplatz
- **Notice:** Please be there 30 minutes prior tour departure.

Route:

① **Mirabell Gardens**

You will certainly have heard about Mirabell Gardens where the song "Do-Re-Mi" was filmed. After or before joining the tour, we warmly recommend you see the gardens for yourself and [②] the Pegasus Fountain as well as the Do-Re-Mi steps.

② **Leopoldskron Palace**

You will have a photo stop at the lake where the famous boating scene was filmed. You will see the Captain's backyard and private palace gardens.

③ **Hellbrunn Palace, Gazebo**

Visit the gardens of Hellbrunn Palace and find the gazebo which was moved from Leopoldskron Palace to the current location for the fans of the movie after the movie was made—you certainly will remember the song "16 going on 17" scene and the kissing scene of Maria and Baron von Trapp.

④ **Nonnberg Abbey**

You will have a photo stop at the foot of the mountain, to get a view at Nonnberg Abbey which is still an active convent today. This is where the "real" Maria was a novice and where she and Baron von Trapp got married in real life. The Abbey does not allow visits within its walls.

⑤ **Salzburg Lake District Area - St. Gilgen**

After your film-location tour within the town of Salzburg, you will drive out into the Lake District, passing Lake Fuschl and Lake Wolfgang, where panorama shots and scenes of the picnic were filmed. Enjoy the wonderful view down onto St. Gilgen and Lake Wolfgang!

⑥ **Mondsee - Wedding Chapel**

In Mondsee you have the chance to see the famous church, where the wedding of Maria and Baron von Trapp was filmed in the movie "The Sound of Music." Afterwards you will have a little break to 　②　 this little town by yourself.

(26) Choose the most appropriate word for 　①　 .

　　a) staples 　　　b) landmarks 　　c) contents 　　　d) replicas

(27) Choose the most appropriate word for 　②　 .

　　a) qualify 　　　b) assure 　　　c) contain 　　　d) explore

(28) What scene was filmed at Mirabell Gardens?

　　a) The famous boating scene.

　　b) The song "16 going on 17" scene.

　　c) The picnic scene.

　　d) The song "Do-Re-Mi" scene.

(29) Which is TRUE about the Sound of Music tour?

    a) The tour starts at 9:15 pm and disbands at 2:00 pm.

    b) The tour price is shown in Euros.

    c) The last tour of the day starts at 4:00 pm.

    d) Participants should be at the meeting place at 9:15 am.

(30) Which is FALSE about the Sound of Music tour?

    a) 映画の有名なボートのシーンが撮影された湖に写真を撮影するために立ち寄る。

    b) ヘルブルン宮殿には映画ファンのために新設された建物がある。

    c) ノンベルク修道院はマリアとトラップ大佐が実際に結婚式を挙げた場所である。

    d) ザルツブルグ市内観光のあとはピクニックシーンなどが撮影された湖水地方へ向かう。

[Part B] Read the following information sheet and answer the questions from (31) to (35) by choosing the most appropriate answer for each question from among the four alternatives; a), b), c) and d). Blacken the letter of your answer on the answer sheet.

OTSUKA MUSEUM OF ART

Over 1,000 pieces of powerful works of Western art! The world's first ceramic board art museum reproducing masterpieces in their original dimensions using ceramic boards.

Main Entrance

Sistine Hall

Modern exhibition room

The Banquet Hall of the Mysteries

The Otsuka Museum of Art is a "Ceramic board masterpiece art museum" with the largest permanent ⎡ ① ⎤ space in Japan (total floor of 29,412 square meters), built to commemorate the Otsuka Group 75th anniversary in Naruto City, Tokushima Prefecture. Inside, there are more than 1,000 replicas of priceless masterpieces of Western art selected by a committee of 6, from ancient murals to modern paintings in the collection of more than 190 art museums in 26 countries worldwide. These masterpieces are reproduced to their original size using special techniques by the Otsuka Ohmi Ceramics Co., Ltd.

Unlike the paintings in art books or textbooks, visitors will able to ② the true artistic value of the original works, and experience art museums of the world while in Japan.

Furthermore, while the original masterpieces cannot escape the damaging effects of today's pollution, earthquakes and fire, the ceramic reproductions can maintain their color and shape for over 2,000 years, and this is a large contribution in the nature of preserving the history of cultural treasures. This is a groundbreaking experiment where we have reproduced "Guernica," now considered too fragile to move, and El Greco altarpiece, which have been dispersed during war. We received many endorsements and compliments from Picasso's son, Miro's grandchildren and art museum directors and curators from all over the world who came to check the quality of these 1,000 works. The Otsuka Museum of Art can be considered as the world's first and only ceramic board masterpiece art museum, both technically and philosophically.

Basic Information

Location: Naruto Park, Naruto-cho, Naruto-shi, Tokushima 772-0053
　　TEL / + 81-88-687-3737　FAX / +81-88-687-1117　e-mail / info@o-museum.or.jp
Museum opening hours: 9:30 am to 5:00 pm
　　Closed on Monday (If a public holiday falls on Monday, the Museum will be closed the following day)
　　* The museum will be closed consecutively in January, and will be open throughout August.
Museum Admission: Elementary, junior high school and high school students 550 Yen
　　University students 2,200 Yen
　　Adults 3,300 Yen　(All inclusive of consumption tax)
　　* Ticket counter closes at 4:00 pm.
　　* 10% discount for groups of 20 or more.
　　* Students must show their student ID at the entrance.
　　* Visitors with a disability permit can visit the museum for a discounted fee.

p.27　画像提供：大塚国際美術館（写真は大塚国際美術館の展示作品を撮影したものです）

(31)　Choose the most appropriate word for ☐ ① ☐.

    a）prohibition   b）compensation

    c）participation   d）exhibition

(32)　Choose the most appropriate word for ☐ ② ☐.

    a）appreciate   b）describe   c）enclose   d）consume

(33)　Otsuka Museum Art was founded by _____.

    a）a private company   b）Tokushima Prefecture

    c）the government of Japan   d）Tokushima City

(34)　Which is FALSE about Otsuka Museum of Art?

    a）A collection of all more than 1,000 original masterpieces has been assembled.

    b）Each masterpiece is reproduced in its original size.

    c）The children of some artists came to check the quality of works.

    d）The ceramic reproduction can last for over 2,000 years.

(35)　Which is TRUE about Otsuka Museum of Art?

    a）月曜日と正月、お盆の 5 日間が休館日である。

    b）最終入館時間は 5 時である。

    c）チケット代金に消費税は含まれていない。

    d）学生は入場の際に学生証を見せなくてはならない。

[Part C] Read the following English conversation, and answer the questions from (36) to (40) by choosing the most appropriate answer for each question from among the four alternatives; a), b) ,c) and d). Blacken the letter of your answer on the answer sheet.

istockphoto / petesphotography

Tour Guide: Okay, we're almost there. We'll be getting off at the next station called Yui Rail, Kenchomae Station.

Tourist A: So, what is this we're going to see again?

Tour Guide: This festival is the Naha Great Tug-of-War. It is one of the oldest festivals in Okinawa. This festival dates back to about the 17th century and was originally a thanksgiving-style celebration after the harvest season.

Tourist B: I can already hear the noise from the crowd ....

Tour Guide: There will be about 300,000 people out today. Highway Route 58 in this part of the city is shut down today, just for this festival. This is a day everyone in Okinawa looks forward to. We've missed the parade at the beginning but even that parade attracts huge crowds. There is Okinawan music, karate demonstrations .... But that's OK. We are here for the main event. Can you see the rope now?

Tourist A: That's amazing! How big is that rope?

Tour Guide: The rope itself is about 200 meters long and weighs over 40 __(36)__ . The Guinness Book of Records __(37)__ it as one as the largest straw ropes in the world a few years ago.

Tourist B: What are they doing now?

Tour Guide: They are tying the rope together. Do you see that part of the rope? That team is the West team. Their rope is called the *Minna* or female rope. That other part is the East team. Their part is called the *Ozuna*, the male rope. There is a big stick in the middle __(38)__ both ropes called a *Kanuchi-bou*. Can you guess how much that stick weighs? Over 300 kilograms!

Tourist A: Unbelievable. The noise from the crowd is amazing! Who are those two people on the platforms being carried over the rope?

Tour Guide: Those are the leaders, or captains you might call them, of the West and East teams. They are the kings of their team. When the Tug-of-War starts, the kings will be trying to __(39)__ their team to pull that rope about five meters over the finish line to win. The actual contest can take 20 or 30 minutes. At the end, all the participants are pretty __(40)__ ! When the contest is over we'll go down and try to get a piece of rope. It's considered good luck.

Tourist B: The crowd is really cheering now. It looks like they're going to start ... this is going to be incredible!

(36) Choose the most appropriate word for __(36)__ .

   a) tonnes   b) length

   c) height   d) width

(37) Choose the most appropriate word for __(37)__ .

   a) qualified   b) renovated

   c) certified   d) interpreted

(38) Choose the most appropriate word for ____(38)____ .

  a）separating   b）connecting

  c）adjoining   d）cutting

(39) Choose the most appropriate word for ____(39)____ .

  a）lead   b）replace

  c）explore   d）increase

(40) Choose the most appropriate word for ____(40)____ .

  a）exhausted   b）exchanged

  c）worried   d）waiting

[**Part A**] Read the following descriptions from (41) to (45) and choose the best answer to complete the sentences with blank parts from among the four alternatives: a), b), c) and d). Blacken the letter of your answer on the answer sheet.

(41) The _____ is a rocky islet connected by a causeway with the mainland. It is well-known as the most famous place of pilgrimage in France. Construction of a Gothic-style Benedictine abbey was begun in 708 by a bishop in accordance with a revelation from Archangel St. Michael. It was completed in the 16th century. The extraordinary architecture of the abbey and its bay make it the most famous tourist attraction with many visitors each year.

a) Côte d'Azur (French Riviera)

b) Val de Loire (Loire Valley)

c) Ile-de-France (Island of France)

d) Mont-Saint-Michel (Mount St Michael)

(42) _____ National Park, located in the northwestern Wyoming, was the first national park created by the US government in 1872. The last remaining herd of wild bison (buffalo) in the USA still peacefully roams the meadows. Visitors can easily spot a wide variety of native American wildlife from their cars as they drive through the gorgeous scenery of this park.

a) Grand Canyon　　　　b) Mesa Verde

c) Yosemite　　　　d) Yellowstone

(43) The _____ was built inside the Vatican Palace in 1473 for Pope Sixtus Ⅳ. On the ceiling of the _____, Michelangelo painted scenes from the Old Testament. Michelangelo's wonderful frescoes of the "Creation" on the barrel-vaulted ceiling and "Last Judgement" on the end wall have both been restored. It took him four years to paint the ceiling; 24 years later he painted the extraordinary "Last Judgement."

   a) Milan Cathedral   b) San Marco Basilica

   c) Sistine Chapel   d) St. Peter's Basilica

(44) _____ china is a type of porcelain is famous for having a high level of whiteness. In addition, since it is very strong, it can be sued to make more delicate tableware than other types of porcelain. It was developed in England in 1748. It is often associated with sophisticated English culture, and some of the most famous brands are well-known internationally, including, Royal Doulton, and Wedgewood.

   a) Bone   b) Afternoon tea

   c) Wool   d) Lace

(45) Rio de Janeiro is the third largest city in brazil. The Rio de Janeiro's _____ takes place for four days before Lent. The most spectacular event during the period is the samba parade. The _____ Festivities reach their climax when samba dancers in bright costumes swayed at the Sambadrome. _____s similar to the world-famous Rio _____ in Brazil are held every year around South America.

   a) Carnival   b) Easter   c) Halloween   d) masquerade

[Part B] Read the following descriptions from (46) to (50) and choose the best answer to complete the sentences with blank parts from among the four alternatives: a), b), c) and d). Blacken the letter of your answer on the answer sheet.

(46) _____ Temple was converted from the Fujiwara villa into a Buddhist temple in 1052. The Phoenix Hall, built in 1053, is the only original remaining building and is considered one of the most beautiful buildings in Japan. The body is represented by the central hall, the wings by the lateral corridors and the tail by the rear corridor. Inside is an image of Amida Buddha, seated in the lotus position.

   a) Byodo-in   b) Chion-in

   c) Jakko-in   d) Nanzen-ji

(47) The Sanriku Fukko National Park is one of Japan's most beautiful seacoast parks. The park extends for 220km from Aomori Prefecture through Iwate Prefecture to Miyagi Prefecture. It is nicknamed the "Alps of the Sea" because of the beauty of the coastal natural park. _____ Beach gives a beautiful contrast between long, white beaches and precipitous oddly shaped rocks as well as fresh green pine trees.

   a) Jodoga-hama   b) Katsura-hama

   c) Kujukuri-hama   d) Shichiriga-hama

(48) _____ Temple is the largest temple of the Tendai set of Buddhism in the Tohoku District. It was founded in 860 by the Buddhist priest Ennin (Jikaku-Daishi) as a branch of Enryaku-ji Temple in Kyoto. This temple is a mountaintop monastery with an ascent that involves a steep climbing of 1,015 stone stairs. The temple is a popular site for viewing cherry blossom in spring and colorful foliage in fall.

a) Chuson-ji   b) Motsu-ji   c) Risshaku-ji   d) Zuigan-ji

(49) _____ is a highly-stylized traditional Japanese play performed with unique classical costumes and masks. It has three performances blended into one with harmony— refined dance (*mai*), dramatic chant (*utai*) and instrumental accompaniments (*hayashi*). Its theory was perfected by Kanami and Zeami into its present form in the early Muromachi period under the patronage of the shogun Ashikaga Yoshimitsu.

a) Bunraku   b) Kabuki   c) Gagaku   d) Noh

(50) The _____ Night Festival features a parade of four gorgeously-decorated festive floats bedecked with lanterns (*yatai*) and two huge carts decorated with beautiful carvings (*kasaboko*). The climax of the festival is at night when four dashi floats and two *kasaboko* carts climb the steep slope of the hill (called dango-zaka) in one spurt with a portable shrine. At night numerous paper lanterns are lit on the festival floats, creating the beautiful sight.

a) Nachi-no-Himatsuri   b) Chichibu-Yomatsuri

c) Yamaga-Toro-Matsuri   d) Yoshida-no-Himatsuri

リスニング試験 ├────────────────────────────────────

6

Listen to the four descriptions for each picture from (51) to (55). Choose the statement that best describes what you see in the picture from among the four alternatives: a), b), c) and d). Blacken the letter of your answer on the answer sheet. The descriptions will be spoken just once.

1-02 (51)

1-03 (52)

1-04 (53)

1-05 (54)

1-06 (55)

7

Listen to the four descriptions for each illustration from (56) to (60). Choose the statement that best describes what you see in the illustration from among the four alternatives: a), b), c) and d). Blacken the letter of your answer on the answer sheet. The descriptions will be spoken just once.

1-07 (56)

Free-To-Use Smartphone **handy** Introduction

`handy' is a free rental smartphone for the private use of our guests.

Main Functionary

 Unlimited domestic and international calls (to 6 selected countries).

📶 The free internet connection, both inside and outside the hotel.

▢ You can download and use applications from the google Play Store.

1-08 (57)

Thank you
Palm Beach

As you have requested, your linen has not been changed. Should you prefer to have your linen changed tomorrow, please remember to place this card on the bed again.

Your every effort helps with environmental protection.

◀》1-09 (58)

BANGKOK TASTE

Join us for lunch and enjoy great Thai Cuisine at
10% Off!
(Beverages not included)

Offers valid with printed coupon only.
Not valid with any others or discounts.
Valid with lunch entree only.

◀》1-10 (59)

Superior Twin 33.0 m²

Number of persons per room: 2 to 3

Bed size: 122cm × 195cm

Bed sharing:
A child under 6 years old is allowed.
(One child per bed.)

It has an entire view of Tokyo Disneyland, and is coordinated by a tone of quiet colors, full of the park-atmosphere. (For the use of 3, Sofa-beds are used.)

◀》1-11 (60)

8

Listen to the first sentences from (61) to (70) and complete each dialog by choosing the best response from among the four alternatives: a), b), c) and d). Blacken the letter of your answer on the answer sheet. The sentences will be spoken twice.

1-12 (61) a) Sure. Will you proceed this way, please?
　　　 b) Of course. We look forward to seeing you.
　　　 c) Yes. I'd like to book a table for Sunday at twelve noon.
　　　 d) Yes, in the name of Stevens. I'm staying at the hotel.

1-13 (62) a) OK, let's make it another day.
　　　 b) Where can I wait for the pick-up bus?
　　　 c) All right. How long does the performance last?
　　　 d) Yes, and can we get the return tickets at that time?

1-14 (63) a) You need one hour to make your connection.
　　　 b) Please look at our home page for further information.
　　　 c) Oh, you should change your e-mail address as soon as possible.
　　　 d) I'm sorry, there's been trouble all morning with getting online.

1-15 (64) a) I think 50 dollars is my limit.
　　　 b) Well, I want you to keep my valuables.
　　　 c) Yes. It costs more than I expected.
　　　 d) Let me see. Can I change 100 dollars?

1-16 (65) a) Be sure to boil the water.
　　　 b) The kitchen is on the first floor.
　　　 c) There is a comfortable bed in the room.
　　　 d) I'm afraid there is no cooking permitted in the rooms.

◀1-17 (66) a) Thank you, but a tip is not necessary.

b) Yes, the taxi stand is out the lobby doors.

c) Certainly. Where did you find it?

d) Please go to lost-and-found counter over there.

◀1-18 (67) a) The subway runs the length of the city.

b) There is a shuttle bus stop near the station.

c) Trams leave every 15 minutes from Central Street.

d) Public transportation is a convenient and cheap way to get around.

◀1-19 (68) a) You're welcome. Please come again.

b) Yes, go straight and you'll see it on the left.

c) Certainly. Shall we charge that to your room?

d) Certainly. The restaurant re-opens for dinner at 4:00 pm.

◀1-20 (69) a) Because it was the last one.

b) Because the bedding was dirty.

c) Because I saw he had injured foot.

d) Because it was across the street.

◀1-21 (70) a) Not many calories.

b) If it's on time.

c) Just to the airport.

d) I'd like a hybrid car.

9

Listen to the conversations from (71) to (80) and choose the most appropriate answer for the question following each conversation from among the four alternatives: a), b), c) and d). Blacken the letter of your answer on the answer sheet. The conversations and the questions will be spoken twice.

1-22 (71) a) He has motion sickness.
       b) He lost his train ticket.
       c) He ran out of medicine.
       d) He forgot his bag on the bus.

1-23 (72) a) The number of SNS followers.
       b) The amount of trash.
       c) An important sports game.
       d) A volunteer experience.

1-24 (73) a) More wine.
       b) Separate bills.
       c) The dessert menu.
       d) A new pasta set.

1-25 (74) a) The tourist cannot get a reservation.
       b) The tourist waited too long to book.
       c) The hotel will undergo special repairs.
       d) The hotel is making a special offer.

1-26 (75) a) A visit to a gallery.
       b) A visit to a cathedral.
       c) A special concert.
       d) A ghost tour.

◀)1-27 (76) a) Claiming a table.

　　　　 b) Making a complaint.

　　　　 c) Asking for the manager.

　　　　 d) Being rude to the staff.

◀)1-28 (77) a) Use the fitness center.

　　　　 b) Access the business center.

　　　　 c) Take a hot-spring bath.

　　　　 d) Go shopping for clothes.

◀)1-29 (78) a) Getting photographed.

　　　　 b) Visiting a museum.

　　　　 c) Taking a history tour.

　　　　 d) Renting costumes.

◀)1-30 (79) a) Get free in-flight Wi-Fi.

　　　　 b) Get a seat upgrade.

　　　　 c) Use air miles.

　　　　 d) Use her credit card.

◀)1-31 (80) a) Safety precautions.

　　　　 b) Ways to save money.

　　　　 c) Calling the police.

　　　　 d) An alternative taxi service.

Listen to the following descriptions **[Part A]** and **[Part B]**, and answer the questions from (81) to (90). Choose the most appropriate answer for each question from among the four alternatives: a), b), c) and d). Blacken the letter of your answer on the answer sheet. The descriptions and the questions will be spoken twice.

1-32 **[Part A]**

(81) a) In southern California.
  b) In central California.
  c) In western Rhode Island.
  d) In eastern Rhode Island.

(82) a) $30,000km^2$
  b) $3,000km^2$
  c) $80km^2$
  d) $18km^2$

(83) a) Its location.
  b) Its size.
  c) Its hotel.
  d) Publicity.

(84) a) 37,000
  b) 370,000
  c) 3,700,000
  d) 37,000,000

(85) a) Traffic problems.
  b) Accessibility problems.
  c) Financial problems.
  d) Environmental destruction.

◀)1-33 **[Part B]**

(86) a) Ancient times.

b) The mid-8th century.

c) The 12th century.

d) The 14th century.

(87) a) 15 sites.

b) 16 sites.

c) 17 sites.

d) 18 sites.

(88) a) Around 13,000.

b) Around 30,000.

c) Around 130,000.

d) Around 300,000.

(89) a) Buddhism.

b) *Fujiko*.

c) *Shugendo*.

d) *Ukiyo-e*.

(90) a) To control volcanic activity.

b) To promote tourism development.

c) To limit the number of climbers.

d) To assist in local education.

筆記試験

1 観光用語の問題

【Part A】

(1) **正解** **a)** 「**別送手荷物**がたくさんある場合には税関職員に申告する必要がある」

解説 **unaccompanied baggage**「別送手荷物」。反意語は accompanied baggage「携帯手荷物」。飛行機旅行のとき、手荷物許容量（baggage allowance）を超えた分を別便で送る場合の荷物のこと。本人の搭乗便とは異なる便で輸送され、別送品のあるときは税関申告書（customs declaration form）が必要である。通常は次のようなものがある。家庭電気製品 (household electric appliance)、楽器類 (musical instruments)、スポーツ用品 (sports goods [equipment]) など。通称「アナカン」 ☞ **Column 01　手荷物** (p.51)

参考 b)「受託手荷物」checked [registered] baggage
　　　c)「紛失手荷物」lost [missing] baggage
　　　d)「超過手荷物」excess [overweight] baggage

(2) **正解** **d)** 「旅行が2時間以上遅れる場合、チケットの全額を**補償します**」

解説 **compensate**「補償する」(= make up for; make compensation for; pay for) ▶ Can you *compensate* me for this damaged bag?「この損傷したバッグを補償してもらえますか」I'll talk to the manager about how we may *compensate* you for the damaged shirt.「損傷したシャツをどのように弁償できるかを支配人にお話してみます」☆ compensation「弁償」▶ make *compensation* for (the lost baggage)「（紛失荷物の）弁償をする」

参考 a)「（小切手）を換金する」cash (a check); change money
　　　b)「（贈り物）を交換する」exchange (gifts); trade
　　　c)「（切手）を発行する」issue (stamps); publish

（3） **正解** **d）** 「欧州の航空会社の多くは短距離便で**無料**提供する飲み物を廃止している」

解説 complimentary (beverage service)「無料の（飲み物サービス）」。名詞の前に用いる。▶ *complimentary* meal「（機内食のように）無料で提供される食事」 *complimentary* newspaper [paper]「（ホテルでの）無料提供の新聞」 *complimentary* refreshments「（会合での）軽い飲食物」 *complimentary* magazine「無料提供の雑誌」☆同音異義語のcomplementary「補足的な」と混同しないこと。

参考 a）「追加の（料金）」additional (charge)
b）「前払いの（支払い）」prepaid (payment)
c）「贈呈用の（箱）」gift (box)

（4） **正解** **a）** 「警察庁は法改正における**あおり運転手**の免許取消処分を決めた」

解説 tailgaters「あおり運転手」。tailgate は前の車の後ろにぴったりついて走行すること。▶ The car behind me [following vehicle] is *tailgating* me for a while.「しばらくの間、僕の後ろの車［後続車］はあおり運転をしている」。☆ malicious tailgating（悪質なあおり運転）▶ The accident was caused by the *malicious tailgating* of a brutal driver.「その事故は凶悪ドライバーの悪質なあおり運転によって引き起こされた」☆改正道路交通法（2020年6月執行）によると、懲役3年以下か罰金50万円以下・免許取消（欠格期間2年）、著しい危険を生じる場合は懲役5年以下か罰金100万円以下・免許取消（欠格期間3年）である。

参考 b）「飲酒運転手」a drunk(en) driver
c）「無謀運転手」a reckless driver
d）「無免許運転手」an unlicensed driver

（5） **正解** **c）** 「富山湾は晴天の日に近場の海岸で見られる**蜃気楼**という珍しい自然現象で知られている」

解説 mirages「蜃気楼」▶ A *mirage* sometime shows up in Toyama Bay.「富山湾には時々蜃気楼が現れる」 *Mirages* are often seen on the streets on sunny days.「蜃気楼は晴れた日の路面によく見られる」☆ 2020年11月3日4年に1度の米大統領選挙の開票日に「レッドミラージュ（赤い蜃気楼）」(red mirage) という用語が何度も使用された。赤、つまり共和党の優勢が、開票が進むにつれて、消えていくことである。

参考 a）「波の花」sea [ocean] foam; the crest of a wave
b）「流氷」an ice floe; a drift ice; a floating ice
d）「虹」a rainbow

【Part B】

(6) **正解** **d)** I had the worst experience with **turbulence** during the flight.

解説 turbulence「乱気流」。air turbulence とも言う。▶ clear-air turbulence [CAT]「晴天の乱気流」。ジェット機などの通過に伴う急激な温度の変化で起きる乱気流。 Please keep your seatbelt on against sudden *turbulence*.「突然の乱気流に備えて座席ベルトをお締めください」

参考 a) air-conditioning「空気調節」 b) oxygen shortage「酸欠」 c) sudden descent「急降下」

(7) **正解** **d)** According to my **travel itinerary**, the overnight train arrives in Amsterdam early in the morning.

解説 travel itinerary「旅程日程表」。itinerary「旅程」(= tour schedule) ▶ What's next on our *itinerary*?「私たちの観光の予定で次はどこですか」(**予定**) What does the *itinerary* say?「旅程では何と書いてありますか」(**内容**) ☆ revised itinerary「改訂（後の）旅程」▶ We'd like you to send us the *revised itinerary* by return fax.「折り返しファックスで改訂旅程を送ってください」

参考 a) e-ticket receipt「E チケット受領書」☆ E-ticket [e-ticket]「E チケット」、electronic airline ticket「電子航空券」
   b) flight information「飛行機情報」
   c) travel account「旅行記」

(8) **正解** **d)** I'm looking for the Japanese **Consulate** General in Rome.

解説 consulate「領事館」。consulate general「総領事館」▶ You can get a visa at the *consulate*.「ビザ [査証] は領事館で受け取れます」☆ consular **形**「領事の」▶ *consular* section「(大使館の) 領事部」 *consular* agent「領事代理」 *consular* assistant「領事官補」

参考 a) Ambassador「大使」☆直接の呼びかけは Your Excellency「閣下」、間接的な呼びかけは His Excellency「閣下」と言う。▶ the *ambassador* in [at] Washington「ワシントン駐在大使」 *ambassador* of friendship「親善大使」 *ambassador* of goodwill「親善使節」(= goodwill ambassador) acting *ambassador*「代理大使」
   b) Embassy「大使館」
   c) Consul「領事」▶ *consul* general「総領事」 acting *consul*「代理領事」

(9) **正解** **d)** The Kurobe **Ravine** is noted for the beauty of rugged mountains and the rushing waters of the river Kurobe.

解説 **Ravine**「峡谷」（= a canyon; a valley）。ravine「両側が絶壁となっている谷間」▶ Kurobe *Ravine*（黒部渓谷）。canyon「深く切り立った絶壁の谷間」▶ Grand *Canyon*（グランドキャニオン）。valley「両側を山に囲まれたなだらかで広い平地で，その中を川が流れる谷間」▶ Akikawa *Valley*（秋川渓谷）☆【日本三大峡谷】The Three Largest Gorges in Japan ① 黒部峡谷（富山県・中部山岳国立公園内にある）② 大杉谷（三重県・吉野熊野国立公園内にある）③ 清津峡（新潟県・上信越高原国立公園内にある）

参考 a) Cliff「断崖」▶ perpendicular *cliff*「切り立った絶壁」
b) Moat「堀・濠」▶ the *moat* around a castle「城の周辺の堀」
c) Rapids「急流」（複数形で）☆【日本三大急流】the Three Fastest Rapids in Japan ① 最上川（山形県：229km）② 富士川（静岡県・山梨県・長野県：128km）③ 球磨川《熊本県：115km》

(10) **正解** **b)** Tottori Sand **Dunes** stretch along the Japan Sea coast for 16 km from east to west and 2 km from north to south.

解説 (Sand) **Dunes**「砂丘」▶ coast(al) *dune*「海岸砂丘」 desert *dune*「砂漠砂丘」 inland *dune*「内陸砂丘」☆【日本三大砂丘】the Three Noted Sand Dunes in Japan ① 鳥取砂丘（鳥取県）② 南遠大砂丘（静岡県）③ 吹上浜砂丘（鹿児島県）

参考 a) Cape「岬」
c) Plateau「高原」
d) (Sand) Spit「砂嘴」（湾［岸］の一方から細長く突き出た砂堤状の地形）▶ The *sand spit* in the Notsuke(zaki) Peninsula「野付崎の砂嘴」（長さ約 28km の分岐砂嘴で，日本最大）

Column 01

手荷物

　米国では **baggage**、英国では **luggage** と区別する傾向があるが、英国でも飛行機や船舶の手荷物は baggage を用いている。また米国でも航空会社関係者が luggage を用いることもあり、空港の掲示物にもよく見かけられる。

　baggage の個数を表すときは How many pieces of baggage do you have?（荷物はいくつですか）、または How much baggage do you have? と表現する。How many baggages [luggages] do you have? とは言わない。また I have three pieces of baggage [luggage] with me.（手荷物を 3 個持っています）であって、three baggages [luggages] とは言わない。「少しの荷物」は a little baggage（a few baggages ではない）、「たくさんの荷物」は much [a lot of] baggage（many baggages ではない）と言う。

　空港でのチェックイン（搭乗手続）カウンターで処理する荷物は主として**機内持ち込み手荷物** (accompanied baggage；carry-on baggage; unchecked baggage) と**委託［別送］手荷物** (unaccompanied baggage；checked baggage) の 2 種に大別される。

【Part A】

(11) 正解 **a)** A：到着するのに 4 時間も遅れるなんて信じられません。私が利用する乗継便に乗り遅れたこと知っていますか。私は今何をすべきですか。

B：はい、理解できます。**ご迷惑をおかけしてもう一度お詫び申し上げます。**ホテル宿泊のクーポン券を提供し、次回利用できる便を確約致します。

解説 空港 A（乗客）は、飛行機が 4 時間遅れて到着したため、接続便に乗り損ねたと苦情を述べている。空港でよく経験する状況である。B は補償を約束しているので空港職員と推測できる。苦境対応としてまずすることは謝罪と考えられる。したがって a) が正解。

参考 b)「お話する時にはマネージャーに謝ってもらいたいです」

c)「前もって電話をして飛行機は予定どおりかどうかを調べます」

d)「幸いにも会議には間に合うようになっています」

☆ connecting flight「接続便」 provide（人）with（物）「（人）に（物）を提供する」 apologize for (inconvenience)「（不便を）詫びる、謝る」

---

(12) 正解 **d)** A：12 月 13 日と 14 日に予約をしたいのです。ツインまたはダブルを希望します。

B：申し訳ございませんが、その日取りは満室です。今後は、いつでもウェブサイトで利用可能かどうかチェックしてご予約いただくことができます。失礼ながら、**またいつの日かご利用いただけることを心待ちにしております。**

解説 ホテル A（宿泊者）は、12 月に部屋を予約しようとする。B（受付）は、その希望する日取りが無理であることを告げる。予約を断る際に告げるお詫びの文言が最適。したがって d) が正解。

参考 a)「数枚チケットが残っているだけです」

b)「宴会場はすべて利用できます」

c)「支払いはクレジットカードあるいは現金でも結構です」

☆ be filled to capacity「定員がいっぱいである、満室［満席、満員］である」 look forward to (doing)「（するのを）楽しみに待つ」

---

(13) 正解 **d)** A：半日ツアーは 26 ユーロ、そして終日ツアーはランチ込みで 50 ユーロです。ツアーは午後 6 時には戻ります。非常に楽しいツアーです。

B：**終日ツアーにする時間は十分にはとれません。**午前ツアーの大人 1 枚と子供 2 枚のチケットを頂けるでしょうか。

解説 旅行代理店　A（受付）は半日ツアーと終日ツアーを案内し終日ツアーをお薦めしている。B（観光客）は午前の半日ツアーにすると言っており、その理由を述べていると推測できる。したがって d) が正解。

参考 a)「おお、本当に素敵なようです」
　　　 b)「全員で4人になります」
　　　 c)「よろしければ昼食を自参しようと思います」
　　　 ☆ half-day tour「半日ツアー」　full-day tour「終日ツアー」

(14) **正解** **d)**　A： 富士山は通常この季節は非常に美しいと聞き及んでいます。でも、東京からはかなり遠いようです。どの鉄道路線を利用すればよいのかよくわかりません。
　　　　　　　　B： 実際にはそこに行くにはそれほど難しくはないのです。**最も簡単な方法は新宿から急行バスに乗ることです。**

解説 観光　A（外国人）は、富士山を見に行きたい様子である。しかし電車での行き方がわからないと嘆いている。B（日本人）は、行くのは難しくないと言っているので簡単な行き方を告げると予測できる。したがって d) が正解。

参考 a)「実際にはこの季節は路線も短時間で行けます」
　　　 b)「最も安い方法を利用すれば多く節約できます」
　　　 c)「東京に着く最も賢い方法は電車を利用することです」
　　　 ☆ figure out「理解する、計算する」　get to (Tokyo)「（東京に）着く」

(15) **正解** **c)**　A：祇園祭は初めてですか。
　　　　　　　　B：はい。**大通りに沿って進む山車**を見るのを本当に楽しみにしています。

解説 観光　A（日本人）は、B（外国人）に京都の祇園祭を見るのは初めてかどうかを尋ねる。Bは、見るのは初めてであり、あるものを見ることを楽しみにしていると返答している。祇園祭で見ることのできるものは、選択肢 c) が適当である。

参考 a)「最新のアニメ」
　　　 b)「空中に舞う色彩豊かな鯉幟」
　　　 d)「夜川に浮かぶ提灯」
　　　 ☆ carp streamer「鯉幟」　festive float「山車」　proceed「進む、進行する」　float (in the river)「（水上に）浮かぶ」

【Part B】

(16) **正解** **c)** A：私共のツアーメンバーの1人は明日医者に診察してもらう必要があります。彼女は数分前にもまた吐きました。胃腸炎のようです。

　　　　　　　　B：食中毒のことですか。インフルエンザではないでしょうか。

　　　　　　　　A：そんなはずはないです。ここ数時間で**彼女は4回もおう吐した**のです。彼女には熱がありません。

解説 **観光** Aは、ツアーメンバーの1人が病気になり再度食べ物を吐く病状を告げる。Bは「インフルエンザではないか」と返答する。Aは、彼女は熱がないのを告げており、インフルエンザではない病状を説明していると考えられる。したがってc) が正解。

参考 a)「彼女はサービスについて不満を言った」

　　　b)「彼女は乗り継ぎに間に合わなかった」

　　　d)「彼女はたくさん食べていた」

　　　☆ vomit「吐く」　infection「感染」　food poisoning「食中毒」　flu「流感、インフルエンザ (influenza)」　(have) a fever「熱 (がある)」　complain「不満を言う」　connection「接続、乗り継ぎ」　throw up「おう吐する」

(17) **正解** **a)** A：今日町の広場に行き、下町を少し散策しながら買い物をするつもりです。

　　　　　　　　B：そうね、**混雑した場所ではスリには用心しなさい**。最近では特に財布や携帯電話の盗難が多発しています。しっかり両手でバッグを握ってなさいよ。

　　　　　　　　A：ありがとう。そのようにします。

解説 **外国での観光** A（日本人）は、町に買い物に行くことを告げる。B（外国人）は、盗難が多発していることと、その予防対策を助言しているのでスリに気をつけるべきと忠告していると考えられる。したがってa) が正解。

参考 b)「顧客に不当な値段を請求するレストランには用心しなさい」

　　　c)「天候の急変には気をつけなさい」

　　　d)「治療を要する怪我を避けるように注意しなさい」

　　　☆ theft「盗難」　pickpocket「スリ」　beware of「用心する」　watch out「気をつける」　take care「注意する」　avoid「避ける」　medical attention「治療」

(18) **正解** **b)** A：この周辺に（ペット）ボトルに入った飲料水が入手できる場所がありますか。レストランでの水は飲みたくないのです。

　　　　　　　　B：実は、この国では**水道水**はかなり安全です。またかなり美味しいとの定評です。

さらには無料です。

A：本当ですか。

解説 **観光**　A（外国人）は、ペットボトル入りの水を探している。レストランの水は警戒している様子である。B（日本人）は、当地の水は安全で無料だと告げている。推定できる正解は b)。

参考 a)「ミネラルウォーター」　c)「炭酸水」　d)「缶詰の水」
☆ bottled water「ペットボトルに入った水」　tap water「水道水」

---

(19) **正解** **c)**　A：滞在中**自由に選択できる素敵な料理が多数**あります。

B：いろいろ食べてみるのを本当に楽しみにしていたのでとても嬉しいです。

A：特にランチタイムには懐石料理が本当にお薦めです。しかし地元名物のようなもの食べたいならば、ラーメンを試すのもよいでしょう。駅周辺には素敵な小さい店が多数あります。長蛇の列をなすところを探してみてください。

解説 **観光**　A（日本人）はB（外国人）に対して、ランチの懐石料理やラーメンを食べることをお勧めしていることから話題は食事に関することと考えられる。したがって c) が正解。

参考 a)「希望する観光地すべてを訪れることができます」
b)「私たちはあなたのために豪華な宿泊施設を選びました」
d)「ハイライトは間違いなくヘリへの搭乗です」
☆ try (the *ramen*)「（ラーメンを）試食する」　look for「〜を探す」　options「選択肢」

---

(20) **正解** **b)**　A：山頂で燃える大きな漢字が見られる日本の祭りを見物したいのです。

B：「大文字焼き」のことだと思います。実のところ日本周辺には多数の祭りがあります。最も有名なものはおそらく京都です。しかしその祭事は**お盆行事の一環として夏季に行われます。**

A：残念だな。次回はその季節に来るようにします。

解説 **観光**　A（外国人）は、山頂に燃える大きな漢字を見たいと言っている。B（日本人）は、大文字五山の送り火のことだと言う。この祭事は8月16日に京都で行われる日本古来の祖先崇拝の行事なので b) が正解。

参考 a)「現在、可燃物を使用することは禁止されています」
c)「年中週末ごとに行われます」
d)「友人や家族用のお土産として購入できます」
☆ flammable (materials)「可燃（物）」　take place「行われる」

(21) 正解 a) Europe is the most **popular tourism destination** in the world.
ヨーロッパは世界で最も人気のある観光目的地である。

解説 the most「最も、いちばん」は many、much の最上級で、形容詞・副詞を修飾する。選択肢を見ると形容詞は popular「人気のある」のみである。in は the world と関連し、in the world「世界中で」となる。「観光地」のことは英語で tourist destination、「観光目的地」は tourism destination。定番である。☆ ① the most beautiful city「最も美しい都市」② a most difficult question「とても［非常に］難しい質問」③ eat most of food「ほとんどの食べ物を食べる」

---

(22) 正解 d) Many of the tourists who visit European countries **come** from **faraway places** like North America, Japan, or increasingly, China.
ヨーロッパを訪れる多くの観光客は北米、日本、あるいは増加途上の中国といったような遠い国々からやって来る。

解説「主語（tourists）＋動詞（come）」の基本文型に着眼する。あとは副詞句を検討する。from は come と関連し come from「～から来る」を構成する。faraway は far「遠い」と away「離れて」が結合した形容詞である。そして名詞の前にのみ使用する（限定用法）。したがって come from faraway places となる。

---

(23) 正解 c) Well, many people visit European countries to see old things: old **buildings such as cathedrals** or castles, old museums with old paintings or artifacts, or old monuments.
大勢の人々は、大聖堂や城塞、古来の絵画や工芸品を収蔵した古い博物館、あるいは古代記念物といったような昔の建造物を観光するためヨーロッパ諸国を訪れる。

解説 such as の語句に関する知識を問われている。such as は「～のような」と例を挙げるときに使い、such as に続くのは名詞または動名詞である。buildings「建物」の例として cathedrals「大聖堂」が挙げられているので、buildings such as cathedrals となる。
▶ She carries a bag *such as* a suitcase.「彼女はスーツケースのようなカバンを運んでいる」

---

(24) 正解 a) Many years ago, few **people** could travel.
何年も前のことだが、旅行できる人々は少なかった。

解説 「主語（people）＋動詞（travel）」の基本文型である。この文のポイントは few「ほとんどない」に関する知識である。few は名詞の前につき、否定（negative）の意味となる。▶ There are *few* students in the classroom today.「今日の教室には生徒はほとんどいない」☆ a few は肯定（positive）の意味である。▶ There are *a few* students in the classroom today.「今日の教室には生徒は何人かいる」

---

(25) **正解** **b)** That **is one reason** why Italy, especially Rome became so popular and famous.

このことがイタリア、特にローマが非常に人気を博して有名になった**理由の 1 つである。**

解説 This is the reason why S+V.「それが、S が V だという理由である」の慣用句の知識である。▶ *This is the reason why* he took an English proficiency test.「これが、彼が英語検定試験を受験した理由です」また、For this reason, he sat for a test. もっと簡潔には That's why he took an exam. と表現する。

【Part A】

(26) 「 ① に該当する最も適切な単語を選びなさい」

正解 **b)** **landmarks** 「ランドマーク、名所旧跡」

解説 空所前を読むと、ツアーではサウンド・オブ・ミュージックの見所の他に、その町や湖水地方の歴史的、建築的な何かを見ることができるとわかる。観光で訪れる場所は名所旧跡と考えられる。したがって b) が正解。

参考 a) staples 「主要産物、基本食料品」

　　　 c) contents 「内容（物）、趣意」

　　　 d) replicas 「レプリカ、原作の写し」

　　　 ☆ landmark 「（地上の）目印、陸標、史跡」。その土地［地域］の目印や象徴にあるような建造物。日本三大ランドマーク（観光スポット）は金閣寺、伏見稲荷大社、原爆ドーム（すべてユネスコ世界遺産）と言われる。

(27) 「 ② に該当する最も適切な単語を選びなさい」

正解 **d)** **explore** 「探検［探求］する、散策する」

解説 空所の後には場所を表す語句がきている。その場所で何をするか考えると、最適なものは d)「探検する、散策する」である。

参考 a) qualify 「資格を与える［得る］」

　　　 b) assure 「保証する」

　　　 c) contain 「含蓄する」

　　　 ☆ explore 「散策する」　▶ *explore* the street of Nottingham 「ノッティンガム路地を散策する」

(28) 「ミラベル庭園で撮影されたシーン（映画場面）は何ですか」

正解 **d)** **The song "Do-RE-Mi" scene** 「『ドレミの歌』を歌うシーン」

解説 ① **Mirabell Gardens** の 欄 に は、You will certainly have heard about Mirabell Gardens where **the song "Do-Re-Mi"** was filmed. 「**ドレミの歌**が撮影されたミラベル庭園についてきっと聞かれたことがおありでしょう」と記載されている。したがって d) が正解。

参考 a) 「有名なボートのシーン」

　　　 b) 「『もうすぐ17歳』の歌を歌うシーン」

　　　 c) 「ピクニックのシーン」

(29)「サウンド・オブ・ミュージック・ツアーに関する**正しい記述**はどれですか」

正解 **b)** 「ツアー価格はユーロで提示されている」

解説 • Price: €40 Adult €20 Child (4-12)「価格：40 **ユーロ** 大人　20 **ユーロ** 子供（4-12 歳）」と記載されている。したがって b) が正解。

参考 以下すべて**正しくない記述**である。

 a)「ツアーは午後 9 時 15 分に出発し、午後 2 時に解散する」ツアーの開始時刻は午前 9 時 15 分と午後 2 時で、所要時間は 4 時間である。

 c)「当日の最後のツアーは午後 4 時に出発する」ツアーは午前 9 時 15 分と午後 2 時に始まる 2 回のみ。

 d)「参加者は午前 9 時 15 分に集合場所にいること」参加者はツアー開始 30 分前に集合する。

(30)「サウンド・オブ・ミュージック・ツアーに関する**正しくない記述**はどれですか」

正解 **b)** ヘルブルン宮殿には映画ファンのために新設された建物がある。

解説 ③ **Hellbrunn Palace, Gazebo** の欄には、the gazebo which was moved from Leopoldskron Palace to the current location「映画ファンのためにレオポルズクローン宮殿から現在地に移転させたパビリオンの一種であるガゼボ（gazebo）」と記載されている。新設した建物ではない。ちなみに、このガゼボでは長女リーズルと恋人ロルフが『もうすぐ 17 歳』（Sixteen Going on Seventeen）を歌い相互の愛を確かめる。また主人公マリアとトラップ大佐ゲオルクが『何かいいこと』（Something Good）を歌い、相互の愛を告白する。

参考 以下すべて**正しい記述**である。

 a) 映画の有名なボートのシーンが撮影された湖に写真を撮影するために立ち寄る。

 c) ノンベルク修道院はマリアとトラップ大佐が実際に結婚式を挙げた場所である。

 d) ザルツブルグ市内観光のあとはピクニックシーンなどが撮影された湖水地方へ向かう。

【Part B】

(31)「 ① に該当する最も適切な単語を選びなさい」

正解 **d)** **exhibition** 「展示」

解説 大塚国際美術館が持つ日本最大級のものが何かを選択肢から考える。permanent exhibition で「常設展示」。したがって d) が正解。

参考 a) prohibition「禁止」

 b) compensation「補償」

c) participation「参加」

---

(32)「　　②　　に該当する最も適切な単語を選びなさい」

正解 **a) appreciate**「鑑賞する」

解説 空所前後から、来館者が原作の芸術的価値を真に味わうためにどうするのか選択肢から考える。したがって a) が正解。

参考 b) describe「記述する」
c) enclose「取り囲む」
d) consume「消費する」

---

(33)「大塚国際美術館は ＿＿＿＿＿＿ によって創業された」

正解 **a) a private company**「民間企業」

解説 The Otsuka Museum of Art is a "Ceramic board masterpiece art museum" with the largest permanent exhibition space in Japan (total floor of 29,412 square meters), built to commemorate the Otsuka Group 75th anniversary in Naruto City, Tokushima Prefecture.「大塚国際美術館は、国内最大級の常設展示スペースを有する陶板名画美術館であり、大塚グループの創立 75 周年記念事業として徳島県鳴門市に設立された」の内容から大塚国際美術館は、他選択肢の国や自治体が創立したのではないことがわかる。したがって a) が正解。

参考 b) Tokushima Prefecture「徳島県」
c) the government of Japan「日本政府」
d) Tokushima City「徳島市」

---

(34)「大塚国際美術館に関する**正しくない記述**はどれですか」

正解 **a)** 「1,000 を越えるオリジナルの傑作が収集されている」

解説 本文には、there are more than 1,000 replicas of priceless masterpieces of Western art「西洋芸術における不朽の傑作の 1,000 以上のレプリカがある」と記載されている。特に These masterpieces are reproduced to their original size using special techniques by the Otsuka Ohmi Ceramics Co., Ltd.「これらの名作は、大塚オーミ陶業株式会社の特殊技術によってオリジナル作品と同じ大きさに複製している」とあり、オリジナルの収集ではない。したがって a) が正解。

参考 以下の記載は**正しい記述**である。

b)「各傑作は原型サイズで複製されている」

c)「芸術家の子供は作品の品質を調べるために来館した」

d)「陶板複製画は 2000 年以上に及んで持続できる」

(35)「大塚国際美術館に関する**正しい記述**はどれですか」

正解 d) 学生は入場の際に学生証を見せなくてはならない。

解説 Basic Information 欄 の 文 尾 に、Students must show their student ID at the entrance.「学生は入り口で学生証を提示する必要がある」と明記されている。したがって d) が正解。

参考 以下すべて**正しくない記述**である。

a) 月曜日と正月、お盆の 5 日間が休館日である。8 月中は開館していると記載されている。

b) 最終入館時間は 5 時である。開館時間は午前 9 時 30 分から午後 5 時までである。

c) チケット代金に消費税は含まれていない。消費税込の価格が記載されている。

【Part C】

(36)「　(36)　に該当する最も適切な単語を選びなさい」

正解 a) tonne(s)「メートルトン」(meter [metric] ton)。略 t。(40t)

解説 ガイドは手綱の大きさを説明している。空所前には weigh over 40 とあることから重さを表す単位を選択肢から選ぶ。したがって a) が正解。

参考 b) length「長さ」 c) height「高さ」 d) width「幅」

(37)「　(37)　に該当する最も適切な単語を選びなさい」

正解 c) certified「認定する」(certify)

解説 空所前後は「ギネスブックが手綱を世界最大のものと _____ した」という意味である。「認定する」というような意味を持つ単語が入ると推測できる。したがって c) が正解。
☆1997年ギネスブック(正式名所 Guinness World Records)では「手綱」だけでなく「15,000人の挽き手」を認定記録した。

参考 a) qualified「資格を与える」(qualify)

b) renovated「刷新する」(renovate)

d) interpreted「通訳する」(interpret)

(38) 「 (38) に該当する最も適切な単語を選びなさい」

正解 **b) connecting**「結合する」

解説 空所前のガイドの説明 (They are tying the rope together.) で、女綱と男綱を結んでいることがわかる。tie（結ぶ）と似た意味を持つ選択肢を選ぶ。したがって b) が正解。

参考 a) separating「分離する」
c) adjoining「合併する」
d) cutting「切断する」

(39) 「 (39) に該当する最も適切な語句を選びなさい」

正解 **a) lead**「指揮する」

解説 空所前のガイドの説明で、東西チームにはそれぞれリーダーがいることがわかる。そのリーダーが各自のチームに何をするのか考えると解答を選ぶことができる。したがって a) が正解。

参考 b) replace「交換する」
c) explore「探求する」
d) increase「増加する」

(40) 「 (40) に該当する最も適切な単語を選びなさい」

正解 **a) exhausted**「疲れきった」

解説 空所前のガイドの説明 (The actual contest can take 20 or 30 minutes.) で、大綱挽きの勝負がつくまでに 20 〜 30 分かかることがわかる。どの参加者も疲れてへとへとになると推測できる。したがって a) が正解。

参考 b) exchanged「交換する」
c) worried「苦悩する」
d) waiting「待機する」

5　海外観光と国内観光の問題

【Part A】

(41) **正解**　**d)**　**Mont-Saint-Michel（Mount St. Michael）**「モン・サン＝ミシェル」。
1979 年ユネスコ世界遺産に登録。

和訳　モン・サン＝ミシェルは、築堤道によって本土と繋がっている岩の小島である。フランスにおける有名な巡礼地としてよく知られている。708 年に大天使聖ミカエルの啓示（お告げ）に従って司教によってゴシック様式のベネディクト修道院の建築が始まり、16 世紀に完成された。修道院の壮観な建物と湾は毎年多数の来訪者を惹きつける有名な観光名所となっている。

解説　解法のカギは、「大天使聖ミカエルのお告げを受けて建造された修道院」があること。
☆「ミカエル」はフランス語で「ミシェル」(Michel)、英語で「マイケル」(Michael) と言う。

参考　以下はフランスの由緒ある観光地である。
- a) Côte d'Azur (French Riviera)「コート・ダジュール」。南フランスにある、風光明媚な保養地として知られる海岸。バカンス（長期休暇）が楽しめる国際的に有名な観光地。
- b) Val de Loire (Loire Valley)「ロワール渓谷」。フランスのロワール川流域に広がる渓谷。シャンボール城（世界遺産）といったような名城が多数点在する。
- c) Île-de-France (Island of France)「イル・ド・フランス（地域区）」。フランスの首都パリを中心とした由緒ある地区のこと。

(42) **正解**　**d)**　**Yellowstone**「イエローストーン（国立公園）」。世界遺産に登録。

和訳　イエローストーン国立公園はワイオミング州北西部に位置し、1872 年米国政府によって指定された最初の国立公園である。アメリカ最後の野生バイソン(バッファロー)の群れが牧草地をのどかに歩き回っている。来園者は公園の美しい景色の中をドライブしながら多種多様なアメリカ先住の野生動物を容易に見つけることができる。

解説　解法のカギは、「ワイオミング州」と「米国政府によって指定された最初の国立公園」、そして「バイソンの群れ」である。

参考　以下アメリカ屈指の国立公園、そしてユネスコ世界遺産に登録。
- a) Grand Canyon「グランド・キャニオン（国立公園）」。アリゾナ州北部にある峡谷。展望橋 (skywalk) からの眺望は圧巻。
- b) Mesa Verde「メサ・ヴェルデ（国立公園）」。コロラド州南西部にある集落遺跡群。断崖をくり抜いた 12 世紀頃の住宅遺跡群が点在する。
- c) Yosemite「ヨセミテ（国立公園）」。カリフォルニア州中央部にある国立公園。グレーシャーポイントからは多数の滝や峡谷が一望できる。

(43) **正解** **c)** **Sistine Chapel**「システィーナ礼拝堂」

和訳 **システィーナ礼拝堂**は、1473 年にバチカン宮殿内にローマ教皇シクストゥス 4 世のために建立された。ミケランジェロは**システィーナ礼拝堂**の天井に、旧約聖書に登場する場面を描いた。ヴォールト（かまぼこのようなアーチ状の）天井にある『創世記』と末端壁にある『最後の審判』のミケランジェロの優れたフレスコ画は修復された。天井画には 4 年を要し、24 年後には『最後の審判』を描いたのである。

解説 解法のカギは、ミケランジェロの傑作である「天地創造」と「最後の審判」のフレスコ画である。

参考 以下はイタリア有数の壮観な大聖堂である。
- a) Milan Cathedral「ミラノ大聖堂」（= Duomo di Milano）。ロンバルディア州都ミラノにある大聖堂。世界最大級のゴシック建築である。135 本の尖塔がある。
- b) San Marco Basilica「サン・マルコ寺院（大聖堂）」。ヴェネト州の州都ヴェネツィア（英語ではベニス）で最も有名な大聖堂。世界遺産「ヴェネツィアとその潟」の観光名所。
- d) St. Peter's Basilica「サン・ピエトロ大聖堂」。世界遺産「バチカン市国」にある大聖堂。世界最大級の教会堂建築である。

---

(44) **正解** **a)** **Bone** (china)「ボーン（チャイナ）」

和訳 **ボーンチャイナ**とは、高レベルの白色度で有名な陶磁器の一種である。さらには、非常に強度なため、一般の陶磁器よりデリケートな食器を製造するのに使用されている。1748 年英国で発展し、洗練された英国文化を連想させる。最も有名なブランドには、ロイヤルドルトン、それにウェッジウッドといったようなものがあり、国際的にもよく知られている。

解説 解法のカギは、china（小文字で書く。陶器の意味）である。bone は「骨」の意味で、この磁器の原料の粘土に牛の骨を焼いた骨灰が多数含まれているため、ボーンチャイナは「骨灰磁器」とも言われる。

参考 b) Afternoon tea「午後の紅茶」
c) Wool「ウール、羊毛、毛糸」
d) Lace「レース、締め［組み］紐」

---

(45) **正解** **a)** **Carnival**「カーニバル（謝肉祭）」

和訳 リオデジャネイロはブラジル第 3 の都市である。リオの**カーニバル**は四旬節の期間に入る前に 4 日間行われる。この期間中で最も壮観なイベントはサンバ・パレードである。派手な衣装を纏ったサンバダンサーたちがサンバドロームで身体を揺らす時**カーニバル**の祭りは最高潮に達する。世界的に有名なブラジルのリオの**カーニバル**と同様に**カーニバル**が毎年、南米各地で開催される。

解説 解法のカギは、「リオデジャネイロ」「サンバ」である。

参考 以下いずれも世界有数の祭典である。

    b）Easter「イースター」（復活祭）。十字架上で死去したイエス・キリストが三日目に復活したことを記念するキリスト教の祝日。カトリック教会で「復活の主日」とも言う。

    c）Halloween「ハロウィン」。10月31日のハロウィンは、秋の収穫を祝い、先祖の霊を迎えるとともに悪魔を追い払うお祭りである。

    d）masquerade「マスカレード」（仮面舞踏会）。イタリアのヴェネツィアが発祥地で、仮面をかぶって年に一度開催されるヴェネツィア・カーニバルは世界的に有名。

【Part B】

(46) 正解 a) Byodo-in「平等院」（ユネスコ世界遺産）

和訳 平等院は、1052年に藤原家の別荘から仏閣に転じたものである。1053年に建立された鳳凰堂は、唯一の現存物であり、日本で最も美しい建造物の1つとされている。（名前の由来の鳳凰の）胴は中央の本堂によって、翼は側面の廊下によって、そして尾は後部の廊下によって表現されている。内陣には蓮の形に座した阿弥陀像が安置されている。

解説 解法のカギは、内陣に阿弥陀像を安置した「鳳凰堂」があることである。

参考 以下すべて京都市にある寺院。

    b）Chion-in「知恩院」。東山区にある浄土宗総本山の寺院。開基（創立者）は法然上人。三門（国宝）は現存するものとして国内最大級の寺門。

    c）Jakko-in「寂光院」。左京区大原にある天台宗の寺院。開基は聖徳太子と伝わる。『平家物語』ゆかりの地として知られる尼寺。

    d）Nanzen-ji「南禅寺」。左京区にある臨済宗南禅寺派大本山の寺院。開基は亀山法皇。三門は国内最大級の高さを誇る。

(47) 正解 a) Jodoga-hama「浄土ヶ浜」

和訳 三陸復興国立公園は、日本の最も美しい海浜公園の1つである。公園は青森県から岩手県を経て宮城県までの220kmにも及んでいる。海岸の自然公園の美しさから、別名「海のアルプス」と呼ばれている。浄土ケ浜は長くて白い海岸と断崖絶壁の奇岩、緑の松林が美しいコントラストをなしている。

解説 三陸復興国立公園は当初1955年「陸中海岸国立公園」に指定された。その後2011年の東日本大震災と津波によって被災した三陸地域の復興に寄与するため2013年には「三陸復興国立公園」に改称された。☆「浄土ヶ浜」岩手県宮古市。三陸海岸（陸奥・陸中・陸前）の中で大部分は岩手に属する。海岸線が屈曲し、数多くの湾入と岬が続くリアス式海岸として知られる。浄土ヶ浜は三陸復興国立公園の代表的な景勝である。奇岩怪石の中でもロー

ソク岩（Candle Rock）と潮吹穴（Salt Spraying Hole）は特に有名。

参考 下記は日本有数の海浜である。

    b) Katsura-hama「桂浜」。高知県にある太平洋に臨む海岸。昔から月の名所で知られる。海辺には太平洋を望んで立つ坂本龍馬の銅像がある。

    c) Kujukuri-hama「九十九里浜」。千葉県にある太平洋沿岸に面する日本最大級の砂浜海岸（全長66km）。

    d) Shichiriga-hama「七里ヶ浜」。神奈川県鎌倉市にある浜。鎌倉幕府の滅亡と関連する稲村ケ崎古戦場（国の史跡）として有名な浜。

(48) **正解** c) **Risshaku-ji**「立石寺」

和訳 立石寺は、東北地方における天台宗最大の寺である。京都の延暦寺の別院として860年に円仁（慈覚大師）によって創建された。1,015段の急な石段を登った山頂にある寺である。ここは春の桜と秋の紅葉の名所でもある。

解説 解法のカギは、「東北地方天台宗最大の寺」「円仁（慈覚大師）」。立石寺は山形県山形市にある天台宗の寺院。山号は宝珠山、本尊は薬師如来。この寺に不朽の名句を詠んだ俳人芭蕉が（1689年に旅の途中に）訪れたことでもよく知られている。「閑さや岩にしみ入る蝉の声」。

参考 下記は東北地方にある由緒ある寺院である。

    a) Chuson-ji「中尊寺」。岩手県にある天台宗東北大本山の寺院。開基は藤原清衡。清衡が建立した阿弥陀堂・中尊寺金色堂（国宝）がある。（世界遺産）

    b) Motsu-ji「毛越寺」。岩手県にある天台宗の寺院。境内には平安時代の優美な浄土庭園（国の特別史跡）がある。（世界遺産）

    d) Zuigan-ji「瑞巌寺」（国宝）。宮城県にある臨済宗妙心寺派の禅宗寺院。伊達家の菩提寺で、桃山時代の真髄を表す荘厳な建物である。日本三景の1つである松島の古刹。

(49) **正解** d) **Noh**「能」

和訳 能は古典的な能衣装や能面をまとって演じるハイセンスな日本古来の演劇。「舞い」・「謡」・「囃子」の見事な三位一体をなす。室町時代初頭に足利義満の支援のもと観阿弥と世阿弥が能の理論を確立する。

参考 a) Bunraku「文楽」

    b) Kabuki「歌舞伎」

    c) Gagaku「雅楽」 ☞ **Column 02 文楽・歌舞伎・雅楽**（p.68）

(50) **正解** **b)** **Chichibu-Yomatsuri**「秩父夜祭」

和訳 秩父夜祭の特色は提灯で華麗に飾られた「屋台」4台と美しい彫刻を刻んだ「笠鉾」2台の行列。クライマックスは夜に山車と笠鉾が神輿とともに一気に急な坂（団子坂）を上るところ。夜に山車の提灯がともされ幻想の世界に一変する。

解説 解法のカギは、豪華な「屋台」と華麗な「傘鉾」である。特に夜に「山車」が団子坂を上る壮観な様相が特徴である。

参考 下記は、夜に行われる日本屈指の祭典である。

a) Nachi-no-Himatsuri「那智の火祭」。和歌山県・熊野那智大社の火祭（400年の伝統祭事）。ハイライトは石段を上る、大松明12本を持つ白装束の僧侶の一団と、熊野那智大社から下る、扇神輿12基を担ぐ一団との出会いである。火の海のような壮観な光景を呈する。

c) Yamaga-Toro-Matsuri「山鹿灯籠祭」。熊本県山鹿市・大宮神社の祭（700年の伝統祭事）。千人の浴衣姿の女性が五重塔型の金銀の燈籠を頭にのせて、夜から朝までゆるりと踊る千人灯籠踊りが続く。頭の上でゆっくりと優雅にゆらぐ灯火灯籠は幻想的である。

d) Yoshida-no-Himatsuri「吉田の火祭」。山梨県・富士吉田市の祭。別名「鎮火大祭」「富士浅間神社火祭り」。富士山の山じまいの祭り。日中は富士山の形をした神輿の渡御。夜には大きな松明80本余に点火される。

文楽・歌舞伎・雅楽

以下の芸能は能楽を含め、ユネスコ無形文化遺産（UNESCO Intangible Cultural Property）に登録されている。

① **Bunraku**「文楽」the classical puppet theater

The Japanese classical puppet show created through the narrative reciting of the *tayu* [narrator] and *shamisen* accompaniment. Bunraku features large costumed puppets which are manipulated by puppeteers on stage, three puppeteers who manipulate dolls on stage, and a narrator who speaks all the lines to the accompaniment of the *shamisen*.

「太夫」の語りと「三味線」の伴奏によって演出される操り人形の日本古来の芝居である。その特徴は衣装を装った大型の操り人形、舞台上の３人の人形遣いそして全台詞を語る「太夫」（a chanter who recite the story）の三業の調和である。

② **Kabuki**「歌舞伎」

KABUKI is a highly-stylized traditional Japanese play with singing and dancing. Kabuki was originally performed in Kyoto in 1603 by a miko shrine maiden at the Izumo-Taisha Shrine (known as Izumo no Okuni) as a religious dance with a prayer to Buddha (nenbutsu). After the Tokugawa shogunate prohibited women from playing in public because of concerns over public morals, the Kabuki has been performed exclusively by actors including female impersonators.

歌舞伎は、歌謡と舞踊を伴う日本古来の伝統的な劇である。1603 年 出雲大社の巫女（出雲の阿国）が「念仏踊り」（仏への祈りを込めた踊り）として京都で演じたのが歌舞伎の始まりとされる。徳川幕府は風紀の乱れを懸念して女性が公然と演技するのを禁止して以来、歌舞伎は女形を含め男優のみが演じるようになった。

③ **Gagaku**「雅楽」

Gagaku includes three forms of performances, which are the orchestral music performed with percussion, wind and string instruments (*Kangen*), an ancient court dance and music (*Bugaku*), and vocal music (*Kayo or utaimono*). Its venues include not only ceremonies at the Imperial court but also religious rites of both Buddhist temples and Shinto shrines.

雅楽には３つの演奏形式があり、打楽器・管楽器・絃楽器が演奏される「管弦（かんげん）」、宮廷を中心に行われる舞いを伴う「舞楽（ぶがく）」、そして声楽歌を主とする「謡物（うたいもの）/歌物」から成る。雅楽は皇居の儀式だけでなく寺社の祭祀などでも演じられる。

『和英：日本の文化・観光・歴史辞典［改訂版］』（山口百々男著、三修社）より

リスニング試験

6 「写真」による状況把握

音声の内容

1-02 (51) a) Each steeple of the church has a cross on the top.

b) The Romanesque architecture is magnificent.

c) There are many elaborate statues in front of the church.

d) A lot of high-rise buildings are towering in the sky.

1-03 (52) a) People are evacuating from a dangerous event.

b) The view of the powerful waterfall attracts a lot of tourists.

c) People are standing in torrential rain.

d) People are crossing the river against the rapids.

1-04 (53) a) The sign shows that smoking is allowed in a designated area.

b) A man with his luggage is talking to a station clerk.

c) Trains are standing on both platform 2 and 3.

d) A man with a child is checking the departure time of the trains.

1-05 (54) a) The rice paddy after harvesting is tranquil.

b) Art works of straw are exhibited in the garden.

c) Falling trees are supported by wooden poles.

d) Straw belts are wrapped around the trees.

1-06 (55) a) The gallery in the theater has no chairs.

b) A program is displayed above the stage.

c) Cedar trees are drawn on the back wall of the stage.

d) The museum houses important cultural assets.

解答と解説

(51) **正解** **a)** 「教会の各尖塔の頂上には十字架がある」

解説 欧米の教会 (church) また大聖堂 (cathedral) には十字架のある尖塔 (steeple) がある場合が多い。尖塔はロマネスク様式またゴシック様式の聖堂建築に多い。

b)「ロマネスク様式の建築は壮観である」

c)「教会の前には精巧な像が多数ある」

d)「多数の高層ビルが空高くそびえ立っている」

☆ steeple「尖塔」 magnificent「壮観な」 elaborate「精巧な」

---

(52) 正解　b)　「迫力ある滝の景観が大勢の観光客を魅了している」

解説 壮観な滝（waterfall）を眺めたり写真を撮っている観光客（tourists）がいる。a) 避難 (evacuate)、c) 集中豪雨 (torrential rains)、d) 川を横断 (cross the river) している様子はない。

参考 a)「大勢の人は危険なイベントから避難している」

c)「大勢の人は集中豪雨の中に立っている」

d)「大勢の人は急流に逆らって川を横断している」

☆ evacuate「避難する、疎開する」 torrential rain「集中豪雨」 rapids「急流」

---

(53) 正解　c)　「電車は2番線と3番線の両ホームに停車している」

解説 ターミナル駅の2番線と3番線のプラットホーム（platform）に電車が停車（stand）している。他の選択肢は駅舎の状況とは合致しない。☞ **Column 03 電車の種類**

参考 a)「看板は喫煙が指定場所で許可されていることを表示している」

b)「手荷物を持った男性が駅員に話している」

d)「子供と一緒にいる男性は列車の出発時刻を調べている」

☆ designated (area)「指定（地域）」

---

(54) 正解　d)　「わらの帯は樹木の周りを包んでいる」

解説 晩秋の頃、害虫から保護するためわらで作られた帯状の束（straw belts）を樹木の周りに巻きつける習慣がある。他の選択肢は写真の趣旨に合致しない。

参考 a)「収穫後の田んぼは平穏である」

b)「わらの芸術品が庭園に展示されている」

c)「倒れそうな樹木は木製の棒で支えられている」

☆ rice paddy「田んぼ」 harvest「収穫」 tranquil「静寂な」 wrap「包む」

---

(55) 正解　a)　「劇場の天井桟敷（さじき）には椅子がない」

解説 gallery は「美術館、画廊」の意味で理解する場合が多いが、この写真では「天井桟敷」（劇場内の後方にある安価な観覧席）の意味である。他の選択肢は写真の内容に合致しない。

参考 b)「プログラムは舞台の上に提示されている」

c)「杉の木が舞台の背壁に描かれている」

d)「美術館には重要文化財が収蔵されている」

☆ cedar (tree)「杉（の木）」 important cultural assets「重要文化財」

Column 03 — 電車の種類

★下線の単語は日本での英語表記である。

普通電車［普］

《日》a **Local** train (which stops at every station)

《米》an accommodation train; a coach; a way train 　《英》a slow train

各駅電車

《米》all stations train 　《英》an omnibus train

準急電車

《日》a **Semi-Express** train; a local express train

快速電車［快］

《日》a **Rapid** train (which skips some stations)

《米》a rapid-transit train 　《英》an intercity train

急行電車［急］

《日》an **Express** train (which stops at even fewer stations than a rapid train); a fast train

特急電車［特］

《日》a **Limited Express** train (which stops only at major stations)

《英》special express train

新幹線 the Shinkansen; an Super Express train; a superfast train（超特急列車）; a bullet train（弾丸列車）

市街［路面］電車 《米》a streetcar 　《英》a tram; a tramcar

☆市街電車の停留所《米》a streetcar stop 　《英》a railway station

郊外電車 suburban train	**通勤電車** commuter train
内周り電車 inbound train	**外回り電車** outbound train
不定期運行電車 irregular train	**定期運行電車** regular train
始発電車 (the) first train	**最終電車［終電］** (the) last train

満員電車 crowded train; full train; jam-packed train

回送電車 《米》deadhead train《日》out-of-service train

除雪車 snow plow [wedge] train

音声の内容

🔊 1-07 (56) a) The smartphone 'handy' can be used only inside the hotel.

b) Guests can make domestic calls with 'handy' free of charge.

c) Hotel guests can get 'handy' at a reduced price.

d) The hotel offers a smartphone as a souvenir.

🔊 1-08 (57) a) The hotel changes linens every other day.

b) The guest is not interested in the eco-program.

c) The guest declined the change of linen yesterday.

d) The hotel doesn't change linens during the stay.

🔊 1-09 (58) a) This coupon is valid for beverages ordered with the lunch menu.

b) Customers can download this coupon from the website.

c) Customers can save 10% of the total amount with this coupon.

d) Two or more kinds of discounts cannot be used at the same time.

🔊 1-10 (59) a) The superior twin room accommodates up to four adults.

b) Bed sharing is not allowed in this room.

c) The sofa turns into a bed when three people use the room.

d) The room is decorated with a lot of Disney characters.

🔊 1-11 (60) a) A Japanese passport bears the mark of a chrysanthemum on it.

b) Japanese wisteria is illustrated on the cover of a Japanese passport.

c) A hydrangea is adopted as the mark on the Japanese passport.

d) A Dandelion is the official flower in Japan.

解答と解説

(56) **正解** **b)** 「客は 'handy' スマホを用いて無料で国内電話がかけられる」

解説 Smartphone handy（個人使用するための無料のレンタル・スマートフォン）に関する記載である。記事には、Free-To-Use Smartphone handy「無料で使えるスマートフォン handy」、また Main Functionary の項目には **Unlimited domestic** and international **calls**「**無制限の国内**および**国際電話**」と記載されている。したがって b) が正解。

参考 a)「'handy' スマートフォンはホテル内のみで使用できる」
  c)「ホテル宿泊客は 'handy' スマートフォンを割引価格で入手できる」
  d)「ホテルはスマートフォンを土産物として提供している」
  ☆ free of charge「無料で」 at a reduced price「割引価格で」

(57) **正解** **c)** 「昨日客はリネンの交換を断った」

解説 ホテルにおける宿泊客に対するメモである。As you have requested, **your linen has not been changed**.「要望どおり、**お客様のリネンは交換しておりません**」と記載されている。ちなみに、「希望する場合は、このカードをベッド上に置くこと」になっている。したがって c) が正解。

参考 a)「ホテルは 1 日おきにリネンを交換する」
  b)「客はエコプログラム（自然保護）には関心がない」
  d)「ホテルは滞在中リネンを交換しない」
  ☆ linen「リネン、リンネル」。シーツ・枕カバー・タオル類など、リンネル製品の総称。元来は「麻で作られた布」のこと。

(58) **正解** **d)** 「2 種以上の割引は同時には使用できない」

解説 **Not valid with any others or discounts.**「**他の物あるいは割引との併用はできない**」と記載されている。通常、併用できない割引券クーポンには、Not valid with any other coupon. などと記載された文言をよく見かける。つまり「割引クーポンは 1 枚ずつしか使うことができない」という意味である。したがって d) が正解。

参考 a)「このクーポン券はランチメニューと一緒に注文する飲み物に有効である」
  b)「顧客はこのクーポン券をウェブサイトでダウンロードできる」
  c)「顧客はこのクーポン券で総額の 10％を節約できる」
  ☆ valid「有効な」 save「節約する」

(59) **正解** **c)** 「3人で部屋を使用する時、ソファーはベッドになる」

解説 最後に、**For the use of 3, Sofa-beds are used.**「3人使用の場合、ソファーベッドになる」と記載されている。他の選択肢には該当する内容がない。したがって c) が正解。

参考 a)「スーペリア・ツインルーム（上級ツイン部屋）には大人4人まで宿泊できる」
b)「この部屋では添い寝は許されていない」
d)「部屋は多数のディズニーのキャラクターで装飾されている」
☆ accommodate「収容する」 bed sharing「ベッドの共有」

(60) **正解** **a)** 「日本の旅券には菊の紋章が付いている」

解説 日本の旅券の表紙に描かれた花を問う質問である。ここでは花に関する英語が問われる。日本の旅券に描かれているのは菊である。したがって a) が正解。☞ **Column 04** 日本の旅券（p.75）

参考 b)「日本の旅券の表紙に日本の藤の絵が入っている」
c)「紫陽花は日本の旅券に紋章として採用された」
d)「蒲公英は正式の国花である」
☆ illustrate「（絵・図解など）入れる」 adopt「採用する」

Column 04　日本の旅券

The new passport (issued in 2020) features the woodblock works of ukiyo-e master of Katsushika Hokusai (1760-1849). The passport has the iconic "The Great Wave off Kanagawa" among other pieces from the series "Thirty-six views of Mt. Fuji" printed on the page as an anti-forgery measure.

新型旅券（2020年発行）の特徴は浮世絵師である葛飾北斎（1761-1849）の代表作の木版画である。旅券には「富嶽三十六景」浮世絵揃物から抜粋された象徴的な「神奈川沖浪裏」が偽造防止対策としての頁にプリントされている。☆旅券は、海外へ渡航する際、自分の国籍を保証また自分自身を判明させる身分証明書と同時に政府が発給する渡航の許可書である。

① **生体確証旅券[パスポート]** biometric(al) passport; passport containing biometric date

☆身体的な特徴［生体測定情報］を記録した旅券。biometrics「生体認証」とは人間の身体的特徴（生体器官）や行動的特徴（癖など）の情報を用いて行う個人認証技術である。指紋採取（finger prints）、掌形採取（palm print）、顔写真撮影（facial recognition photographs）など空港での出入国（immigration）にて行う認証手段として採用されている。

② **IC旅券** IC (integrated circuit) passport

▶ The new passport has more secure IC chips, making it harder for holder's personal data to be stolen. 「新型旅券にはさらに安全なICチップ機能が内蔵され、個人情報を不正に読み取られないにように強化されている」

☆ 国籍や氏名・生年月日などの旅券面の身分事項のほか、所持人などの顔写真を電磁的に記録したICを搭載した旅券のこと。生体確認（biometrics）技術を個人情報記録のために利用する。これにより旅券の偽造また他人による不正使用が防止される。旅券発行手数料はICチップ（IC chips）の実費（千円）が上乗せになる。バイオメトリック・パスポート（Biometric Passport）また電子旅券［パスポート］（e-passport）などとも言う。ちなみに、ICとは「集積回路」（整流・増幅・演算などが一体として結合されている超小型の回路）の意味である。

8 「対話」に関する内容把握

音声の内容

📢1-12 (61) Welcome to our restaurant. Do you have a reservation, sir?

📢1-13 (62) The performance starts at 7:00. So can you pick up the tickets by 6:30 at the latest?

📢1-14 (63) I've been trying to send an e-mail, but I can't seem to get connected.

📢1-15 (64) May I ask what price range you have in mind?

📢1-16 (65) Is there a microwave oven in the room?

📢1-17 (66) I've lost my camera. Can you help me?

📢1-18 (67) Excuse me, could you tell me which bus goes to the outlet mall?

📢1-19 (68) We'd like the family pack of tickets for the water park, please.

📢1-20 (69) Why did you give your seat up?

📢1-21 (70) What kind of car did you want to rent?

解答と解説

(61) **問い** 「いらっしゃいませ。予約はございますか」

正解 d)「はい、スティーブンという名で予約しています。当ホテルに滞在しています」

解説 レストラン　レストランに入ってくる顧客に対する係員の第一声である。顧客は予約に関して何らかの返答が問われる。「スティーブン名で（in the name of Stevens）予約している」という返答が適切。したがって d) が正解。

参考 a)「承知しました。どうぞこちらにお越しくださいますか」
　　　 b)「もちろん。あなたにお会いすることを楽しみにしています」
　　　 c)「はい、日曜日の正午 12 時にテーブルを予約したいのです」
　　　 ☆ look forward to（+ 動名詞）「（〜することを）楽しみにする」

(62) 問い 「公演は7時開始です。遅くとも6時30分までにはチケットを入手できますか」

正解 c) 「承知しました。公演はどれくらい続きますか」

解説 劇場 係員は来客に公演の開始時間を知らせ、開始30分前までにチケットを引き取れるかどうか聞いている。返答として、追加で公演に関して質問をしている c) が正解。その他の選択肢は話題にしているものがずれている。

参考 a) 「いいよ、別の日にしましょう」

b) 「どこで迎えのバスを待ちますか」

d) 「はい、その時に帰りの切符を貰えますか」

☆ pick up (the ticket) 「(チケットを) 手に入れる」 pick-up bus 「送迎用バス」

---

(63) 問い 「Eメールを送ろうとしたのですが、なかなか接続しそうにありません」

正解 d) 「申し訳ございません。午前中ネット接続にトラブルが続いています」

解説 ホテルなど Eメールを送ろうとしたがアクセス不能の状態であると言っている。ネット接続のトラブル (trouble with getting online) について述べている d) が正解。

参考 a) 「接続するのに1時間を要します」

b) 「さらなる情報を得るにはホームページをご覧ください」

c) 「できるだけ早くEメールアドレスを変えるべきです」

☆ get connected (to the Internet) 「(ネットに) つながる」 get online 「ネットに接続する」

---

(64) 問い 「ご予算を伺ってもよろしいでしょうか」

正解 a) 「50ドルが限界だと考えています」

解説 買い物 店員が顧客に対して念頭においている (in mind) 予算幅 (price range) を聞いている。予算範囲の金額を提示 (Fifty dollars is my limit.) している a) が正解。

参考 b) 「そうね、貴重品を預かってください」

c) 「はい。思った以上に費用がかかります」

d) 「そうですね。100ドルを換金できますか」

☆ valuables 「貴重品」

---

(65) 問い 「部屋には電子レンジがありますか」

正解 d) 「恐縮ですが部屋での料理は許可されておりません」

解説 ホテル 宿泊客が部屋に電子レンジ (microwave oven) が備っているかどうかを尋ねている。電子レンジの有無ではないが、部屋での料理は There is no cooking permitted 「禁

止されている」と返答している d) が最適。

(66) **問い**　「カメラをなくしました。どうすればよいのでしょうか」

　　 正解　**d)**　「そこの遺失物取扱所に寄ってください」

解説 **空港**　カメラをなくした人が途方に暮れ、その対処法を尋ねている。選択肢を見ると遺失物取扱所 (lost-and-found counter) の語句がある。したがって d) が正解。

(67) **問い**　「すみませんが、どのバスがアウトレットモールに行くのでしょうか」

　　 正解　**b)**　「シャトルバスの停留所は駅近くにあります」

解説 **バスターミナル**　アウトレットモール（高級ブランド品を安く買える商業施設）に行くシャトルバスを探し、その停留所を尋ねている。選択肢を見ると near the station「駅近く」にあると告げ、場所を教えている b) が最適。

(68) **問い**　「水上公園行きの家族用パックのチケットが欲しいのです」

　　 正解　**c)**　「承知しました。部屋にツケ払いにしましょうか」

解説 **ホテル**　水上公園に行くためのチケットを入手しようとしている。購入する場合通常は金銭を支払う。しかし選択肢には金銭授受の内容はない。ホテルでは部屋にツケ払い (charge it to one's room) する場合が多い。したがって c) が正解。

☆ charge (the drinks to one's room)「(飲み物を部屋の) ツケ払いにする」

(69) 問い 「なぜお席を譲られたのですか」

正解 c) 「彼が足を負傷したことが分かったからです」

解説 車内 車内で座席を譲った理由を尋ねている。理由として適切なのは「足を負傷している男性に気がついたから」(I saw he had injured foot) と返答している c) である。

参考 a)「それが最後であったからです」
b)「寝具類が汚れていたからです」
d)「それが道路を横切ったところにあったからです」
☆ injure「傷つく、負傷する」

(70) 問い 「どのような車種を借りたかったのですか」

正解 d) 「ハイブリッド車が欲しかったのです」

解説 レンタカー 借りたかった車種について尋ねている。選択肢を見ると、車種はハイブリット車 (a hybrid car) のみが提示されている。したがって d) が正解。

参考 a)「カロリーは少なめ目に」
b)「時間どおりであれば」
c)「ちょうど空港の方に」
☆ on time「時間どおり」

音声の内容

■1-22 (71) F : Are you OK?

   M: I'm fine. I always get like this when I ride a bus. You know, a little dizzy, a little nausea.

   F : Maybe you should have taken the train.

   M: I still get it a little on trains, and cars, too. But buses are the worst. But the bus is much cheaper, so I still take it. Actually, I have some medication, but I forgot it today.

   F : Well, I hope you feel better soon.

   Question: What is the man's problem?

■1-23 (72) F : The sign over there says, "No Littering." But there's litter all over the square.

   M: Well, there was a big football game yesterday, and the local team won, so people went a little crazy. It's pretty filthy now, isn't it? But workers will be by to clean it up later today. That's what usually happens.

   F : I'm going to take a picture now and put in on the web. This is unbelievable!

   Question: What are they talking about?

■1-24 (73) F : How was everything this evening? Would you like some dessert?

   M: Wonderful. Everything was great. I think we'll skip dessert, though. We're all pretty full. And, if it's possible, we'd like to get separate checks. Is that OK?

   F : Sure. What should I do about the bottle of wine?

   M: Can you put it on my bill? I had the set with pasta with uni and cucumber.

   Question What is the guest asking for?

■1-25 (74) F : I just got a letter from the hotel I reserved in Amsterdam. It said that they had experienced some flooding and that they are forced to cancel all reservations for the last week of June in order to do the repairs.

M: Does that affect you?

F : Well, my reservation is for the first week of July. But they said if an unexpected problem occurs, they may need to cancel all bookings that week as well.

M: What are you going to do?

F : Just wait and hope it's OK. I doubt I can get anything else at this time.

Question　What is the problem?

01-26 (75) F : Did you manage to make a reservation for that tour you wanted to go on?

M: Yes, and it is going to be great. We meet at a haunted pub at 11:00 at night and the guide tells us some scary stories of ghosts that people have seen. They have all these pictures on the wall of people who used to frequent the pub and who've been seen there after they died. And then we walk over to the graveyard of the historical local church, where visitors regularly see spirits walking around at midnight.

F : Sounds terrifying. I can't believe you enjoy that kind of thing.

Question　What are they talking about?

01-27 (76) M: Good evening, ma'am, I'm the manager. What seems to be the problem?

F : I would like to make a complaint. The staffs here are unbelievably rude. I cannot accept the way they've been speaking with me.

M :I'm sorry that you've had a bad experience, ma'am. Could you give me some more details so I can better understand what happened? Then we can try to get this sorted out. And I'll see if I can offer some sort of compensation for your discomfort.

Question　What is the guest doing?

◀))1-28 (77) **F :** Is the gym open at this time?

M: It's open 24 hours.

F : Do I need to do anything to use it?

M: Just show your room key card to the attendant. We require appropriate footwear. If you don't have any with you, you can rent some there.

F : Are towels provided as well?

M: Yes, they are.

Question What is the guest planning to do?

◀))1-29 (78) **F :** Where is the place we can rent them?

M: The pamphlet says that there is a place just on the main street here. It must be a fairly big building. It says they have a huge range of period costumes we can choose from.

F : Should be fun. I'm going to go crazy taking pictures probably.

M: Yeah. Won't my friends love to see me dressed as a samurai walking around in old Edo!

Question What are the tourists talking about?

◀))1-30 (79) **F :** Is there Internet access on this flight?

M: Yes.

F : In all classes? I'm seated in economy.

M: Let me just check ... yes, there is.

F : Is it free or is there some sort of charge?

M: There's a small surcharge. You can pay by credit card on board the flight.

F : Oh, OK. I think I'll do that. I wish it were free, though.

Question What was the tourist hoping to do?

◀))1-31 (80) **F :** Can we get a cab here?

M: I've already called one. I've got one of those peer-to-peer ride-sharing apps on my phone.

F : Isn't it dangerous?

M: I don't know. I used them a lot the last time I was here. I never had any trouble.

F : Are they cheaper?

M: Yes. And faster. It should be here soon.

Question　What are the tourists talking about?

対策

会話は 2 回放送される。

「1 回目の放送」では、会話の内容を一言一句に拘泥せずにしっかりと「全体像」を把握すること。そのためには会話の「**場面・状況**」をキャッチすること。最後に「**質問**」(QUESTION) を的確に理解すること。

「2 回目の放送」では、質問を念頭におきながら、問題冊子にある 4 つの「**選択肢**」を見ながら適切な解答を探ること。解答となる重要な「**語句**や**文**」に合致する内容が必ずあるので、その文脈を理解しながら会話の内容を把握すること。

この設問は「会話の流れ」を的確に把握することが問われている。以下の各設問の 解説 では、会話の流れがわかるように主旨を述べた。

解答と解説

(71) 質問 「男性が問題にしているのは何ですか」

正解 a） 「彼は乗り物に酔った」

解説 **バス車中**　女性は男性に対して Are you OK?「気分はどうですか」と尋ね、男性は I'm fine. I always get like this when I ride a bus. You know, a little dizzy, a little nausea.「大丈夫です。バスに乗ればいつもこんな調子で、ちょっぴりフラフラして、むかつきます」と返答する。女性は Maybe you should have taken the train.「電車に乗るべきだったかもしれないですね」と言う。男性は I still get it a little on trains, and cars, too. But buses are the worst. But the bus is much cheaper, so I still take it. Actually, I have some medication, but I forgot it today.「電車や車でも酔うのですがバスは最悪です。でもバスは非常に安いのでいつも利用するのです。薬を持っているのですが今日は忘れました」と返答する。女性は男性に対して Well, I hope you feel better soon.「すぐに回復すればいいですね」と元気づける。

参考 b） 「彼は電車の切符を失った」

c）「彼は薬を切らした」

d）「彼はバスにバッグを忘れた」

☆ motion sickness「乗り物酔い」

---

(72) 質問 「彼らが話し合っているのは何ですか」

正解 **b)** 「ごみの量」

解説 日常会話 女性は The sign over there says, "No Littering." But there's litter all over the square.「向こうにある標識には『ごみを捨てるな』と書かれています。でも街区一面ごみだらけです」と嘆いている。男性は Well, there was a big football game yesterday, and the local team won, so people went a little crazy. It's pretty filthy now, isn't it? But workers will be by to clean it up later today. That's what usually happens.「昨日フットボールの試合があり、地元チームが勝利したので大勢の人がちょっぴり熱狂したのですね。今となってはかなり汚れ放題です。でも作業員らは今日の夕方には清掃することになっています。いつものことです」と言う。女性は I'm going to take a picture now and put in on the web. This is unbelievable!「写真を撮ってウェブサイトに載せます。信じられないです」と返答する。

参考 a)「SNS のフォロワーの数」

c)「重要なスポーツの試合」

d)「ボランティアの経験」

☆ trash「ごみ、がらくた」

---

(73) 質問 「顧客が依頼するのは何ですか」

正解 **b)** 「別々の勘定書」

解説 レストラン 女性は How was everything this evening? Would you like some dessert?「今晩の料理はいかがでしたか。デザートはいかがでしょうか」と尋ねる。男性は Wonderful. Everything was great. I think we'll skip dessert, though. We're all pretty full. And, if it's possible, we'd like to get separate checks. Is that OK?「おいしかったです。どれもみな最高でした。でもデザートは結構です。みんな満腹です。そしてできれば、別々の会計したいのです。OK ですか」と聞く。女性は Sure. What should I do about the bottle of wine?「かしこまりました。ワインボトルはいかがなさいますか」と尋ねた。男性は Can you put it on my bill?「それは僕の勘定書に入れておいてください」と返答する。

参考 a)「ワインのおかわり」

c)「デザートのメニュー」

d)「新しいパスタ・セット」

☆ bill「勘定書」(= check)　ask for「依頼する」

---

(74) 質問 「何が問題ですか」

正解 c) 「ホテルは特別な大修理を行う」

解説 日常会話 女性が I just got a letter from the hotel I reserved in Amsterdam. It said that they had experienced some flooding and that they are forced to cancel all reservations for the last week of June in order to do the repairs.「アムステルダムで予約したホテルから手紙を受け取りました。手紙によればホテルは洪水氾濫を受け、その修理のため6月最終週に受けたすべての予約を余儀なく取り消しているようです」と言っている。男性は Does that affect you?「あなたには影響しているのですか」と聞くと、女性は Well, my reservation is for the first week of July. But they said if an unexpected problem occurs, they may need to cancel all bookings that week as well.「私は7月第1週に予約をしました。しかし不測の事態が起これば、ホテルはその週の予約もすべて取り消すかもしれません」と言っている。男性は What are you going to do?「どうするつもりですか」と聞くと、女性は Just wait and hope it's OK.「待って問題ないことを希望するのみです」と返答した。

参考 a)「観光客は予約ができない」
　　 b)「観光客は長く待たされ予約ができない」
　　 d)「ホテルは特別な提供をしている」
　　 ☆ too+ 形 + to + 動 「形すぎて動できない」　undergo repairs「修理する」

---

(75) 質問 「彼らが話し合っているのは何ですか」

正解 d) 「ゴースト (幽霊) ツアー」

解説 日常会話 女性は Did you manage to make a reservation for that tour you wanted to go on?「あなたが行きたがっていたあのツアーをなんとか予約できましたか」と尋ねた。男性は Yes, and it is going to be great. We meet at a haunted pub at 11:00 at night and the guide tells us some scary stories of ghosts that people have seen. They have all these pictures on the wall of people who used to frequent the pub and who've been seen there after they died. And then we walk over to the graveyard of the historical local church, where visitors regularly see spirits walking around at midnight.「はい、うまくいきそうです。夜11時に化け物 [幽霊] パブで会い、ガイドさんが大勢の人

が見たと言うゴースト（お化け）の怖い話をします。その中には、壁に飾られた、パブによく通い、死後もそこで目撃された人たちの写真の話もあります。その後由緒ある地元の教会の墓地に歩いて行きます。そこでは深夜になると見学者が霊が歩き回るのをたびたび目撃しています」と言っている。

参考 a)「ギャラリー（画廊）を訪ねること」
　　 b)「カテドラル（大聖堂）を参拝すること」
　　 c)「特別コンサート」
　　☆ ghost「幽霊」　cathedral「大聖堂」

---

(76) 質問 「客がしているのは何ですか」

　　 正解 **b)** 「苦情を述べること」

解説 ホテル 男性は I'm the manager. What seems to be the problem?「私はマネージャーです。何が問題となっているのでしょうか？」と問う。女性は I would like to make a complaint. The staffs here are unbelievably rude. I cannot accept the way they've been speaking with me.「苦情を言いたいのです。ここのスタッフは信じられないほど無礼な振る舞いをしています。私との話し方は気にいりません」と返答する。男性は Could you give me some more details so I can better understand what happened? ... And I'll see if I can offer some sort of compensation for your discomfort.「何が起きたかよく理解するためにもう少し詳しくお話しいただけませんか。……お客様の不快感に関して何か補償できるかどうか検討します」と言っている。

参考 a)「テーブルを要求すること」
　　 c)「マネージャー（支配人）に要請すること」
　　 d)「スタッフ（従業員）に無礼な振る舞いをすること」
　　☆ make a complain「苦情を述べる」　rude「無礼な」　claim「請求［要求］する」

---

(77) 質問 「観光客は何をしようとしていますか」

　　 正解 **a)** 「フィットネス・センターを利用する」

解説 ホテルのジム 女性は Is the gym open at this time?「この時間にジムは開いていますか」と尋ねると、男性は It's open 24 hours.「終日開いています」と返答する。女性は Do I need to do anything to use it?「ジムを利用するには何か必要ですか」と聞くと、男性は Just show your room key card to the attendant. We require appropriate footwear. If you don't have any with you, you can rent some there.「係員に部屋のカードキーを見せるだけです。相応の履物が求められます。持参していない場合はレンタルできます」また

Are towels provided as well「タオルも備わっていますか」という女性の質問に対し、Yes
と返答している。

参考 b)「ビジネス・センターに行く」

c)「温泉に入る」

d)「衣服の買い物に行く」

☆ clothes「衣服」

---

(78) **質問**「観光客が話し合っているのは何ですか」

正解 d)「衣装を借りること」

解説 観光 女性は Where is the place we can rent them?「それらを借りられる場所は
どこでしょうか」と尋ねている。男性は The pamphlet says that there is a place just on
the main street here. It must be a fairly big building. It says they have a huge range
of period costumes we can choose from.「パンフレットによれば、この大通りにあり、
かなり大きなビルです。幅広い時代衣装が揃っていて、そこから選べるようです」と返答し
ている。女性は I'm going to go crazy taking pictures probably.「たぶん写真を撮るの
に夢中になるでしょう」と言う。男性は Won't my friends love to see me dressed as a
samurai walking around in old Edo!「侍の格好をした私が江戸を歩き回るのを友人たちは
見たいでしょう」と言う。

参考 a)「写真に撮ってもらうこと」

b)「博物館を訪れること」

c)「歴史ツアーに参加すること」

☆ photograph「写真を撮る」(= take a picture)

---

(79) **質問**「観光客は何をしたかったのでしょうか」

正解 a)「機内での無料 Wi-Fi を取得すること」

解説 機内 女性は Is there Internet access on this flight?「機内ではインターネット接
続はありますか」と尋ね、男性は Yes.「あります」と返答する。女性は In all classes? I'm
seated in economy.「どのクラスにもあるのですか。私はエコノミークラスに座っています」
と言う。男性は yes, there is「はい、エコノミーにもあります」と返答する。すかさず女性
は Is it free or is there some sort of charge?「無料ですか、有料ですか」と尋ねる。男性
は There's a small surcharge.「小額の追加料金がかかります」と返答する。女性は Oh,
OK. I think I'll do that. I wish it were free, though.「OK です。やむを得ません。でも、無

料であればいいんですがね」と言う。

参考 b）「座席をアップグレードさせること」

　　　c）「航空マイレージ（ポイント）を使用すること」

　　　d）「クレジットカードを使用すること」

　　　☆ upgrade「等級を上げる」

(80) **質問**　「観光客は何について話していますか」

　　　正解　**d）**　「新しいタクシーサービス」

解説 **観光**　女性が Can we get a cab here?「ここでタクシーを拾うことができます
か」と聞いている。男性は I've already called one. I've got one of those peer-to-peer
ride-sharing apps on my phone.「もうすでに 1 台呼んでいます。僕の電話で P2P 型ラ
イドシェアリング（車の相乗り）のアプリを使っての 1 台です」と返答する。女性は Isn't
it dangerous?「危険じゃないですか」と聞くと、男性は I used them a lot the last time I
was here. I never had any trouble.「以前来た時にも何度も利用したけれども、どんなトラ
ブルもなかったです」と返答する。女性は Are they cheaper?「それは安いのですか」と聞くと、
男性は Yes. And faster. It should be here soon.「安いし、そのうえ速いです。もうすぐこ
こに着きますよ」と返答した。したがって d) が正解。☆ peer-to-peer [P2P] とは peer（仲
間）同士が直接繋がるデータを通信する仕組みのこと。

参考 a）「安全対策［予防策］」

　　　b）「貯金の方法」

　　　c）「警察への連絡」

　　　☆ precaution「予防」　save (money)「（金銭を）節約する」　alternative「代わりとなる、新しい」

10 「観光事情」に関する内容把握

[Part A]

音声の内容

01-32　F：Yosemite National Park is a United States National Park located in east central California. The park covers an area of more than 3,000 square kilometers, about the same size as the state of Rhode Island, though most visitors only spend time in the Yosemite Valley, an 18 square kilometer section of the park.

The park has always been popular, in part because of its amazing scenery and in part because of the publicity efforts of early developers. As early as 1855, magazine articles began appearing that contained drawings of Yosemite's famous rock cliffs and descriptions of its beautiful natural scenery. One early attraction was the Mariposa Grove of giant Sequoia trees, including the Wawona tree, a tree so large that a tunnel was cut through it in 1881. Visitors enjoyed driving carriages or cars through it until the tree fell down in 1969. One reason for Yosemite's present popularity is that it is close enough to San Francisco to be accessible as a day tour. Tourists can visit using one of the many tours available using either bus or train. Or they can rent a car and drive themselves. Last year, about 3.7 million people visited the park and many people are now complaining that it has become too popular and too crowded. Most people visit in summer and only visit those parts of the park that are accessible by car, so traffic congestion and parking are serious problems.

If you can, it is highly recommended that you visit in any other season than summer and that you stay in the park for a night, taking time to walk or hike and really enjoy the natural beauty.

Questions

(81) Where is Yosemite National Park located?

(82) How large is the park?

(83) Why did Yosemite originally become famous?

(84) About how many people visit the park annually?

(85) What problems is the park experiencing recently?

解答と解説

(81) 質問 「ヨセミテ国立公園はどこにありますか」

正解 b) 「カリフォルニア州中央部に」

解説 冒頭に Yosemite National Park is ... located in east central California. 「ヨセミテ国立公園はカリフォルニア州東中央部に位置している」と放送されている。したがって b) が正解。

参考 a) 「カリフォルニア州南部に」
b) 「ロードアイランド州西部に」
c) 「ロードアイランド州東部に」

(82) 質問 「公園の広さはどれくらいですか」

正解 b) 「3,000km²」

解説 冒頭の文に続き、The park covers an area of more than 3,000 square kilometers. 「ヨセミテ国立公園は 3,000 平方キロメートル以上のエリアに広がっている」と放送されている。したがって b) が正解。

参考 a) 「30,000km²」 c) 「80km²」 d) 「18km²」

(83) 質問 「ヨセミテが有名になった理由はなぜでしょうか」

正解 d) 「広報［宣伝］活動」

解説 前半で ... in part because of its amazing scenery and in part because of the publicity efforts of early developers. 「1 つには驚異的な景観のため、また 1 つには初期開拓［開発］者の宣伝努力があったため（有名になった）」と放送されている。したがって d)

が正解。

参考 a)「その所在地」 b)「その規模」 c)「そのホテル」

---

(84) 質問 「毎年公園に訪れる人の数はどのくらいですか」

正解 c) 「3,700,000 人」

解説 数字を正確に聴解することが問われる。後半で、about 3.7milion people visited the park と放送されている。

参考 a)「37,000 人」 b)「370,000 人」 d)「37,000,000 人」

---

(85) 質問 「公園が最近経験するのはどのような問題ですか」

正解 a) 「交通問題」

解説 最後の方で、traffic congestion and parking are serious problems.「交通渋滞と駐車が深刻な問題である」と放送されている。したがって a) が正解。

参考 b)「アクセス性の問題」 c)「財政問題」 d)「環境破壊」

【Part B】

◀))1-33 **F:** Since ancient times, Mt. Fuji has been honored as a mountain where the gods dwell and has served as an object of faith for people. Sengen-jinja Shrine was built at the foot of the mountain after the mid-8th century in order to pray for volcanic activity to be calmed. Around the 12th century, it became a hall for the practice of *Shugendo*, a type of Buddhism. A mountain trail was opened in the 14th century (Muromachi period) and Mt. Fuji became widely known among the general public as a sacred mountain. In addition, *Fujiko* (a Shinto sect dedicated to the worship of Mt. Fuji) became a popular religious faith among ordinary people during the Edo period, and many people came to visit the mountain during the time. Even now, many people—regardless of age—climb Mt. Fuji. Mt. Fuji soothes the spirits of Japanese people.

Mt. Fuji has long served as the subject of a wide range of creative activities, including *waka* poetry, *monogatari* (narrative tales), *haiku*, and paintings. The famous paintings of Mt. Fuji include *ukiyo-e* from the Edo period. The most renowned of such prints include the "Thirty-six Views of Mt. Fuji" by Katsushika Hokusai and a series of the same name by Utagawa Hiroshige.

On June 22nd, 2013, Mt. Fuji was approved as a UNESCO World Heritage site, becoming the country's 17th to make the list. The above-mentioned cultural influence of Mt. Fuji shows why UNESCO registered Mt. Fuji not as a natural heritage site but as a cultural heritage site; the peak was not treated as a mere natural scene.

However, there remain a number of problems to overcome. For example, around 300,000 people climb Mt. Fuji every year, and now that it is listed as a World Heritage site, the number is expected to rise further, resulting in more possible damage to the environment. To limit the number of climbers, the governments of Yamanashi and Shizuoka prefectures where the mountain is situated, have decided to charge an entrance fee of 1,000 yen per climber on a trial basis for a certain period this summer.

Questions

(86) Since when has Mt. Fuji served as an object of faith for people?

(87) How many UNESCO World Heritage sites are there in Japan, including Mt. Fuji?

(88) About how many people currently climb Mt. Fuji every year?

(89) What was the name of the Shinto sect that worshipped Mt. Fuji, starting in the Edo period?

(90) Why have Yamanashi and Shizuoka prefectures decided to charge an entrance fee to climb Mt. Fuji this summer?

解答と解説

(86) 質問 「富士山はいつ頃から信仰の対象とされてきましたか」
　　　正解 a) 「古来（から）」

解説 冒頭で、Since ancient times, Mt. Fuji has been honored as a mountain where the gods dwell and has served as an object of faith for people.「古来、富士山は神が宿る山として崇敬され、人々にとって信仰の対象とされてきた」と放送されている。したがってa) が正解。

参考 b) 「8世紀中頃」　c) 「12世紀」　d) 「14世紀」

(87) 質問 「富士山を含め日本のユネスコ世界遺産はいくつありますか」
　　　正解 c) 「17物件」（富士山—信仰の対象と芸術の源泉）

解説 中頃で、On June 22nd, 2013, Mt. Fuji was approved as a UNESCO World Heritage site, becoming the country's 17th to make the list.「2013年6月22日、富士山はユネスコ世界遺産に承認され、国内17番目にリストアップされた」と放送されている。したがって c) が正解。☆ 2021年現在、日本には「文化遺産」19件、「自然遺産」4件、合

計23件のユネスコ世界遺産がある。

---

(88) **質問** 「現在では富士山に何人ほどが毎年登山しますか」

正解 **d)** 「約30万人」

解説 後半で、For example, around 300,000 people climb Mt. Fuji every year「例えば、年間30万人ほどが富士山に登山する」と放送されている。したがって d) が正解。

参考 a)「約1万3千人」 b)「約3万人」 c)「約13万人」

---

(89) **質問** 「江戸時代に始まった富士山を崇拝する神道の一派の名は何ですか」

正解 **b)** 「富士講」

解説 中頃で、Fujiko (a Shinto sect dedicated to the worship of Mt. Fuji) became a popular religious faith among ordinary people during the Edo period「江戸時代になると庶民の間で富士講（富士山を崇拝する神道の一派）という信仰が大衆化された」と放送されている。したがって b) が正解。

参考 a)「仏教」 c)「修験道」 d)「浮世絵」

---

(90) **質問** 「山梨県と静岡県は、この夏に富士山を登山するためには有料と決めたのはどうしてですか」

正解 **c)** 「登山者の人数を制限するため」

解説 最後の方で、To limit the number of climbers, the governments of Yamanashi and Shizuoka prefectures where the mountain is situated, have decided to charge an entrance fee of 1,000 yen per climber on a trial basis for a certain period this summer.「登山者の人数を制限するため、富士山の所在地である山梨と静岡の行政は、この夏には一定期間試行的に1,000円の入山料を課すことと決めた」と放送している。したがって c) が正解。

参考 a)「火山活動を管理するため」

b)「観光業の発展を促進するため」

d)「地元教育を支援するため」

---

1. 最初に筆記試験（試験時間は60分）、引き続きリスニング試験（試験時間は約30分）が行われます。試験監督者の指示に従ってください。
2. 問題冊子は試験監督者から開始の合図があるまで開かないでください。
3. 解答用紙（マークシート）の記入欄に、氏名・生年月日・受験番号等を記入してください。
4. 試験開始の合図後、最初に問題冊子のページを確認してください。もし乱丁や落丁がある場合は、すみやかに申し出てください。
5. 解答は全て、解答用紙の該当するマーク欄を黒鉛筆で塗りつぶしてください。
   - 黒鉛筆またはシャープペンシル以外は使用できません。
   - 解答用紙には解答以外の記入をいっさいしないでください。
6. 辞書・参考書およびそれに類するものの使用はすべて禁止されています。
7. 筆記用具が使用不能になった場合は、係員にすみやかに申し出てください。
8. 問題の内容に関する質問には、一切応じられません。
9. 不正行為があった場合、解答はすべて無効になりますので注意してください。

【筆記試験について】

1. 試験監督者が筆記試験の開始を告げてから、始めてください。
2. 各設問は1から50までの通し番号になっています。
3. 試験開始後の中途退出はできません。（リスニング試験が受けられなくなります。）

【リスニング試験について】

1. 各設問は51から90までの通し番号になっています。
2. リスニング中に問題冊子にメモをとってもかまいませんが、解答用紙に解答を転記する時間はありませんので、注意してください。
3. 放送が終了を告げたら、筆記用具を置いて、係員が解答用紙を回収するまで席を立たないでください。

全国語学ビジネス観光教育協会

筆記試験

1 観光用語の問題

[Part A] Read the following English statements from (1) to (5) and choose the most appropriate Japanese translation for each underlined part from among the four alternatives: a), b), c) and d). Blacken the letter for your answer on the answer sheet.

(1) I have the opportunity to take a short tour in the city, while waiting for the <u>connecting flight</u> for JAL.

    a) 帰国便   b) 出国便   c) 直行便   d) 接続便

(2) You should show a <u>boarding pass</u> or passport when you buy something at a duty-free shop.

    a) 航空券   b) 搭乗券   c) 入場券   d) 乗車券

(3) Before checking out of a hotel, tour members must pay for their <u>incidental charge</u> individually.

    a) 施設利用料   b) 臨時支払い   c) 個人勘定   d) サービス料

(4) *Seishun-Juhachi-Kippu* is a cheap ticket for unlimited travel on local and <u>rapid</u> trains

    a) 急行   h) 特急   c) 準急   d) 快速

(5) Peace Memorial Park contains a Peace Flame burning near the <u>cenotaph</u> for the Atomic-Bomb victims.

    a) 霊廟   b) 慰霊碑   c) 墳墓   d) 記念碑

[Part B] Read the following Japanese statements from (6) to (10) and choose the most appropriate English translation for each underlined part from among the four alternatives: a), b), c) and d). Blacken the letter of your answer on the answer sheet.

(6) 旅行者は全員<u>税関</u>申告書を提出するように義務付けられている。

All passengers are required to fill out a _____ declaration form.

    a) customs   b) disembarkation   c) embarkation   d) taxation

(7) この食べ物は<u>生</u>ものですので、早めにお召し上がりください。

This is _____ food. Please consume it immediately.

    a) fragile   b) frozen   c) pre-packaged   d) perishable

(8) このクレジットカードは先週で<u>有効期限切れ</u>ですのでお引き受けできません。

I'm afraid we can't accept this credit card because it _____ last week.

    a) aspired   b) expired   c) inspired   d) respired

(9) 渋谷スクランブル交差点で青信号になると大勢の歩行者が同時に<u>交差点</u>を渡る。

In the Shibuya Scramble Crossing, many pedestrians cross over the _____ when the crossing light turns green.

    a) avenue   b) alley   c) detour   d) intersection

(10) 祇園祭の起源は京都に<u>疫病</u>が流行し大勢の人が死亡した 869 年にまでさかのぼる。

Gion Festival originated in 869 when a/an _____ raged in Kyoto and killed many people.

    a) cancer   b) epidemic   c) heatstroke   d) pneumonia

2 英語コミュニケーションの問題

[Part A] Read the following English dialogs from (11) to (15) and choose the most appropriate utterance to complete each dialog from the four alternatives: a), b), c) and d). Blacken the letter of your answer on the answer sheet.

(11) A: I think we'll need to go to the embassy. One of the members of my tour has lost her passport.

   B: I'm afraid that might be difficult. The embassy is in Canberra, _____. Would that be OK to go there?

   a) and I think they have a lost-and-found section

   b) but I have the bill with me

   c) but there is a Consulate General of Japan in Sydney

   d) we can try to register as soon as possible

(12) A: Thank you for waiting. Do you mind if I give you most of the amount in one hundred dollar bills?

   B: Actually, I'd prefer _____.

   a) to use my credit card for shopping

   b) to get at least half of it in smaller denominations

   c) to get the confirmation slip right now if I can

   d) to countersign the traveler's checks

(13) A: I don't see any prices for the cocktails in the menu. Could you tell me how much they are?

B: _____ There is no need to show your room key, or pay your server.

a) All alcoholic drinks are prohibited in the hotel.

b) Everyone gets free meal vouchers for their stay.

c) All beverages are complimentary for guests at the resort.

d) Use your key card to open the lockers in the recreation area.

(14) A: Can you recommend some place for sightseeing that has a historical feel, a little bit of nature, and is accessible from Tokyo on a day trip?

B: There are lots of places you could go, but one place I often recommend is Matsumoto. It is _____. You can get there by express train from Shinjuku.

a) near the mountains and has a castle

b) the ancient capital of the country

c) famous for its traditional Heian period gardens

d) within walking distance of Tokyo Station

(15) A: Is consumption tax 10 percent? My guidebook says that consumption tax is 8 percent in Japan.

B: _____

a) It was just raised to 10 percent in April 2019.

b) I'm sorry but the machine is out of order.

c) Go straight and you can find the elevator.

d) There should be an announcement in a few minutes.

[Part B] Read the following English conversations from (16) to (20) and choose the most appropriate utterance to complete each conversation from the four alternatives: a), b), c) and d). Blacken the letter of your answer on the answer sheet.

(16) A: How was the flight?

　　B: Scary! We had a really bad experience with turbulence. Stronger than anything I've ever experienced. Early in the flight, the plane suddenly lost altitude and even the ＿＿＿＿＿＿＿＿＿＿＿＿＿.

　　A: Wow! That must have been frightening!

　　a) lavatories were occupied

　　b) boarding passes were issued

　　c) emergency vehicles appeared

　　d) the oxygen masks dropped

(17) A: Can I use this train with this ticket?

　　B: No, that's an express train. All seats on it are reserved and tickets are not sold on the train. You need to get a special ticket ＿＿＿＿＿＿＿＿＿＿＿＿. You can get one at the ticket office down those stairs and on your right.

　　A: Thank you.

　　a) to exchange your money

　　b) to check the timetable

　　c) after you get on

　　d) before you board

(18) A: Excuse me. This is Tanaka in room 405. It seems I was given a room that is different from what I reserved. The room itself is fine, but it overlooks the garden and the pool, and I specifically requested a room overlooking the sea.

B: Yes, sir. Just a moment, sir ... I'm very sorry, sir. I've got a room on the third floor available and I'll send the bell staff to help you move.

A: That'll be fine, so long as _____.

a) on a higher floor

b) away from the street

c) quieter than this one

d) it's an ocean-view room

(19) A: OK. We're going down to the large communal outdoor bath now. Do you want to come?

B: I don't think I should. _____

A: Oh, it'll be no problem at all. Everyone does it in Japan. Come on. It'll be fun.

a) I'm really looking forward to sharing this moment.

b) I'm a little embarrassed to get naked with other people.

c) It's a traditional part of the local culture.

d) Be sure to wash yourself outside the tub first.

(20) A: Look in there! What are those people doing in that noisy, smoky hall?

B: They're playing pachinko. It's _____. Do you want to give it a try?

A: No, thanks, especially on a nice day like today. I'd rather be outside.

a) a game that is a little like pinball, but with more balls

b) a type of celebration where everyone watches the game

c) a traditional local festival involving a competition

d) a ritual in which only adult males participate for honor

3 英文構成の問題

Read the following English paragraphs which contain incomplete sentences.
To complete the sentence, put each word into the best order. When you have finished, blacken letter on your answer sheet from among the four alternatives: a), b), c) and d) for the word in the position of the blank that has the question numbers from (21) to (25).

    Ancient Rome is easy to find in the modern Italian capital. If you go down practically any street, you are likely to _____ (21) _____ _____ reminders of the past. The Roman Forum and the Colosseum are the most famous of these ruins and they _(22)_ _____ _____ _____ annually. You can buy one ticket that can be used for admission to both sites. Buying a ticket for all three can save time because ticket lines can get very long, particularly in the hot summer when Rome is full of tourists.

    The Colosseum, originally known as the Flavian Amphitheater,was _____ _____ _____ (23) of eight years in the first century C.E. It was the site of games that included fights with men and animals. Modern people would be shocked by this type of entertainment, but when the stadium was at its peak, 5,000 lions, tigers and elephants were killed in it each year. And so were many gladiators, the men who fought for the entertainment of the large crowds. Today in the old stone stadium there are only crowds of tourists. Standing next to the building, you can not only feel the power of old Rome, but you can feel the power of the busy, modern Rome with cars, taxis, and buses constantly whizzing by.

    The Roman Forum today is only a wide area _(24)_ _____ _____ _____ and pieces of broken buildings, but it was originally a vibrant city square at the center of a powerful city. Many, many years ago, the square was _____ (25) _____ _____ monuments.

    Now, almost nothing is left standing. Now it is almost unrecognizable. If you try to go on your own, you may find the Forum disappointing.

Guided tours are available in English and many other languages and are well worth the price.

(21) a) see   b) ruins   c) other   d) or

(22) a) tourists   b) millions   c) of   d) attract

(23) a) period   b) over   c) a   d) built

(24) a) covered   b) old   c) with   d) roads

(25) a) temples   b) and   c) with   d) lined

4

[Part A] Read the following information sheet and answer the questions from
(26) to (30) by choosing the most appropriate answer for each question from
among the four alternatives; a), b), c) and d). Blacken the letter of your answer
on the answer sheet.

Vatican Museums Bus Tour

Highlights: Vatican Museums
Sistine Chapel
St. Peter's Basilica

Route:

The tour begins by coach passing through **Piazza della Repubblica** with the
Fountain of the Naiads and following the ancient **Aurelian Walls** which once
surrounded the ancient city.

From **Piazza del Popolo** where you will see an Egyptian obelisk dating back to the
time of Ramses II. Finally, on arrival at the Vatican Walls, your guide will then lead
you into the **Vatican Museums** taking the beautiful **Spiral staircase** and continuing
through the **Gallery of the Tapestries** and the **Gallery of the Geographical Maps**
before arriving in the famous **Sistine Chapel** with its magnificent fresco of the
Last Judgement by Michelangelo. At the end of the tour you'll have some free
time to visit **St. Peter's Basilica**.

> This tour is available in English, Italian, Spanish, German and French.

No drop off at the hotels but stop at: Via Veneto, Piazza Barberini, Piazza Venezia, Piazza
Cavour, Piazza della Repubblica, Rome Termini railway station and Green Line's Terminal.

Tour in the morning:
Every day (except on Sundays and on Catholic holidays) at 8:00 am.
From November 1st to March 31st only on Monday and Friday.

Tour in the afternoon:
Every day (except on Sundays and on Catholic holidays) at 2:30 pm.
From November 1st to March 31st from Tuesday to Saturday.

| ① | : Four hours

Price: Euro 61,00 per person including transportation, guide, and entrance fees.

Note:
• Admission fees for Vatican museums and Sistine Chapel are included in the tour price.
• There is a dress code for this tour: knees and shoulders must be covered and men must wear full-length trousers.
• It is absolutely ② to bring into the museums backpacks, umbrellas or metal objects.

(26) Choose the most appropriate word for ① .

    a) Duration   b) Derivation

    c) Division   d) Exclamation

(27) Choose the most appropriate word for ② .

    a) appointed   b) forbidden

    c) hesitated   d) recognized

(28) Which of the following is NOT mentioned in the tour advertisement?

    a) The Spiral staircase is located in the Vatican Museums.

    b) The participants can appreciate the Last Supper by Michelangelo.

    c) In the Piazza del Popolo, the participants can see an obelisk.

    d) The participants will pass a fountain early in the tour.

(29) Which is TRUE about the Vatican Museums Bus Tour?

    a) The morning tour starts at noon from Tuesday to Saturday.

    b) When visiting the Vatican Museums, knees and shoulders must be covered.

    c) Admission fee for the Sistine Chapel is not included in the tour price.

    d) The tour is available in English, Italian, Portuguese, German, and French.

(30) Which is FALSE about the Vatican Museums Bus Tour?

    a) ツアーバスは古代アウレリアヌス城壁を通過する。

    b) ツアーバスはローマ・テルミニ鉄道駅に停車する。

    c) 交通費はツアー料金に含まれている。

    d) 午後のツアーは 12 月 1 日より実施される。

[Part B] Read the following information sheet and answer the questions from (31) to (35) by choosing the most appropriate answer for each question from among the four alternatives; a), b), c) and d). Blacken the letter of your answer on the answer sheet.

YUFUIN

Yufuin, a popular hot spring resort, located about 10 kilometers inland from Beppu, another, much larger and more developed hot spring resort. Yufuin has a ┌─①─┐ of art museums, cafes and boutiques, and many travelers come to the city just to ┌─②─┐ about town for the day.

The ryokan and hotels of Yufuin are spread out around town, and not clustered along the main street like in many other resort towns. Instead, the main street is lined with cafes, boutiques and small museums, giving Yufuin an atmosphere more like a trendy shopping area than a traditional onsen town. Nonetheless, there are a large number of lodgings with hot spring baths, some of which open their baths to non-staying guests during daytime.

Tsuka no Ma

Daytime Hours: 9:30 to 18:30
Daytime Admission: 800 yen
Overnight Stay: From 18,000 yen

Tsuka no Ma is located on a hillside in the northern part of Yufuin where large steam clouds from hot spring sources can be seen rising into the air. The ryokan has large, gender separated outdoor baths with bluish-looking water, untypical for Yufuin.

Musoen

Daytime Hours: 10:00 to 14:30
Daytime Admission: 900 yen
Overnight Stay: From 19,000 yen

The views of Mount Yufu from Musoen's outdoor baths are considered among Yufuin's best. The ryokan is located slightly above town to the south and has large, attractive baths that are gender separated. The ryokan grounds are quite attractive, as well.

Sansuikan

Daytime Hours: 12:00 to 16:00
Daytime Admission: 700 yen
Overnight Stay: From 15,000 yens

Located just a short walk from Yufuin Station, the Sansuikan offers some of the most easily accessible baths to tourists without private means of transportation. The large ryokan's gender separated bathing facilities feature multiple outdoor and indoor pools, a scented bath and a sauna.

Shitanyu Public Bath

Hours: 10:00 to 22:00
Admission: 200 yen

The Shitanyu is a very simple, old-fashioned public bath house at the shore of Lake Kinrinko with two small pools. It is gender mixed without dedicated changing rooms and very limited facilities. The bath house opens towards the back, giving bathers a view onto some greenery.

japan-guide.com の湯布院のページ（https://www.japan-guide.com/e/e4750.html）より転載

(31) Choose the most appropriate word for ① .

    a) advance   b) details   c) alley   d) wealth

(32) Choose the most appropriate word for ② .

    a) export   b) stroll   c) expire   d) evacuate

(33) If a tourist visits Yufuin for short time, which facility is the most convenient for daytime bathing?

    a) Tsukanoma   b) Musoen

    c) Sansuikan   d) Shitanyu public bath

(34) Which is FALSE according to the Yufuin information?

    a) Less than 1,000 yen allows tourists daytime bathing.

    b) There is a facility open until late for non-staying guest.

    c) All facilities listed are accommodations.

    d) One of the facilities opens just four hours for daytime bathing.

(35) Which is TRUE according to the Yufuin information?

    a) 束の間は湯布院には珍しい青みがかったお湯で有名である。

    b) 下ん湯の露天風呂からは眼下に街を眺めることができる。

    c) 山水館は高台に位置しており、露天風呂からは由布岳を望むことができる。

    d) 下ん湯は混浴であるが、脱衣所は男女別に設けられている。

[Part C] Read the following English conversation, and answer the questions from (36) to (40) by choosing the most appropriate answer for each question from among the four alternatives; a), b), c) and d). Blacken the letter of your answer on the answer sheet.

Guide: On behalf of the Saga International Balloon Festa, I would like to welcome you all to Saga, Japan! Could I ask everyone to please look at the event   (36) ? Thank you! Now, as you can see, this event is held over the next five amazing days.

Tourist A: Excuse me? May I ask a question?

Guide: Certainly, go ahead.

Tourist A: You said, "international." How many different countries are   (37)   in the event this year?

Guide: There are over 25 foreign balloons from countries such as Poland, Hungary, Germany, Korea, China, and more.

Tourist B: Don't forget Japan, and we're here from Australia!

Guide: Yes, that's correct. You'll be able to meet everyone at the General Briefing this morning. Would you like to hear a little more about the event?

Tourist B: Yes, please.

Guide: As you may know, this is the biggest international hot air balloon event in Japan. It's   (38)   here on the Kase River bank, at the beginning of November, every year. Competitions are   (38)   in the early morning and the evening when air currents are stable. In the afternoon non-competing balloons in funny shapes appear in the sky for enjoyment and they offer further excitement to the Festa.

Tourist C: And what is the light up event called again? Something French?

Guide: Good question. The "La Montgolfier Nocturne" is a special night-time event in which hot air balloons are illuminated by their burner flames and create fantastic scenes.

Tourist B: Wow, that event sounds like something we don't want to miss!

Guide: Indeed. Once we've had a chance to review all the events, I'll ask you to ___(39)___ for the events you would like to attend. Remember, some events have limited space and are available on a ___(40)___ basis.

(36) Choose the most appropriate word for ___(36)___.

    a) travel documents   b) envelope

    c) receipt   d) brochure

(37) Choose the most appropriate word for ___(37)___.

    a) delivering   b) organizing

    c) participating   d) playing

(38) Choose the most appropriate word for ___(38)___.

    a) exchanged   b) compared

    c) detained   d) held

(39) Choose the most appropriate word for ___(39)___.

    a) appreciate   b) revise

    c) register   d) write

(40) Choose the most appropriate word for ___(40)___.

    a) first-come-first-served   b) last-in first-out

    c) first-in last-out   d) no service

第2回試験

5

[Part A] Read the following descriptions from (41) to (45) and choose the best answer to complete the sentences with blank parts from among the four alternatives: a), b), c) and d). Blacken the letter of your answer on the answer sheet.

(41) Located on the island of central Java, the magnificent _____ temple is one of the greatest South-East Asian Buddhist Monuments in Indonesia. It is an enormous construction covering a hill 42km from Jogjakarta City. The temple consists of six square bases topped by three circular ones. The central dome is surrounded by 72 Buddhist statues seated inside a perforated stupa. It was constructed in the early 9th century AD.

    a) Angkor Wat   b) Angkor Thom

    c) Borobudur   d) Wat Arun (Temple of Dawn)

(42) Nobody can forget the picture of the snow-covered shape of the mountain. It is _____ that means a maiden virgin in German. Whenever you see a guide to Switzerland, you cannot miss the name of this 4,158-m-high mountain. It is one of the main peaks in the European Alps. If the weather is very clear, you can enjoy a panoramic view of several peaks over 3,000-m high from the observatory at the top of the mountain.

    a) Mont Blanc   b) Mount McKinley

    c) Mt. Kilimanjaro   d) the Jungfrau

(43) The _____ (formally called Sultan Ahmet Mosque) is an historical mosque in Istanbul, Turkey. The mosque was built between 1609 and 1616 years during the rule of Sultan Ahmed I. The mosque has six minarets (towers), a main dome and four secondary domes. It contains a tomb of the founder, a madrasa (educational institution),

and a hospice. Today it attracts large numbers of tourist visitors.

a) Blue Mosque   b) Jameh Mosque of Isfahan

c) Jameirah Mosque   d) Prophet's Mosque

(44) A _____ is an outer garment worn by some Iranian women when they venture out in public. It is a full-body-length semicircle of fabric that is open down the front. It is thrown over the head and held shut in front. Muslim women may follow the Islamic dress code.

a) chador   b) chima   c) mantilla   d) sari

(45) Some countries in Europe specialize in a special form of entertainment. The French chanson, Spanish flamenco, Italian canzone or Portuguese _____. It will be among unforgettable memories of tourists. The _____ is a form of a melancholy folksong characterized by mournful tunes. It was registered as a UNESCO Intangible Cultural Heritage in 2011.

a) fado   b) mazurka   c) polka   d) yodel

[Part B] Read the following descriptions from (46) to (50) and choose the best answer to complete the sentences with blank parts from among the four alternatives: a), b), c) and d). Blacken the letter of your answer on the answer sheet.

(46) _____ Grand Shrine was founded in 768 as a tutelary shrine for the Fujiwara clan. The shrine with vermilion-colored pillars is famous not only for the numerous rows of more than 2,000 stone lanterns of various sizes and shapes that are lined on both sides of the approach to the shrine precincts but also for about 1,000 metal lanterns that are suspended from the eaves of its corridors.

    a) Fushimi-Inari Taisha   b) Kasuga Taisha

    c) Kumano-Nachi Taisha   d) Izumo Taisha

(47) _____ Onsen is located in the northern foothills of Mt. Shirane in Gunma Prefecture. It has a long history and an atmosphere all its own, because of its Yuba, hot-water field, which is full of steam from the boiling water gushing out of the earth. This spa is well-known for "Yumomi", a traditional method of cooling down hot spring water gushing directly from the source, while singing a local folk song.

    a) Arima   b) Dogo   c) Gero   d) Kusatsu

(48) Beyond the Nijubashi (Double Bridge) are seen the _____ Yagura (about 13.0m tall turret) of the former Edo Castle and stone walls running along the moat. It is the most beautiful two-story turret remaining from the former Edo Castle. It is flanked by two galleries (*tamon*) and is the last remaining Edo Castle fortified tower.

    a) Fujimi   b) Fushimi   c) Tamon   d) Tatsumi

(49) _____ porcelain ware is produced in Saga Prefecture. It was also called Imari porcelain ware because it was once exported from the port of Imari. Its origin dates back to the 16th century when the first porcelain was made in Saga Prefecture by a Korean potter named Li Sanpei. It is characterized by high-quality of blue designs on a white background (*sometsuke* design). It was exercised as a powerful influence on Europe.

    a) Arita-yaki   b) Mino-yaki   c) Oribe-yaki   d) Seto-yaki

(50) The _____ is an oblong white silk head hood worn in her traditional coiffure by a bride at her wedding ceremony. According to traditional tales, a woman will have horns on her head when she gets jealous. It is said to hide the horns of jealousy which women might possess, and to assure that the bride will not have horns of jealousy after marriage. It also symbolizes humility in the nuptial pledge before gods.

    a) Okoso-zukin   b) Shiromuku
    c) Takashimada   d) Tsuno-kakushi

6

Listen to the four descriptions for each picture from (51) to (55). Choose the statement that best describes what you see in the picture from among the four alternatives: a), b), c) and d). Blacken the letter of your answer on the answer sheet. The descriptions will be spoken just once.

🔊 1-35 (51)

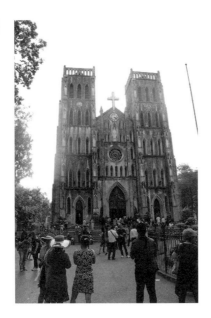

🔊 1-36 (52)

1-37 (53)

1-38 (54)

1-39 (55)

7

Listen to the four descriptions for each illustration from (56) to (60). Choose the statement that best describes what you see in the illustration from among the four alternatives: a), b), c) and d). Blacken the letter of your answer on the answer sheet. The descriptions will be spoken just once.

■))1-40 (56)

■))1-41 (57)

Please Help Us Make a Difference

Our Hotel policy is to change bed linens every three days and at end of stay.

Place this card on the bed if you would like your bed linens changed.
Only towels placed on the floor or the tub will be replaced.

Palace Hotel

Afternoon Tea

£ 21.95 per person

**Served Monday to Friday
12:00 noon to 4:30 p.m.
Reservation in advance is required**

Scones with Jam and Cream

Finger Sandwiches

Selection of Macaroons

**Your Choice of Tea
Green, Herbal, Fruit and Black Tea**

Sparkling Apple Juice

Toshogu Main Parking Area

(1) Open year round
(2) Charge (per vehicle per day)

Motorcycles	¥400
Passenger cars	¥600
Compact buses	¥1,200
Large buses	¥2,000

*Passenger cars: 200 spaces available.
*Compact / large buses: Spaces limited, reservations required 7 days in advance.
Spaces are not available on weekends and holidays.

8

Listen to the first sentences from (61) to (70) and complete each dialog by choosing the best response from among the four alternatives: a), b), c) and d). Blacken the letter of your answer on the answer sheet. The sentences will be spoken twice.

◀1-45 (61) a) All right. I'll pay by Visa.
　　　 b) Please give me more information.
　　　 c) Can I open a new bank account here?
　　　 d) May I have your name card, please?

◀1-46 (62) a) Don't worry. It doesn't take long to fix it.
　　　 b) I'm terribly sorry. Would you fill out this form, please?
　　　 c) I'm sorry, but fragile items are not covered by insurance.
　　　 d) I'll have our security officer investigate the case immediately.

◀1-47 (63) a) That'll be $180 including consumption tax.
　　　 b) We'll be there about a half past five.
　　　 c) We have some small banquet rooms accommodating 7 to 10 people.
　　　 d) We're filled to capacity at that time. Could you make it for 7:00 p.m.?

◀1-48 (64) a) There are 33 trains per day.
　　　 b) The fare is 10 euro per person.
　　　 c) The journey time is 1 hour 57 minutes.
　　　 d) Distance from Paris to Lyon is 393 km.

◀1-49 (65) a) They're open every day.
　　　 b) Please ask at the front desk.
　　　 c) We don't accept traveler's cheques.
　　　 d) The taxi stand is next to the post office.

(66) a) You can rent a swimsuit if you want.

　　　 b) Water from the tap is safe to drink.

　　　 c) I'm sorry. I'm afraid there's been a mistake.

　　　 d) I'm sorry, I'll be right back with a bottle of sparkling water.

(67) a) Sure. Could you tell me when you plan to go?

　　　 b) Let me see, I'm afraid I can't find your name.

　　　 c) Well, would you please be at gate 14 by 10:40?

　　　 d) OK. How long do you want to stay in the Netherlands?

(68) a) It takes about three and a half hours.

　　　 b) It's an express train, so it makes only two stops.

　　　 c) Every ten minutes. The next train will soon be here.

　　　 d) The last train for South Station leaves platform 5 at 10:00 a.m.

(69) a) We have five banquet rooms.

　　　 b) We are fully booked on that day.

　　　 c) We have a business center on the second floor.

　　　 d) We have valet parking for an additional charge.

(70) a) Just one hour is too short to enjoy shopping.

　　　 b) There are many souvenir shops around the hotel.

　　　 c) There are several outlets in the suburbs of the city.

　　　 d) On the way back to the hotel, we can enjoy shopping there.

第2回試験

9

Listen to the conversations from (71) to (80) and choose the most appropriate answer for the question following each conversation from among the four alternatives: a), b), c) and d). Blacken the letter of your answer on the answer sheet. The conversations and the questions will be spoken twice.

◀》1-55 (71) a) He can't find the duty-free shop.
      b) He needs to pick up his items soon.
      c) His purchases were misplaced.
      d) His flight was delayed.

◀》1-56 (72) a) A waiter.
      b) A police officer.
      c) A security guard.
      d) An airline customer service rep.

◀》1-57 (73) a) She can't find the bus stop.
      b) She doesn't have exact fare.
      c) Her directions were wrong.
      d) Her glasses are broken.

◀》1-58 (74) a) She missed a good shot.
      b) She was charged for a photo.
      c) She had her camera stolen.
      d) She had to pay for the dress.

◀》1-59 (75) a) To make a reservation.
      b) To cancel a reservation.
      c) To explain a payment problem.
      d) To return the man's credit card.

(76) a) Go directly to their hotel.
   b) Put their bags in a locker.
   c) Send their luggage to their hotel.
   d) Have their duty-free items delivered.

(77) a) Lift weights.
   b) Go for a run.
   c) Eat a light breakfast.
   d) Try cherry-blossom viewing.

(78) a) No tables are available now.
   b) They lost their reservation.
   c) Parties are seated out of order.
   d) The terrace is being closed.

(79) a) Safety features.
   b) Baggage handling.
   c) Boarding procedures.
   d) In-flight entertainment.

(80) a) Temple admission charges.
   b) The way to the destination.
   c) How to pay for the transfer.
   d) Whether to take the expressway.

第2回試験

10

Listen to the following descriptions **[Part A]** and **[Part B]**, and answer the questions from (81) to (90). Choose the most appropriate answer for each question from among the four alternatives: a), b), c) and d). Blacken the letter of your answer on the answer sheet. The descriptions and the questions will be spoken twice.

◀)1-65 **[Part A]**

(81) a) It is old.

　　 b) It has historic buildings.

　　 c) It is huge.

　　 d) It is compact.

(82) a) Public transport.

　　 b) Taxis.

　　 c) Boats.

　　 d) Bicycles.

(83) a) About 200 yen.

　　 b) About 1,200 yen.

　　 c) About 2,000 yen.

　　 d) About 2,100 yen.

(84) a) Concerts.

　　 b) Museums.

　　 c) A canal tour.

　　 d) City Hall.

(85) a) Rembrandt's house.

　　 b) The Rijksmuseum.

　　 c) The Concert Hall.

　　 d) The Bridge of 15 Bridges.

[Part B]

(86) a) In the southernmost part.
　　 b) In the northernmost part.
　　 c) In the easternmost part.
　　 d) In the central part.

(87) a) In the 6th century.
　　 b) In the 10th century.
　　 c) In the 15th century.
　　 d) In the 18th century.

(88) a) The male senior high school students and teachers.
　　 b) The female senior high school students and teachers.
　　 c) The male college students and teachers.
　　 d) The female university students and teachers.

(89) a) Many dead senior high school students and teachers.
　　 b) Many noted dead soldiers.
　　 c) Many well-known dead civilians.
　　 d) Many unknown war dead.

(90) a) It is the site of the fiercest battle of the war.
　　 b) It is the site of the beautiful scenery.
　　 c) It is the site of many unknown war dead.
　　 d) It is the site of traditional Ryukyu architecture.

筆記試験

1　観光用語の問題

【Part A】

（1）**正解** **d）**　「JAL の**接続便**を待機する間、短い市内観光をするチャンスがある」

解説 **connecting flight**「接続便、乗り継ぎ便」（= connecting plane）　▶ You had better check your reservation for the *connecting flight* and confirm your booking on arrival. 「乗り継ぎ便の予約を確認し、到着してから予約確定したほうがよい」

☆ connecting flight counter「乗り継ぎ便カウンター」　connecting passenger「乗り継ぎ客」（= passenger taking a connecting flight）　minimum connecting time [MCT]「最少乗継所要時間」

参考 a）「帰国便」return [homeward] flight
　　　 b）「出国便」departure [outgoing] flight
　　　 c）「直行便」direct [nonstop] flight

（2）**正解** **b）**　「免税店で何かを購入する時には**搭乗券**あるいは旅券を見せなくてはいけない」

解説 **boarding pass**「搭乗券」。boarding card、embarkation ticket とも言う。乗客搭乗手続きカウンターで航空券（flight coupon）を渡し、代わりに搭乗券を受け取る。▶ Here is your *boarding pass* and baggage claim tag. I've clipped your baggage tag to the cover of your ticket. 「搭乗券と手荷物合符をどうぞ。航空券の表に引換券をはっておきました」☆ boarding card「（旅客機の）搭乗カード」は接続便に乗り換えるときに手渡されるカードである。embarkation card「出国（記録）カード」は飛行機［船舶］の乗客が国外へ出る際に出国審査官に提示するカード。反意語は disembarkation card「入国カード」。

参考 a）「航空券」a flight [plane; an airline] ticket
　　　 c）「入場券」an admission ticket;（駅舎の）a platform ticket

d)「乗車券」a train [bus; streetcar] ticket

（3） 正解 **c)**「ホテルをチェックアウトする前に、ツアー参加者は**個人勘定**を各自で支払わなければならない」

解説 **incidental charge**「個人勘定」（= incidentals; personal [individual] account）。団体で一括に支払う勘定以外に請求される個人的な雑費の払い（冷蔵庫の飲食物、個人通話、有料映画、ルームサービスなど）　▶ Any *incidental charge* should be paid individually prior to check-out.「個人勘定はチェックアウトの前に個人的に支払わなくてはならない」☆ incidentals「（宿泊料と金銭の精算における）別勘定」

参考 a)「施設使用料」facility usage charge; usage fee of facilities; facility rental rates

　　 b)「臨時支払い」interim payment

　　 d)「サービス料」service charge; cover charge（レストラン用語）

（4） 正解 **d)**「青春18きっぷは、普通電車と**快速**電車が乗り放題の格安切符である」

解説 **rapid** (trains)「快速（電車）」

参考 a)「急行」express trains

　　 b)「特急」limited express trains

　　 c)「準急」semi-express trains

（5） 正解 **b)**「平和記念公園には原爆死没者**慰霊碑**近くに燃える平和の灯がある」

解説 **cenotaph**「慰霊碑」。a cenotaph (built in memory of war dead); a memorial (erected to war victims)「戦没者記念碑（遺骨を埋めた場所とは別に戦死した人を記念して建てた記念碑［塔］）」　☆ cenotaph はギリシャ語で「空の墓」の意。

参考 a)「霊廟」a mausoleum (enshrining an ancestor's spirit) 祖先の霊をまつる所。「廟宇」「廟所」また「御霊屋」などとも言う。▶ the *Mausoleum* of Tokugawa Ieyasu (the founder of the Tokugawa shogunate)「徳川家康の霊廟」☆複数形は mausolea（ラテン語中性名詞の複数形）または mausoleums（英語式）。

　　 c)「墳墓」a grave; a tomb

　　 d)「記念碑」a monument; a cenotaph

【Part B】

(6) **正解** **a）** All passengers are required to fill out a **customs** declaration form.

解説 customs (declaration form)「税関（申告書）」(= customs declaration card)　▶ Please be sure to sign your passenger's *customs declaration form*.「旅客者の税関申告書にサインすることを忘れないでください」☆ customs declaration「税関申告」は口頭申告（oral declaration）と書面申告（written declaration）がある。通常は口頭申告で済む場合が多い。

☆ customs inspection「税関検査」　customs office「税関所」　customs officer「税関検査官、税関吏、税関係官」(= customs official; customs inspector)

参考 b) disembarkation「降機、上陸、下船、入国」▶ *disembarkation* card「入国（記録）カード」(= entry [landing; arrival] card)

c) embarkation「搭乗、乗船、出国」▶ *Embarkation*/Disembarkation card [E/D card]「出入国（記録）カード」

d) taxation「課税」(= duty)

---

(7) **正解** **d）** This is **perishable** food. Please consume it immediately.

解説 perishable「生もの、腐りやすい」。▶ *perishable* food「生鮮食料品」*perishable* goods [items]「腐りやすい食品」(= perishables)【小包表示】PERISHABLE—Keep Away From Heat.「いたみ物ー熱に近づけないこと」☆ perish「腐る」

参考 a) fragile (goods)「壊れやすい（品）」

b) frozen (food)「冷凍（食品）」

c) pre-packaged (food)「レトルト（食品）」

---

(8) **正解** **b）** I'm afraid we can't accept this credit card because it **expired** last week.

解説 expired「有効期限切れの」　▶ *expired* ticket「有効期限切れの切符」My passport *expired* because I did not renew it.「旅券は更新しなかったので失効した」My visa *expired* on the first of May.「5月1日にビザが切れました」The validity term of your ticket *expired*.「あなたの切符は有効期限切れです」☆ expire「有効期限が切れる」(= run out)

参考 a) aspired (job)「志望の（仕事）」

c) inspired (poet)「天来の（詩人）」

d) respired (air)「呼気」

(9) **正解** **d)**　In the Shibuya Scramble Crossing, many pedestrians cross over the **intersection** when the crossing light turns green.

解説 **intersection**「交差点」(= junction, crossroads)　▶ I'm looking for the museum. —Straight down this way, third *intersection*.「博物館を探しています—こちらをまっすぐに行き、三番目の交差点です」☆「青信号」は a green light [signal] と言い、a blue light (青色) とは言わない。▶ cross the road on the *green* light「青信号で道路を渡る」「赤信号」は a red light と言い、a danger [warning] signal (危険 [警告] 信号) とも言う。「黄信号」は a yellow light と言い、英国では a amber light (琥珀色) とも言う。

参考 a) avenue「大通り」　b) alley「路地」　c) detour「迂回路」

(10) **正解** **b)**　Gion Festival originated in 869 when an **epidemic** raged in Kyoto and killed many people.

解説 **epidemic**「疫病」(= plague; pestilence)　▶ An *epidemic* has spread all over the country. They were attacked with the *epidemic*.「疫病が全国に蔓延し、彼らは疫病に罹った」 ⤳ **Column 05 祇園祭 (p.134)**

参考 a) cancer「癌(がん)」　c) heatstroke「熱中症」　d) pneumonia「肺炎」

【Part A】

(11) **正解** **c)** A：私たちは大使館に行くべきだと思います。ツアーメンバーの１人がパスポートを紛失しました。

B：それは難しいと思います。大使館はキャンベラにありますが、**シドニーには日本総領事館があります**。そこに行くことでよろしいでしょうか。

解説 **観光** A（観光客）はキャンベラの大使館に行く必要があると言う。しかしB（ガイド）はそこに行くには遠いので紛失したパスポートを対処する別の方法を提案している。

参考 a)「また遺失物取扱所があると思います」

b)「しかし私には請求書があります」

d)「できるだけ早く登録するように努力します」

☆ lost-and-found section「遺失物取扱所」 bill「請求書」 register「登録する」

(12) **正解** **b)** A：お待たせしました。大部分を 100 ドル札で差し上げてよろしいでしょうか。

B：実は、**少なくとも半分は小銭［少額紙幣］で頂ければありがたいのです**。

解説 **両替所** A（係員）は換金するときに 100 ドル札が多くてもよいかどうか尋ねている。B（旅行者）は希望（prefer）の金種を答えることになる。したがって b) が正解。

参考 a)「買い物にクレジットカードを使用したいのです」

c)「できればすぐに確認書を頂きたいのです」

d)「トラベラーズチェックに副署したいのです」

☆ denomination「（通貨の）単位」 confirmation slip「確認［承認］書」 countersign (a check)「（小切手に）副署［連署］する」

(13) **正解** **c)** A：メニューにあるカクテルの料金が見あたりません。おいくらになるかを教えてください。

B：**リゾートでは飲み物すべてをお客様に無料で提供しています**。部屋のカギを見せたり、給仕に支払ったりする必要はございません。

解説 **ホテル** A（宿泊客）はカクテルの料金を尋ねている。B（従業員）はルームキーを見せたり給仕に支払わなくてもよいと伝えているのでサービスであると推測できる。したがって c) が正解。

参考 a)「ホテルではアルコール類の飲み物はすべて禁止です」

b)「どの人も滞在中は無料の食券をもらえます」

d)「キーカードを使用してレクリエーションエリアのロッカーを開けてください」

☆ complimentary (drink)「無料の（飲み物）」

---

(14) **正解** **a)** A：歴史的な情緒があり、少し自然を帯びた観光地、そして東京から日帰り旅行で
行けるようなところをどこか推薦してくださいますか。

B：行けるところは多数ありますが、私がよく薦める場所として松本があります。
そこには山が近くあり、しかもお城があります。 新宿から急行電車で行けると
ころです。

解説 観光案内所　A（観光客）は、東京から日帰り旅行でき、自然のある歴史的な観光地
を紹介してほしいと言っている。B（係員）は松本を推薦している。したがってその場所の特
色が述べられている a) が正解。

参考 b)「その国の古都です」

c)「伝統的な平安時代の庭園で有名です」

d)「東京駅から歩いて行ける範囲です」

☆ accessible「行きやすい」　a day trip「日帰り旅行」

---

(15) **正解** **a)** A：消費税は 10 パーセントですか。ガイドブックでは、日本では消費税は 8 パー
セントと書いています。

B：**2019 年 4 月に 10 パーセントに上がりました。**

解説 観光　A（外国人）はガイドブックを見て、日本での消費税は 8 パーセントと思って
いた。消費税の増税について言及している a) が正解。

参考 b)「申し訳ございませんが機械は故障中です」

c)「まっすぐ行けば、エレベーターがございます」

d)「数分でアナウンスがあるはずです」

☆ consumption tax「消費税」　out of order「故障中」

【Part B】

(16) **正解** **d)** A：飛行機はどうでしたか。

B：恐ろしかったです。乱気流で本当に苦い経験でした。以前経験した以上に強烈でした。飛行して間もなく、飛行機は急に高度を下げ、**酸素マスクが落下しました。**

A：わあ！怖かったに違いないでしょう。

解説 空港　A（迎えの友人）は飛行機の乗り具合を尋ね、B（乗客）は酷い乱気流にあったと返答する。その時の機内の状況に合ったものを選択肢から選ぶ。d) が正解。

参考 a)「化粧室は使用中でした」

b)「搭乗券が発行されました」

c)「緊急自動車が現れました」

☆ turbulence「乱気流」　altitude「高度」　issue「発行する」　emergency「緊急」　oxygen mask「酸素マスク」

(17) **正解** **d)** A：この切符でこの列車に乗れますか。

B：いいえ、それは急行列車です。全席予約制で、切符は車中では売っていません。**乗車前に**特別切符を買うべきです。この階段を降り右側の切符売場で切符を買えます。

A：どうもありがとう。

解説 駅舎　A（乗客）は自分の持っている切符で列車に乗れるかどうかを尋ねている。B（駅員）は全席予約制であり、しかも車内では切符は買えないと返答する。したがって d) が正解。

参考 a)「換金するため」　b)「時刻表を調べるため」　c)「乗車後に」

☆ express train「急行列車」　get on「乗車する」

(18) **正解** **d)** A：すみません。こちらは405号室の田中です。この部屋は予約したものと違うようです。部屋自体はよいのですが、庭園やプールを見渡すだけです。私は海が見渡せる部屋を頼みました。

B：はい、少々お待ちください。……申し訳ございません。3階のお部屋が使用できるようにいたしました。そして部屋への移動を手伝うベルスタッフを送ります。

A：**海が見える部屋でありさえすれば**いいでしょう。

解説 ホテル　A（宿泊客）は海が見える部屋を予約したのに部屋が違うと苦情を述べる。

B（係員）は3階に用意した旨を伝える。Aは「〜であれば (so long as) よい」と言っている。空所には元々希望していた海が見える部屋が最適。したがって d) が正解。

参考 a)「高層階に」 b)「道路から離れて」 c)「この部屋より静かな」
☆ overlook「見渡す」 request「要請する」 quiet (room)「静かな（部屋）」

(19) **正解** **b)** A：それじゃ。今から共同の大露天風呂に行きましょう。行きますか。
B：遠慮したいと思います。**他人様と一緒に裸でいることは少し当惑しますね。**
A：おお。全然大丈夫ですよ。日本では誰でもそうしていますよ。いらっしゃい。おもしろいよ。

解説 露天風呂　A（日本人）は露天風呂に行くことを誘う。B（外国人）は行く気がないと返答しているので空所にはその理由が述べられていることが推測できる。したがって b) が正解。

参考 a)「このひとときを分かち合うことを本当に楽しみにしています」
c)「地元文化の伝統的な一端です」
d)「まずは必ず浴槽外で身体を洗ってください」
☆ communal (bath)「共同（浴場）」　be embarrassed「当惑する」　be sure to (do)「必ず〜（する）」

(20) **正解** **a)** A：内部をごらんよ！あの喧しくて、煙でもうもうとしたホールであの人たちは何をしているのですか。
B：パチンコで遊んでいます。パチンコとは、**少しピンボールに似ていますが、玉が多数あるゲームです。** 試しにやってみたいですか。
A：いいえ、結構です。特に今日のように晴天の日にはごめんですね。屋外にいるほうがはるかにいいですよ。

解説 パチンコ店　A（外国人）が騒々しい煙だらけのホールで大勢の人が何をしているのか知りたがっている。B（日本人）がパチンコだと返答して、その概要を説明する。パチンコの説明として最適なものは a) である。

参考 b)「誰もが試合観戦する一種の祝い事です」
c)「競技を伴う伝統的な地元祭事です」
d)「成人男性のみが名誉のために参加する儀式です」
☆ give it a try「試す」　involve「伴う、関連する」　ritual「儀式」

Column 05

祇園祭

The *Gion Festival* is held on July 1-31 in honor of Yasaka Shrine. This festival reaches its climax with a parade of two kinds of wheeled festive floats on July 17. People erected 66 tall spears [halberds] (*hoko*) representing the provinces of Japan asking for god's protection. Today the original spears [halberds] (*hoko*) have been replaced by big festive floats (called "*hoko*") of the same name. The smaller floats (called "*yama*") carry big life-size figures of famous historical personages. This festival is featured by the *Yama-boko junko* parade of the elaborate festive floats which are carried by many young men through the city to the accompaniment of musicians playing music known as *Gion-bayashi*.

祇園祭は八坂神社を祝って7月1日から31日まで行われ、そのクライマックスは2基の山車巡行が行われる17日である。神の御加護を求めて人々は全国の地方を表す66基の大きな槍（鉾）を建てた。今日では昔の槍（鉾）は同じ名前の大きな山車（「鉾」と呼ばれる）に取り代わる。小さい山車（「山」と呼ばれる）には有名な歴史人物の大きな等身大の人形がある。祭りのハイライトは豪華な山車の「山鉾巡行」で、「祇園囃子」で知られる楽士の音楽に合わせて若者たちが市内を練り歩く。

☆2016年ユネスコ無形文化遺産に登録された。

『和英：日本の文化・観光・歴史辞典［改訂版］』（山口百々男著、三修社）より

(21) **正解** **b)** If you go down practically any street, you are likely to **see ruins or other** reminders of the past.

実際にどの道に行っても、過去の**遺跡やその他**の名残を**見る**ことになるだろう。

解説 「主語（you）＋動詞（see）＋目的語（ruins）」の基本文型に留意すること。other は「他の」といった意味で、限定用法の形容詞として名詞を修飾する。▶ *other* people「他の人たち」。この文中では他の reminders of the past（昔を偲ばせる物）と続く。☆ be likely to「〜しそうだ」▶ He *is likely to* be late for school.「彼は学校に遅れそうだ」

(22) **正解** **d)** The Roman Forum and the Colosseum are the most famous of these ruins and they **attract** millions of tourists annually.

フォロ・ロマーノまたコロセウムはこれらの遺跡の中で最も有名なものであり、毎年**数百万の観光客を魅了して**やまない。

解説 「主語（they）＋動詞（attract）＋目的語（tourists）」の基本文型に留意すること。millions of (people)「数百万の（人々）」。大勢の人や多数の物を表す時に使用する熟語である。関連語に thousands of「何千もの〜」、hundreds of「数百もの〜」などがある。

(23) **正解** **a)** The Colosseum, originally known as the Flavian Amphitheater, was **built over a period** of eight years in the first century C.E.

フラウィウス円形闘技場で知られるコロセウムは 1 世紀において 8 **年の期間**をかけて建設された。

解説 主語が Colosseum の受動態（be ＋過去分詞）の文になっている。選択肢には動詞の過去分詞は (be) built しかない。残る単語の並び順は慣用句の知識が問われる。over a period of は「〜の期間にわたり」の意味である。▶ *over a period of* (eight years [months])「(8 年 [カ月] の期間にわたって」

(24) **正解** **a)** The Roman Forum today is only a wide area **covered with old roads** and pieces of broken buildings, but it was originally a vibrant city square at the center of a powerful city.

フォロ・ロマーノは現在**古代の道路**や崩れた建物の破片で**覆われた**広い場所であるが、当時は有力な都市の中心にある活気あふれた街の広場であった。

解説 選択肢の cover(ed) with に着眼すること。何で覆われているのかを考えると roads である。そしてどのような roads かを再考する。主語のフォロ・ロマーノは古代遺跡であるため old roads となる。最後に covered と関連する単語は area であり、a wide area (which is) covered with old roads と構成することができる。

---

(25) **正解** **c)** Many, many years ago, the square was **lined with** temples and monuments.

何年もの昔のことだが、広場は**寺院や記念物で連**なっていた。

解説 受動態（主語＋ be 動詞＋ PP（過去分詞））の文である。過去分詞に該当する動詞は、選択肢には lined しかない。line with は「〜に沿って（ものを）並べる」の意味である。主語は the square であり、そこに並べられていた（lined）のは temples である。

【Part A】

(26)「 ① に該当する最も適切な単語を選びなさい」

正解 **a）** **Duration**「期間、継続時間」

解説 空所の後に Four hours「4 時間」とあり、バチカン美術館ツアーの所要時間の表示であると考えられる。したがって a) が正解。

参考 b) Derivation「由来、起源」
　　　 c) Division「分類」
　　　 d) Exclamation「感嘆」

---

(27)「 ② に該当する最も適切な単語を選びなさい」

正解 **b）** **forbidden**「禁止する」

解説 空所の後には「美術館にバックパック、傘、金属類を持ち込むこと」と記載がある。作品保護のため傘などは持ち込みが禁止されていることが多い。したがって b) が正解。

参考 a) appointed「任命［指名］された」
　　　 c) hesitated「躊躇する」
　　　 d) recognized「認知された」

---

(28)「次のうちツアー広告に**記載されていない**のはどれですか」

正解 **b）**「参加者はミケランジェロ作の『最後の晩餐』(The Last Supper) を観賞できます」

解説 レオナルド・ダ・ビンチ作の『最後の晩餐』はミラノにあるサンタ・マリア・デッレ・グラツィエ修道院 (Convent in Church of Holy Mary of Grace [Chiesa di Santa Maria delle Grazie]) の食堂にある。バチカン美術館のシスティーナ礼拝堂内ミケランジェロ作の祭壇にあるフレスコ壁画は『最後の審判』(The Last Judgement) である。したがって b) が正解。

参考 以下の内容は記載されている。
　　　 a)「(二重) 螺旋階段はバチカン美術館にある」
　　　 c)「参加者はポポロ広場でオベリスクを見ることができる」
　　　 d)「参加者はツアーの早い段階で噴水を通過する」

(29) 「バチカン美術館バスツアーに関する**正しい記述**はどれですか」

正解 **b)** 「バチカン美術館を来館する時には、膝と肩を覆うこと」

解説 本文最後の**Note**中には、There is a dress code for this tour: knees and shoulders must be covered and men must wear full-length trousers. 「このツアーには服装規定があり、膝（小僧）や肩は覆い、男性は長ズボンを着用すべきである」と記載されている。したがって b) が正解。

参考 以下すべて**正しくない記述**である。

- a) 「午前のツアーは火曜日から土曜日まで正午に出発する」。午前のツアーは毎日（日曜日とカトリックの祝日は除く）
- c) 「システィーナ礼拝堂への入場料はツアー価格に含まれていない」。入場料はバチカン美術館ともに含まれている。
- d) 「ツアーは英語、イタリア語、ポルトガル語、ドイツ語、フランス語で利用できる」。ポルトガル語ではなくスペイン語が利用可能である。

---

(30) 「バチカン美術館のバスツアーに関する**正しくない記述**はどれですか」

正解 **d)** 午後のツアーは 12 月 1 日より実施される。

解説 **Tour in the afternoon**（午後のツアー）の欄に、From November 1st to March 31st. 「11 月 1 日から月 3 月 31 日まで実施する」と記載されている。したがって d) が正解。

参考 以下すべて**正しい記述**である。

- a) ツアーバスは古代アウレリアヌス城壁を通過する。
- b) ツアーバスはローマ・テルミナ鉄道駅に停車する。
- c) 交通費はツアー料金に含まれている。

【Part B】

(31) 「[　　①　　] に該当する最も適切な単語を選びなさい」

正解 **d) wealth** 「豊富」

解説 空所前後から湯布院には、美術館、カフェ、ブティックがあることを伝えたい文とわかる。選択肢を見ると、a wealth of 「たくさんの〜」という熟語をつくることができる。したがって d) が正解。

参考 a) advance「前進」　b) details「詳細」　c) alley「路地」
　　 ☆ wealth「裕福」　▶ a person with a *wealth* of experience「経験の豊かな人」

(32) 「[　　②　　] に該当する最も適切な単語を選びなさい」

正解 **b) stroll** 「散策する」

解説 多くの観光客が湯布院を訪れると記載があり、空所前の to 以下からその目的を説明している。観光客の目的として最適な単語は b) stroll「散策する」。

参考 a) export「輸入する」　c) expire「満期になる」　d) evacuate「避難［退避］する」
　　 ☆ stroll「散策する」（= take stroll）　▶ *stroll* through the countryside「田舎周辺を散策する」

(33) 「観光客が湯布院を短時間訪れるとすれば、昼間に入浴するにはどの施設がいちばん便利ですか」

正解 **c)** 「山水館」

解説 Located just a short walk from Yufuin Station, the **Sansuikan** offers some of the most easily accessible baths to tourists without private means of transportation.「山水館は湯布院駅から少し歩いて行ける所にあり、個人的な交通手段をもたない観光客にとっては非常に行きやすい温泉場である」と記載されている。したがって c) が正解。

参考 a)「束の間」　b)「夢想園」　d)「下ん湯大衆浴場」

(34) 「湯布院の情報に関する**正しくない記述**はどれですか」

正解 **c)** 「記載されているすべての施設は宿泊施設である」

解説 Shitanyu Public Bath だけは宿泊施設ではない。他の3軒の施設は overnight stay（一泊）ができる。したがって c) が正解。

参考 以下の記載は**正しい記述**である。
　　 a)「1,000円未満で観光客は日帰り入浴できる」

b)「宿泊しない客向けに遅くまで開いている施設がある」

d)「1か所の施設は日帰り入浴として4時間だけ営業している」

(35)「湯布院の情報に関する**正しい記述**はどれですか」

正解 **a)** 束の間は湯布院には珍しい青みがかったお湯で有名である。

解説 The ryokan (Tsuka-no-Ma) has large, gender separated outdoor baths with bluish-looking water, untypical for Yufuin.「旅館（束の間）には、湯布院にはめずらしい青みがかった湯の男女別大露天風呂がある」と記載されている。したがって a) が正解。

参考 以下すべて**正しくない記述**である。

b）下ん湯の露天風呂からは眼下に街を眺めることができる。下ん湯の説明に眺望に関する記述はない。

c）山水館は高台に位置しており、露天風呂からは由布岳を望むことができる。山水館ではなく夢想園の説明である。

d）下ん湯は混浴であるが、脱衣所は男女別に設けられている。男女別の脱衣所はない。

【Part C】

(36)「　(36)　に該当する最も適切な単語を選びなさい」

正解 **d)** **brochure**「パンフレット」

解説 ガイドは、イベントの「何か」を見てほしいとお願いし、その後イベントが5日間にわたり開催されることを説明している。イベント日程が記載されているものとして考えるとパンフレット（brochure）が最適。したがって d) が正解。

参考 a) travel documents「旅行書類」　b) envelope「封筒」　c) receipt「領収書」

(37)「　(37)　に該当する最も適切な単語を選びなさい」

正解 **c)** **participating**「参加する」

解説 佐賀インターナショナルバルーンフェスタでは、その名前のとおり、いろいろな国から出場している。空所後の in と結びつく、意味的にも最適な動詞は participate。したがって c) が正解。

参考 a) delivering「配達する」　b) organizing「組織化する」　d) playing「遊ぶ」

(38)「 (38) に該当する最も適切な単語を選びなさい」

正解 **d) held**「開催される」

解説 空所後に佐賀インターナショナルバルーンフェスタが行われる場所や時間帯が記載されている。「行われる」の意味を持つ選択肢を探す。したがって d) が正解。

参考 a) exchanged「交換された」
b) compared「比較された」
c) detained「拘留さえた」

(39)「 (39) に該当する最も適切な語句を選びなさい」

正解 **c) register**「登録する」

解説 参加したいイベントに対して必要なことを選ぶ。また、イベントによってはスペースが限られているという説明があるので、register が最適。したがって c) が正解。

参考 a) appreciate「観賞する」 b) revise「改訂する」 d) write「書く」

(40)「 (40) に該当する最も適切な単語を選びなさい」

正解 **a) first-come-first-served**「先着順に」

解説 空所前には、イベントによってはスペースが限られているとあるので、申込方式として考えられるのは先着順か抽選である。したがって a) が正解。

参考 b) last-in first-out「後入先出法」
c) first-in last-out「先入後出方式」
d) no service「圏外」（携帯電話などの電波がないこと）

5　海外観光と国内観光の問題

【Part A】

(41) 正解 c)　Borobudur「ボロブドゥール」。1991年世界遺産に登録。

和訳 ジャワ島中心部にある壮観な**ボロブドゥール**寺院は、インドネシアにおける東南アジア最大の仏教遺跡のひとつである。ジョグジャカルタ市から42kmのところにある丘陵を覆う壮大な建造物である。寺院は6層の方形壇、さらにその上に3層の円形壇から成る。中央ドームの周辺には穴のあいたストゥーパ(仏舎利塔)に座す72体の仏像がある。寺院は9世紀初頭に建造された。

解説 解法のカギは、まずは「ジャワ島」、次に「インドネシアにあるアジア最大の仏教遺跡」、最後に「全体で9層の階段ピラミッド」である。

参考 以下すべて世界遺産である。
- **a)** Angkor Wat「アンコール・ワット」。カンボジア北西部にある「国都(Angkor)寺院(Wat)」。カンボジア国旗の中央にも描かれている。
- **b)** Angkor Thom「アンコール・トム」。アンコール遺跡の1つで、アンコール・ワットの北部にある都市遺跡。中央付近にあるバイヨン寺院は有名。
- **d)** Wat Arun (Temple of Dawn)「ワット・アルン」(暁の寺)。タイのバンコクにある寺院。三島由起夫の小説『暁の寺』の舞台になった。

(42) 正解 d)　the Jungfrau「ユングフラウ」(標高4,458m)

和訳 雪に覆われたその山の絵画を見た人は誰も忘れることができない。その山とはドイツ語で処女を意味する**ユングフラウ**である。スイスのガイドブックを見る時はいつも4,158mのこの山の名を見落とすことができない。ヨーロッパアルプス山脈の中における主峰の1つである。晴天の日であれば、山頂の展望台から標高3,000m級以上のパノラマのような全景を眺望することができる。

解説 解法のカギは、まず「スイスの山」、次に「アルプス山脈の主峰」、最後に「4,158mの山」である。

参考 下記は世界有数の名峰である。
- **a)** Mont Blanc「モンブラン」(標高4,810m)。フランスとイタリアの国境にあるヨーロッパアルプスの最高峰。「白い(blanc)山(Mont)」の意味。
- **b)** Mount McKinley「マウント・マッキンリー」(6,190m)。北米アラスカ州にある山。北アメリカ大陸の最高峰。2015年より「デナリ」(Denali)が正式呼称。
- **c)** Mt. Kilimanjaro「キリマンジャロ」(標高5,895m)。タンザニア北東部にある山。アフリカ大陸の最高峰。キリマンジャロ・コーヒーは「キリマン」で知られる。

(43) **正解** **a)** **Blue Mosque**「ブルーモスク」

和訳 ブルーモスク（正式名称スルタン・アフメト・モスク）はトルコのイスタンブールにある由緒ある
モスクである。モスクは、（オスマン帝国第 14 代の）スルタン・アフメト 1 世が統治する期間中の 1609
年から 1616 年にかけて建造された。モスクには 6 基のミナレット（尖塔）、大ドーム、そして 4 つの副ドー
ムがある。内部には、創建者（アフメト）の墓、マドラサ（教育施設）そしてホスピス（巡礼者用の宿泊施設）
がある。現在大勢の観光客を魅了してやまない。

解説 解法のカギは、まずは「トルコのモスク」、次に「6 基のミナレット」、最後に「創建者の墓」
があること。☆モスクの内部の壁、天井、柱などを覆う模様が青色（blue）を帯びているこ
とから「ブルーモスク」と呼ばれる。世界で最も美しいモスクと評されている。1985 年世界
遺産に登録された。

参考 中東における由緒ある著名なモスク。
- b) Jameh Mosque of Isfahan「イスファハーンのジャーメ・モスク」。イラン最古の「金曜モスク」。
  2012 年世界遺産に登録。
- c) Jameirah Mosque「ジュメイラ・モスク」。1979 年建造のアラブ首長国連邦のドバイにある
  モスク。
- d) Prophet's Mosque「予言者のモスク」。622 年建造のサウジアラビアにあるイスラム教の礼拝堂。
  予言者ムハンマドの霊廟がある。

(44) **正解** **a)** **chador**「チャードル」☆日本語で「チャドル」とも表記する。

和訳 チャードルはイラン女性が公衆の面前に出る時に着用する衣類である。身体全身を覆う半円の布で、
前が下まで開くようになっている。頭から被って前を閉める。イスラム女性にはイスラム圏において従う
服装規定がある。

解説 解法のカギは、「イラン女性」と「イスラム女性用の服装規定」。

参考 東洋女性が着用する衣装。
- b) chima「チマ」。朝鮮民族の女性用朝鮮衣装チマ・チョゴリにおけるチマのことで、「巻きスカー
  ト」の意味。チョゴリは男女共通の上着のこと。
- c) mantilla「マンティーラ」。スペインやメキシコなどの女性が頭から肩にかけるレースのスカー
  フ。また女性用の短いマントのこと。
- d) sari「サリー」。インド、パキスタンなど、ヒンドゥー教徒の女性が衣装として巻きつける長い
  絹［綿］布の外衣。

(45) **正解** **a)** **fado**「ファド」

和訳 ヨーロッパには特殊なエンターテイメント形式を得意とする国がある。フランスのシャンソン、ス

ペインのフラメンコ、イタリアのカンツォーネ、ポルトガルには**ファド**。ファドは観光客にとって忘れられない思い出になるだろう。**ファド**は哀愁を帯びた旋律が特徴的なメランコリックな民族歌謡である。2011年にはユネスコ無形文化遺産に登録された。

解説 解法のカギは、「ポルトガルの民族的な大衆歌謡」であること。選択肢の中のファドだけがユネスコ無形文化遺産である。☆ Fado はポルトガル語で「運命・宿命」の意味である。あのメランコリックな日本の歌謡曲『異邦人』（作詞・作曲：久保田早紀）はファドが元になっていると言われている。

参考 ヨーロッパで生まれた民族舞曲。
- b) mazurka「マズルカ」。ポーランドの農民から起った民族舞踏・舞曲。
- c) polka「ポルカ」。チェコの民族舞踏・舞曲。2拍子の軽快なリズム。
- d) yodel「ヨーデル」。ヨーロッパ・アルプス地方などで発祥した歌唱法。

【Part B】

(46) **正解** b) **Kasuga Taisha**「春日大社」

和訳 **春日大社**は、768年藤原家の鎮守社として創建された。朱塗りの柱をもつこの神社は、境内に通ずる参道の両側に並ぶ、大小さまざまな形をした2,000以上の石灯籠の列、また回廊の軒下に吊り下げられた約1,000の金属灯籠で有名である。

解説 解法のカギは、「藤原家の鎮守社」、多数の「石灯籠」と「金属灯籠」である。☆奈良県（奈良市春日野町）にある神社。主祭神は春日神。万灯籠祭で有名。大小の3,000基の明かりのもと青銅製や石造の灯籠によって醸し出される幻想的な風景が見られる。1998年には「春日山原始林」を含めユネスコ世界遺産に登録。

参考 日本を代表する大社。
- a) Fushimi-Inari Taisha「伏見稲荷大社」。京都市伏見区にある神社。708年 - 715年に創建。主祭神は稲荷大神。朱塗りの千本鳥居が有名。
- c) Kumano-Nachi Taisha「熊野那智大社」和歌山県那智勝浦町にある神社。317年に創建。主祭神は熊野夫須美大神。那智の滝は有名。2004年世界遺産に登録。
- d) Izumo Taisha「出雲大社」。島根県出雲市にある神社。創建は神代とされる。主祭神は大国主大神。縁結びの神また因幡のしろうさぎ神話で有名。

---

(47) **正解** d) **Kusatsu**「草津（温泉）」

和訳 草津温泉は群馬県白根山の北麓にある。長い歴史と独特な雰囲気をもち、地中から湧き出る熱湯の

蒸気で満ちた「湯場」がある。民謡の歌に合わせながら源泉から直接湧き出る温泉を冷ます伝統的な「湯もみ」でよく知られる。

解説 解法のカギは、「群馬県白根山」、「湯もみ」。☆群馬県吾妻郡草津町に湧出する温泉。日本一の自然湧出量を有する日本を代表する名泉。草津温泉といえば、湯畑のある由緒ある温泉街、そして湯もみと草津節である。

参考 日本三名泉（草津・有馬・下呂）と日本三古湯（有馬・道後・白浜）。
  a) Arima「有馬（温泉）」。兵庫県神戸市北区有馬町に湧出する温泉。江戸時代の温泉番付ではナンバーワンであった。金泉（湧出口では透明だが、空気に触れると赤湯になる）が有名。
  b) Dogo「道後（温泉）」。愛媛県松山市に湧出する温泉。万葉集、また夏目漱石の小説『坊ちゃん』にも描かれる愛媛県を代表する観光地。
  c) Gero「下呂（温泉）」。岐阜県下呂市に湧出する温泉。傷ついた一羽の白鷺が温泉のありかを知らせたという伝説がある。千年以上の歴史を有する古湯。

(48) 正解 b) Fushimi「伏見（櫓）」

和訳 二重橋の向こうには旧江戸城の**伏見櫓**（高さ約 13.0 m）と濠沿いに広がる石垣が目に留まる。伏見櫓は旧江戸城内に残存する最も美しい二重櫓である。左右には 2 棟の多聞で側面を守られ、江戸城の頃から残されている最後の砦であった。

解説 解法のカギは、「二重橋」（正門石橋）の奥に借景となる「二重櫓」である。

参考 旧江戸城遺構として残存する櫓（伏見櫓・富士見櫓・巽櫓・多聞櫓）。
  a) Fujimi「富士見（櫓）」（約 16 m）。中雀門を入って左手の本丸南端に位置する三重の櫓である。櫓上から富士山、秩父連山、筑波山、東京湾などを臨むことができた。
  c) Tamon「多聞（櫓）」。江戸城本丸には 15 棟の多聞櫓があったが、富士見多聞（鉄砲や弓矢が納められている）はその中で唯一の現存遺構である。
  d) Tatsumi「巽（櫓）」。桜田巽二重櫓の略。江戸城の隅角に造られ監視と防御を目的する隅櫓である。江戸城本丸の東南（辰巳＝巽）の方向にあることが名の由来である。

(49) 正解 a) Arita-yaki「有田焼」

和訳 **有田焼**は佐賀県（有田町）で生産されている焼物。焼物の積み出しが伊万里港であるため伊万里焼とも呼ばれる。有田焼の起源は 16 世紀に遡り、朝鮮人陶工である李参平が佐賀県で制作し始めた。良質な「染付」（白色の素地に青色の図柄）が特色の磁器である。欧州にも多大な影響を与えた。

解説 解法のカギは「佐賀県」、「伊万里焼とも呼ばれる」こと。☆佐賀県有田町を中心に焼かれた磁器。有田焼の生みの親、李参平の直系の子孫が現在も磁器の製作活動を行っている。有田町はドイツのマイセン市と姉妹都市であり、ドレスデン博物館には有田焼が多数保管さ

れている。

参考 日本三大焼物（有田・美濃・瀬戸）である。☞ **Column 06** 陶磁器の種類 （p.147）

b) Mino-yaki「美濃焼」。岐阜県の美濃地方にて制作される陶磁器。その起源は、奈良時代の須恵器とも言われる由緒ある焼物。

c) Oribe-yaki「織部焼」。岐阜県土岐市にて制作される陶磁器。美濃焼の一種。

d) Seto-yaki「瀬戸焼」。愛知県瀬戸市にて制作される陶磁器。瀬戸は、千年以上の歴史をもつ、日本屈指の窯業地。瀬戸物は陶磁器の代名詞になった。

(50) **正解** **d）** **Tsuno-kakushi**「角隠し」

和訳 角隠しとは結婚式の時、花嫁が伝統的に結った髪型にまとう、長方形の白い絹布の被り物のことである。女性は嫉妬するとき、その頭上に角が出るのだと昔から言い伝えられてきた。角隠しを着用することは、女性が持つかもしれない嫉妬の角を隠すため、また結婚後、花嫁が嫉妬の角を持つことがないと保証するためだと言われている。また花嫁が神前で行う婚礼の誓約における謙虚さを象徴する。

解説 「角隠し」の由来には諸説がある。古来、女性は嫉妬に狂うと角が生え鬼になるという言い伝えがあった。江戸時代、能楽で女性の生霊（= living ghost　生きている人間の霊魂が体外に出て自由に動き回ること）が嫉妬で鬼形になることから、また激怒の様相が角をはやした鬼に似ていることから、角は女性の嫉妬のたとえに用いられた。

参考 日本女性の代表的な衣装・髪型。

a) Okoso-zukin「御高祖頭巾」。四角い布に紐を付け、目だけ出して頭・顔を包む防寒用頭巾。江戸時代から明治・大正時代にかけて若い女性に流行した。

b) Shiromuku「白無垢」。表裏白一色で仕立てた和服。室町時代から使用され、明治以降は結婚式（神前挙式）で花嫁が着用する伝統的な婚礼衣装となった。

c) Takashimada「高島田」。髪の根元を高く仕立てた島田髷の一種。江戸時代の未婚の女性の代表的な髪型である。明治以降、花嫁日本髪の正装は文金高島田となった。

陶磁器の種類

日本三大陶磁器とは有田焼・瀬戸焼・美濃焼である。

① **有田焼／伊万里焼　Arita [Imari]** porcelain ware 《佐賀県》

Arita porcelain ware is produced in and around the city of Arita in Saga Prefecture. It was also called Imari porcelain ware because it was once exported from the port of Imari. The origin of *Arita-yaki* dates back to the 16th century when the first prorcelain was made in Arita by a Korean potter named Li Sanpei (?-1655). It is characterized by high-quality of blue designs on a white background (*sometsuke* design). It was exercised as a powerful influence on Europe.

佐賀県有田町周辺で生産されている焼物。焼物の積み出しが伊万里港であるため伊万里焼とも呼ばれる。有田焼の起源は 16 世紀に遡り、朝鮮人陶工である李参平が有田で制作し始めた。その特色は良質な「染付」（白色の素地に青色の図柄）の磁器である。欧州にも多大な影響を与えた。★豊臣秀吉の朝鮮出兵後の頃、日本に連行された李参平は有田焼の生みの親である。酒井田柿右衛門（1596-1666）の重要無形文化財色絵磁器（porcelain ware of enamel decorations in shades of a red-persimmon color）は有名である。

② **瀬戸焼　Seto** ceramic and porcelain ware 《愛知県》

Seto ceramic and pottery is produced in and around the city of Seto in Aichi Prefecture. *Seto-yaki* dates back to the 13th century when Kato Toshiro, known as the founder of glazed ceramics (*yutoki*) at the Seto district, brought back glazing techniques from China in the Kamakura period (1185-1333). It is the glazed porcelain with a white translucent body.

瀬戸焼は愛知県の瀬戸市周辺で生産されている焼物である。瀬戸焼の起源は 13 世紀に遡り、瀬戸地域で釉陶器と創始者として知られる加藤藤四郎が、鎌倉時代（1185-1333）に中国からその技法を伝えた。磁器は白く透光性があり、釉薬を塗っている。★瀬戸は日本最古・最大の製陶地（Japan's largest ceramic producing）であり、瀬戸物という場合もある。しかも瀬戸物は陶器を代表する用語となっている。

③ **美濃焼　Mino** ceramic and procelain ware 《岐阜県》

Mino ceramic ware is produced at Mino Province (present cities of Toki and Tajimi) in Gifu Prefecure). *Mino-yaki* dates back in the 16th century when many potters moved to Mino Province from Seto district. They produced various ceramic ware of rustic type, including superb tea utensils, under the protection of Oda Nobunaga (1534-82).

美濃焼は美濃地方（現・岐阜県土岐市・多治見市）で生産される焼物である。美濃焼は 16 世紀に遡り、その頃大勢の陶工たちが瀬戸地区から美濃地方に移り住んだ。彼らは織田信長（1534-82）の保護のもとで、優れた茶器を含め、素朴なタイプの陶器を生産した。★時代が流れ、桃山時代には志野焼（国宝指定の焼物もある）、特に江戸時代には織部焼の優品が生産された。

4 その他の陶磁器

志野焼 **Shino** ceramic ware characterized by thick white glazes (produced in the Mino region, now Gifu Prefecture).

織部焼 **Oribe** ceramic ware characterized by geometrical designs.

伊賀焼 **Iga** ceramic ware characterized by rustic charm (produced in the Iga region of Mie Prefecture).

唐津焼 **Karatsu** ceramic ware characterized by its earthy, simple and natural style (produced in the Karatsu region of Saga Prefecture).

清水焼 **Kiyomizu** porcelain ware [chinaware] produced in the area around Kiyomizu Temple in Kyoto Prefecture.

九谷焼 **Kutani** porcelain ware characterized by its rich decorative pattern (produced in Ishikawa Prefecture).　☆派手な色彩が多い

薩摩焼 **Satsuma** ceramic ware produced in Kagoshima Prefecture.

信楽焼 **Shigaraki** ceramic and pottery characterized by ceramic figurines of raccoon dogs holding sake jugs (produced in Shiga Prefecture).　☆たぬき像は「他を抜く」の意味から店先などによく見かける。また茶器の逸品が多い。

萩焼 **Hagi** ceramic and porcelain ware characterized by rough cracked glaze (produced in the Hagi region of Yamaguchi Prefecture).

備前焼 **Bizen** ceramic ware characterized by natural but lustrous color (produced in Okayama Prefecture).

益子焼 **Mashiko** ceramic and porcelain characterized by round, warm design (produced in Tochigi Prefecture).

リスニング試験

6 「写真」による状況把握

音声の内容

1-35 (51) a) Barriers prevent people from entering the building.

   b) Some people are observing this modern building.

   c) Visitors are admiring this religious building.

   d) The inside of the historic ruins is open to the public.

1-36 (52) a) People are taking pictures of a wooden door.

   b) The unique carvings are attracting attention.

   c) Tourists are photographing the entranceway to the temple.

   d) The windows are decorated with marble carvings.

1-37 (53) a) Due to the heat some people are using parasols.

   b) Some monks are walking away from the temple.

   c) Large crowds are enduring the monsoon rains.

   d) The temple has few visitors during the midday sun.

1-38 (54) a) The screen shows information about optional tours.

   b) People are in a line to go through government procedures.

   c) People have to go through the gate for a security check.

   d) The entrance gate leads to the train platform.

1-39 (55) a) A rowboat is leaving the dock area.

   b) Passengers are enjoying a trip on the river.

   c) A man is using a paddle to move the canoe.

   d) A ship is passing a pole in the water.

第2回試験

解答と解説

(51) 正解 **c)** 「来訪者はこの宗教的な建物に見とれている」

解説 建物の中央上部には十字架（a cross）があるので教会（church）である。大勢の来訪者（visitors）が壮観な宗教建築（religious building）を見て感嘆している。したがって c) が正解。

参考 a)「壁が邪魔して建物に入ることができない」

　　　 b)「この近代的な建物を観察する人が数名いる」

　　　 d)「歴史的遺跡の内部は公開されている」

　　　 ☆ prevent from (doing)「（しないように）防ぐ、～させない」　admire「感嘆する」　(historic) ruins「遺跡（史跡）」

(52) 正解 **b)** 「ユニークな彫刻（物）は注目を浴びている」

解説 日光東照宮の三猿、ユニークな彫刻（unique carvings）である。選択肢にある a) a wooden door、c) the gateway to the temple、d) marble carvings ではない。したがって b) が正解。

参考 a)「木造ドアの写真を撮る人が多数いる」

　　　 c)「観光客は寺院への入口を撮影している」

　　　 d)「窓は大理石の彫刻で装飾されている」

　　　 ☆ entranceway「入り口、通路」　marble (carvings)「大理石（の彫刻）」

(53) 正解 **a)** 「暑さのため日傘をさす人が数名いる」

解説 写真を見ると、東南アジア独特の猛烈な暑さ（the heat）を凌ぐため日傘（parasols）をさす人もいる。選択肢に目を通すと、b)、c)、d) における説明は写真内容に合致しない。したがって a) が正解。

参考 b)「寺院から立ち去る僧侶が数名いる」

　　　 c)「大勢の人がモンスーン期の降雨を耐えている」

　　　 d)「真昼の太陽が照りつける間は寺院への参詣者も少ない」

　　　 ☆ use (parasols)「（日傘）をさす」　monk「僧侶」（= Buddhist priest）

(54) 正解 **d)** 「改札口は電車の（プラット）ホームに通じている」

解説 写真は駅舎の改札口であり、b) また c) における空港ではない。改札口（ticket gate）は当然のことながら電車のホーム（train platform）に通じている。したがって d) が正解。

参考 a)「スクリーン（画面）にはオプショナルツアーに関する情報が表示されている」

　　　b)「大勢の人が渡航手続（CIQ）を通過するために列をなしている」☞ **Column 07** CIQ

　　　c)「人々は保安検査のためゲートを通過しなくてはいけない」

(55) **正解 b)**　「乗客は水上ツアーを楽しんでいる」

解説 写真を見るかぎりでは、水上でのツアー（a trip on the water）を楽しんでいる様子である。選択肢 a)、c)、d) は写真内容とは合致しない。したがって b) が正解。

参考 a)「漕艇は波止場を出発している」

　　　c)「男性はカヌーを漕ぐために櫂を使っている」

　　　d)「船は水中に棹を渡している」

　　　☆ rowboat「漕艇、漕ぎ舟」（=《英》rowing boat）　paddle「櫂」

Column 07

CIQ
[CUSTOMS − IMMIGRATION − QUARANTINE]

　海外渡航をするとき、出入国に際して、customs「**税関**」（荷物・免税品・課税品などの検査）、immigration「**出入国管理**」（旅券・出入国カードなどの検査）、quarantine「**検疫**」（予防接種証明書などの検査）の３つの関所を通過する。諸外国の出入国に際しての必要な検査や手続きのこと。またはこれらに当たる監督庁のことである。これらの手続きを government procedures または **government formalities**「行政手続き」と言う。

音声の内容

◀1-40 (56) a) Liquids are prohibited in the cabin.

b) Liquids in carry-on baggage should be checked separately.

c) 100 milliliters is the total amount allowed in the cabin.

d) Packages of liquids are available at the duty-free shop.

◀1-41 (57) a) The Palace Hotel changes bed linens every other day.

b) If you would like to re-use your towels, please place them on the hook.

c) Towels are exempted from the hotel's eco program.

d) The Palace Hotel is proud of its high quality linens.

◀1-42 (58) a) The afternoon tea menu is available seven days a week.

b) The afternoon tea menu is offered on a first come, first served basis.

c) You can choose your favorite tea from the list.

d) Alcoholic beverages are available at an additional charge.

◀1-43 (59) a) The card game consists of 48 pairs of cards.

b) The picture cards have popular scenes on them.

c) This game contains 100 poems, each one written by a different poet.

d) Playing cards were introduced to Japan during the Edo period.

◀1-44 (60) a) Motorcycles can be parked free of charge in the parking area.

b) The parking area doesn't accept buses on weekends and holidays.

c) Spaces for compact cars are limited, so advance reservation is needed.

d) The charge listed is per vehicle per hour.

解答と解説

(56) 【正解】 **b)** 「機内持ち込み手荷物の中の液体は別々に検査を受けるべきである」

【解説】 空港で Regulations for Hand Luggage（手荷物に関する規定書）をよく見かける。イラストの上部に、There are restrictions on liquids which can be taken the cabin.「機内に持ち込むことができる液体には制限がある」と記載されている。イラストの下部には、Please present separately at the Security Control.「検問［保安検査］では別々に提示してください」と記載されている。したがって b) が正解。

【参考】a)「キャビン（機室）内への液体の持ち込みは禁止されている」
　　　 c)「100 ミリリットルがキャビン（機室）内で許可される総量である」
　　　 d)「液体の包装は免税店で市販されている」
　　　 ☆ carry-on baggage「機内持ち込み手荷物」 available「利用［使用］できる」

(57) 【正解】 **b)** 「タオルを再使用したい場合、ホック（鉤）につるしてください」

【解説】 パレスホテル宿泊者に向けた注意事項である。Only towels placed on the floor or the tub will be replaced.「床または浴槽に置かれたタオルのみが交換される」と記載されている。そのため宿泊者がタオルを再度使用（re-use towels）したいならば床または浴槽に放置せずホック（hook）にかける必要がある。したがって b) が正解。

【参考】a)「パレスホテルはベッドリネン製品（シーツと枕カバー）は隔日に取り替える」
　　　 c)「タオルはホテルのエコプログラムから除外される」
　　　 d)「パレスホテルは高品質のリネン製品を誇りにしている」
　　　 ☆ re-use「再使用」 hook「ホック（掛け）鉤、留め金」 exempt(ed)「除く」

(58) 【正解】 **c)** 「好みのお茶をリストから選べる」

【解説】「英国人は『午後の紅茶』(Afternoon Tea) のために戦争を中断する」という文言は有名である。その「午後の紅茶」かどうかは別として、カフェにおけるお茶の話題である。イラストの下部に Your choice of Tea　 Green, Herbal, Fruit and Black Tea「顧客は緑茶、ハーブ茶、フルーツ茶、紅茶が選べる」と記載されている。したがって c) が正解。

【参考】a)「アフタヌーン・ティーのメニューは週に 7 日利用できる」
　　　 b)「アフタヌーン・ティーのメニューは先着順に受け付ける」
　　　 d)「アルコール飲料は追加料金で利用できる」
　　　 ☆ on a first come, first served basis「先着順に」 additional charge「追加料金」

(59) 正解 a) 「このカードゲーム（歌留多）は 48 組のカードから成る」

解説 いろはカルタは日本で戦国時代から江戸時代にかけて成立した古典的カードゲームを指す総称である。いろは 48 文字を頭字とする語呂のよい短句形のことわざを選び集めたものである。天正カルタ（天正年間［1573-1592］に流行）のように、ポルトガル式の 48 枚から構成されるトランプもある。したがって a) が正解。

参考 b)「絵札には人気のシーン（場面）がある」

c)「このゲームには 100 の詩歌があり、個々異なる詩人によって詠われている」

d)「カード遊びは江戸時代に日本へ導入された」

☆ consist of「〜から成る、構成する」 introduce「導入する、紹介する」

(60) 正解 b) 「バスは週末と祝祭日には駐車場を利用することができない」

解説 東照宮にある駐車場の掲示である。イラスト下部の Compact / large buses の項目には、Spaces are not available on weekends and holidays.「駐車場は週末と祝祭日（休日）には使用できない」と記載されている。したがって b) が正解。

参考 a)「オートバイは駐車場内に無料で駐車できる」

c)「小型自動車の駐車場は制限されているので、事前予約が要る」

d)「提示された料金は 1 車両 1 時間あたりのものである」

☆ free of charge「無料」 advance reservation「事前予約」 per hour「時間単位で」

8 「対話」に関する内容把握

音声の内容

1-45 (61) Three hundred and thirty four dollars in all. How would you like to settle the account?

1-46 (62) Excuse me. My suitcase is badly cracked, and the lock is broken.

1-47 (63) I'd like to make a dinner reservation for three Sunday at 5:00 p.m.

1-48 (64) How long does it take to travel from Paris to Lyon by train?

1-49 (65) Where can we find a rental car agency?

1-50 (66) Excuse me. I think you overcharged us for the water. We didn't have any sparkling water.

1-51 (67) I'd like to get some information about flights to Amsterdam.

1-52 (68) Excuse me. How often does the train for Boston South Station come?

1-53 (69) Are there parking facilities in your hotel?

1-54 (70) Does the tour include shopping at the outlet?

解答と解説

(61) 問い 「総計 334 ドルです。お支払いはどのようになさいますか」

正解 a) 「わかりました。ビザ（カード）で支払います」

解説 買い物 店員は総計 334 ドルを提示し、その支払い方法を尋ねている。買い物客は現金なのか、カードなのかを明示する必要がある。「ビザ（カード）で支払う」（pay by Visa）と返答している a) が正解。

参考 b) 「もっと詳しく情報をください」

c) 「ここで新しい銀行口座を開設できますか」

d) 「名刺を頂けますか」

☆ settle the account「勘定を支払う」 bank account「銀行（貯金）口座」 name card「名刺」（= business card）

(62) **問い**　「すみません。スーツケースにひどいひびが入り、錠前が壊れました」

　　正解　**b)**　「大変申し訳ございません。この書類（用紙）にご記入願えますか」

解説 空港　乗客が飛行機から降り、手荷物受取所でスーツケースが破損しているのに気づいた場面。乗客は荷物の破損状況を係員に告げる。そのような場合、手荷物事故報告書（Property Irregularity Report［PIR］）に記入するように指示される。したがって b) が正解。

参考 a)「心配無用です。すぐに修理できます」
　　　　c)「すみませんが、壊れ物は保険が適用できません」
　　　　d)「その事態をすぐに公安職員に調べさせます」
　　　　☆ cracked「ひびの入った」　lock「錠前、鍵」　fill out「記入する」（= fill in）　fragile items「壊れ物」
　　　　insurance「保険」　security officer「公安職員」　investigate「調査する」　immediately「すぐに」
　　　　（= at once; soon）

---

(63) **問い**　「日曜日の 5 時に 3 名でディナーの予約をお願いしたいのです」

　　正解　**d)**　「その時間帯は満席です。7 時にしていただくことはできますか」

解説 レストラン　顧客はディナーの時間を 5 時として予約する。その時店員は受理できるか否かを返答する必要がある。満席（We're filled to capacity）であり、7 時に変更する（make it for 7:00 p.m.）ことができるかどうか打診している d) が正解。

参考 a)「消費税込みで 180 ドルです」
　　　　b)「5 時半ごろには行けます」
　　　　c)「7 名から 10 名が収容できる小さな宴会場はございます」
　　　　☆ consumption tax「消費税」　accommodate「収容する」　be filled to capacity「満室［満席］
　　　　である」

---

(64) **問い**　「パリからリヨンまで列車で旅行するにはどれくらいかかりますか」

　　正解　**c)**　「旅行（移動）時間は 1 時間 57 分です」

解説 駅舎／旅行代理店　旅行者はパリ・リヨン間の所要時間 (How long ... ?) を聞いている。係員は数字でもって返答すると考えられる。a)「列車の本数」、b)「運賃」、d)「距離」ではない。したがって c) が正解。

参考 a)「1 日につき 33 本の列車があります」
　　　　b)「運賃は 1 人につき 10 ユーロです」
　　　　d)「パリからリヨンまでの距離は 393km です」
　　　　☆ per day「1 日当たり」　fare「運賃」　per person「1 人当たり」

(65) **問い** 「レンタカー営業所はどこにありますか」

正解 **b)** 「フロント（受付）でお尋ねください」

解説 **ホテル** レンタカーを借りようとする旅行者が、その営業所の所在地を探そうとしている。選択肢を見ると、その所在地を答えてはいないものの、フロント（the front desk）へ案内している b) が正解。

参考 a)「毎日営業しています」

　　 c)「トラベラーズチェックは受け付けません」

　　 d)「タクシー乗り場は郵便局の隣にあります」

　　 ☆ agency「代理店」　accept (traveler's cheques〔《米》checks〕)「トラベラーズチェックを受理する」　taxi stand「タクシー乗り場」(=《英》taxi rank)

(66) **問い** 「すみません。水の代金を余計に請求されたと思います。私たちは炭酸水を飲んでいません」

正解 **c)** 「申し訳ございません。手違いがあったようです」

解説 **レストラン** 会計係が顧客に対し金額を余分に請求した（overcharge）場面。会計係は正当なのか、あるいは不当かを返答する必要がある。選択肢を見ると、「間違っていた」(there's been a mistake.) と誤りを認めている。したがって c) が正解。

参考 a)「ご希望であれば水着を借りることができます」

　　 b)「水道水は安心して飲めます」

　　 d)「申し訳ございません。炭酸水 1 瓶をすぐにお持ちして参ります」

　　 ☆ overcharge「(値段を) 余計に請求する」　sparkling water「炭酸水」　water from the tap「水道水」(= tap water)

(67) **問い** 「アムステルダム行きの飛行機に関する情報が欲しいのです」

正解 **a)** 「承知しました。いつ行かれる予定かをお知らせくださいますか」

解説 **旅行代理店** 旅行者はアムステルダム行きの便に関して知りたいことがある。返答する前にまずどの便についての質問か知る必要がある。出発予定日（when you plan to go）を確認している a) が最適。

参考 b)「えーと（そうですね）、お客様のお名前が見つからないようです」

　　 c)「10 時 40 分までには 14 番ゲートに来てくださいますか」

　　 d)「わかりました。オランダにはどれくらい滞在されたいのですか」

　　 ☆ Let me see.「(思案などを示して) はてな」　I'm afraid「(残念ながら)‥～と思う」

(68) **問い** 「すみません。ボストンサウス駅行きの電車はどのくらいの頻度で来ますか」

正解 c) 「10分おきです。次の列車がまもなく当駅に来ます」

解説 **駅舎** 乗客はボストンサウス駅行きの電車が往来する回数・頻度・間隔（How often ...？）を尋ねている。返答も当然頻度に関する内容である。したがって c) が正解。

参考 a) 「約3時間半を要します」

b) 「それは急行列車ですので、たった2回の停車です」

d) 「サウス駅行きの最終列車は午前10時に5番ホームを発車します」

☆ an express train「急行電車」 the last train「最終電車」

---

(69) **問い** 「当ホテルには駐車施設がありますか」

正解 d) 「追加料金を払えば係員付き駐車サービスがあります」

解説 **ホテル** 自動車で上級ホテルなどに来る宿泊者に対して、玄関でのサービスの一環として valet service（係員による客の車の駐車場出入れサービス）がある。駐車について言及している d) が正解。

参考 a) 「5か所の宴会場があります」

b) 「当日は予約で満室です」

c) 「2階にはビジネスセンターがあります」

☆ the second floor「2階」（英国では3階） additional charge「追加料金」

---

(70) **問い** 「このツアーにはアウトレットでの買い物は含まれていますか」

正解 d) 「ホテルに帰る途中、そこでの買い物が楽しめます」

解説 **旅行代理店** 顧客がツアーの旅程内にアウトレットモールでショッピングできる時間があるかどうかを尋ねている。返答者はその有無を知らせる必要がある。「買い物が楽しめる」（we can enjoy shopping there.）と返答している d) が正解。

参考 a) 「1時間だけでは短くて買い物は楽しめません」

b) 「ホテル周辺には土産物店が多数あります」

c) 「その町の郊外にアウトレットが数軒あります」

☆ enjoy (shopping)「(買い物を) 楽しむ」 on the way back to (the hotel)「(ホテルに) 戻る途中で」

音声の内容

1-55 (71) M: Is this the place to pick up duty free items?

F: No, sir. You can pick them up between gates 26 and 28. What time does your flight depart?

M: At 11:30. But they told me at check in that I had to be at the gate at 11:00.

F: You had better hurry. Purchased duty-free items can only be collected up to an hour before departure. It's almost 10:30 now.

M: Oh, OK. Thanks.

Question What is the man's problem?

1-56 (72) M: Is this bottle of water yours?

F: Yes, it is.

M: I'm sorry but you can't take it on the flight.

F: But it's just a bottle of water ... What's the problem?

M: I'm sorry Miss. More than 100 milliliters and it can't fly. You can drink it now or I have to put it in the bin. And could you please remove your coat and step through the x-ray machine?

Question Who is the tourist talking to?

1-57 (73) F: Does this bus go to the Ala Moana shopping center?

M: Yes, it does.

F: Can you break a 10 dollar bill? I don't have any coins with me now.

M: Sorry, I can't do that.

F: Well, what should I do?

M: I'm sorry. Exact change only.

Question What is the woman's problem?

1-58 (74) F: I'm really angry. I just paid 20 euros for a picture.

M: What happened?

F: Well, there were some women standing by the Spanish Steps in lovely costumes. When I took a picture, one woman waved me

第2回試験 解答と解説

over and suggested I take some more pictures with her. So I did.

M: So why are you angry?

F: When I said good-bye she demanded 20 euros for the pictures. I can't believe it.

Question Why is the woman angry?

1-59 **(75) F:** Hello. My name is Diana and I'm the director of sales for the hotel.

M: Yes ....

F: I'm calling to ask you to stop by the front desk. We need to get a form of payment on file for your room.

M: Pardon me. Is there a problem?

F: Apparently there was a problem with your credit card. If you can give us another card number, that would be great.

Question Why is the woman calling?

1-60 **(76) F:** It's great arriving in Osaka on an early flight. But now we have to lug our suitcases around with us all day, before we can check into the hotel.

M: Actually, I heard that instead of carrying our bags with us, we can send them by delivery service ... to our hotel.

F: What? From the airport?

M: Yes. Let's ask about it at the information counter.

Question What are the tourists hoping to do?

1-61 **(77) F:** Does this hotel have a fitness room with running machines?

M: Just a small one. Most of our guests prefer to go jogging outside in this season, though. There's a lovely course along the river, and the cherry blossoms are in bloom now.

F: That sounds nice. I've got a meeting tomorrow morning, but if I get up a little early, I should have time for a run before breakfast.

Question What does the woman want to do?

1-62 **(78) M:** How many people?

F: There are four of us. Can we sit on the terrace?

M: Just a moment while we get your table ready. If you don't mind, I have seats ready inside. I'd like to give them to the next group first.

F: Oh, sure. We'll just wait here then.

M: Thank you.

Question What has happened?

01-63 (79) **M:** There are exits on both sides of the aircraft, and in an emergency, floor lights will help guide you to them. There are also life vests under your seat. In the event of a water landing, you can use them. But don't inflate them until you leave the aircraft. If the cabin loses pressure, oxygen masks will fall.

Question What is the man talking about?

01-64 (80) **F:** Excuse me. How much will a taxi ride cost to Asakusa? We want to go to the temple.

M: I use a meter .... To Asakusa ... maybe 4,000 yen. There is also a toll charge to use the highway. Is that OK?

F: How much is that?

M: About 700 yen.

F: OK. Sure.

Question What are the tourist and taxi driver discussing?

第2回試験

解答と解説

解答と解説

(71) **質問** 「男性が問題とすることは何ですか」

正解 **b)** 「彼は自分の（免税）品をすぐに受け取る必要がある」

解説 空港 男性は Is this the place to pick up duty free items? 「ここは免税品を受け取る場所ですか」と尋ねている。女性は No, sir. You can pick them up between gates 26 and 28. What time does your flight depart? 「違います。26番ゲートと28番ゲートの間で受け取れます。お客様の便が出発するのは何時ですか」と確認する。男性は At 11:30. But they told me at check in that I had to be at the gate at 11:00. 「11時30分です。でも搭乗手続きをする時には11時には搭乗口にいるように言われました」と返答した。女性は You had better hurry. Purchased duty-free items can only be collected up to an hour before departure. It's almost 10:30 now. 「急いだほうがよいです。購入した免税品は出発1時間前までに集められます。現在はもうすぐ10時30分です」と言っている。男性は Oh, OK. Thanks. 「了解です。どうもありがとう」と返答している。

参考 a) 「彼は免税店を見つけることができない」
c) 「彼は購入した物は置き忘れられた」
d) 「彼の搭乗する便が遅れた」
☆ pick up (items) 「（物を）受け取る」 misplace 「置き忘れる」

(72) **質問** 「観光客が話しているのは誰ですか」

正解 **c)** 「警備員」

解説 空港　男性は Is this bottle of water yours?「ペットボトルの水はあなたのものですか」と尋ねている。女性は Yes, it is.「はい、そうです」と返答する。男性は I'm sorry but you can't take it on the flight.「申し訳ないのですが機内に持ち込めないのです」と伝える。女性は But it's just a bottle of water ... What's the problem?「これはただの水が入っているボトルです。何か問題があるのですか」と反論する。さらに男性は More than 100 milliliters and it can't fly. You can drink it now or I have to put it in the bin.「100 ミリリットル以上のものでも、飛行機は飛べないのです。今水を飲んでいただくか、私がゴミ箱に捨てなくてはいけないのです」と告げる。保安上の話題である。

参考 a)「給仕」　b)「警察官」　d)「空港の顧客サービス担当者」
☆ security guard「警備員、ガードマン」　rep [representative]「代表者、担当者、外交員」

(73) **質問** 「女性が問題とすることは何ですか」
正解 **b)** 「彼女はぴったりの運賃を持参していない」

解説 バス停　女性は Does this bus go to the Ala Moana shopping center?「このバスはアラ・モアナショッピングセンターへ行きますか」と尋ねている。男性は Yes, it does.「行きます」と返答する。女性は Can you break a 10 dollar bill? I don't have any coins with me now.「10 ドル札を崩せますか。今小銭を持ち合わせてないのです」と聞くが、男性は Sorry, I can't do that. ... Exact change only.「できません。釣り銭のいらないようにお願いします」と返答する。

参考 a)「彼女はバス停を見つけることができない」
c)「彼女は方向を間違えた」
d)「彼女の眼鏡が壊れた」
☆ bus stop「バス停」　direction「方向」　glasses「眼鏡」

(74) **質問** 「女性はなぜ怒っているのですか」
正解 **b)** 「彼女は写真の代金を請求された」

解説 観光　女性が I'm really angry. I just paid 20 euros for a picture.「ほんとうに呆れます。1 枚の写真に 20 ユーロを支払いました」と言うと、男性は What happened?「どうかしたのですか」と尋ねる。女性が言うには、Well, there were some women standing by the Spanish Steps in lovely costumes. When I took a picture, one woman waved me over and suggested I take some more pictures with her. So I did.「可愛い衣装をまとった数名の女性が（スペイン広場の）スペイン階段に立っていました。私が写真を撮った時、1

人の女性が手を振って、彼女と一緒に写真を撮るようにと持ちかけたのです。そこで、私はそうしました」と言った。男性は So why are you angry?「それで、なぜ怒っているのですか」と尋ねたので、女性は When I said good-bye she demanded 20 euros for the pictures. I can't believe it.「別れ際に、彼女は写真の代金として 20 ユーロを請求したのです。信じられません」と返答した。

参考 a)「彼女は絶好のシャッターチャンスを逃した」

　　 c)「彼女はカメラを盗まれた」

　　 d)「彼女は衣装の代金を払わなければならなかった」

　　 ☆ miss「逃す」　charge「(代金などを) 請求する」

---

(75) **質問**　「女性はなぜ電話をかけているのでしょうか」

　　 正解　c)　「支払い問題を説明するため」

解説 **ホテル**　女性は Hello. My name is Diana and I'm the director of sales for the hotel.「もしもし、こちらはダイアナと申します。ホテルの営業部長です」と内線をする。さらに彼女は I'm calling to ask you to stop by the front desk. We need to get a form of payment on file for your room.「フロントにお立ち寄りいただきたく電話をかけています。お客様の部屋代に関する支払様式を記録する必要があります」と告げる。男性は Is there a problem?「何か問題があるのですか」と尋ねる。女性は Apparently there was a problem with your credit card. If you can give us another card number, that would be great.「お客様のクレジットカードにどこかしら問題があるようです。別のカード番号を頂ければ幸いです」と返答する。

参考 a)「予約するため」

　　 b)「予約を取り消すため」

　　 d)「男性のクレジットカードを返却するため」

　　 ☆ payment problem「支払い問題」

---

(76) **質問**　「観光客が (行動を起こ) したいのは何ですか」

　　 正解　c)　「彼らの手荷物をホテルに送ること」

解説 **空港**　女性は It's great arriving in Osaka on an early flight. But now we have to lug our suitcases around with us all day, before we can check into the hotel.「早便で大阪に着いたのはいいのですが、ホテルにチェックインするまで、終日スーツケースをひきずり回さなくてはいけない」と言っている。男性は Actually, I heard that instead of carrying our bags with us, we can send them by delivery service ... to our hotel. 「実のところ手荷物を自分で運ぶ代わりに、ホテルまで配達サービスに頼んで送ってもらえるらしいですよ」と言いながら、Let's ask about it at the information counter. 「案内所で確認しましょう」と提案する。

参考 a) 「彼らのホテルに直行すること」
　　　b) 「彼らのバッグをロッカーに入れること」
　　　d) 「彼らの免税品を配達してもらうこと」
　　　☆ put (the bag) in (a locker) 「(バッグをロッカー) に入れる」　deliver 「配達する」

---

(77) 質問 「女性が（行動を起こ）したいのは何ですか」
　　　正解 b) 「一走り（ジョギング）すること」

解説 ホテル　女性は Does this hotel have a fitness room with running machines? 「このホテルにはランニングマシンのあるフィットネスルームはありますか」と尋ねる。男性は Just a small one. Most of our guests prefer to go jogging outside in this season, though. There's a lovely course along the river, and the cherry blossoms are in bloom now. 「小さなものはありますが、大半の宿泊客はこの季節には野外でジョギングします。川沿いに素敵なコースがあり、今は桜の花も満開です」と返答する。女性は That sounds nice. I've got a meeting tomorrow morning, but if I get up a little early, I should have time for a run before breakfast. 「それは名案です。明朝は会議がありますが、少し早めに起床すれば朝食前には一走りできます」と言っている。

参考 a) 「ウエイト（重り）を持ち上げること」
　　　c) 「軽く朝食をとること」
　　　d) 「(桜の) 花見をしようとすること」
　　　☆ lift (weights) 「(ウエイト) を持ち上げる」　go for (a walk) 「《英》(散歩に) 出かける」☆《米》take a walk 「散歩する」(行動そのもの)

---

(78) 質問 「何が起きたのですか」
　　　正解 c) 「一行は順不同で着席している」

解説 レストラン／カフェ　男性は人数（How many people?）を聞いている。女性は There are four of us. Can we sit on the terrace? 「4名です。テラスに席を取ってもよいですか」と聞いている。男性は Just a moment while we get your table ready. If you don't mind, I have seats ready inside. I'd like to give them to the next group first. 「テーブルを準備する間少々お待ちください。よろしければ、室内での席は用意されています。まずは

次の団体客に案内するつもりです」と言う。女性は Oh, sure. We'll just wait here then. 「それでは、ここで次を待ちます」と返答している。

参考 a)「現在テーブルは利用できない」

b)「彼らは予約を逃した」

d)「テラスは閉鎖中です」

☆ out of order「順番が間違っている、故障中」

---

(79) **質問** 「男性は何について話していますか」

正解 **a)** 「安全（装置）機能（非常用設備）」

解説 **機内** There are exits on both sides of the aircraft, and in an emergency, floor lights will help guide you to them. There are also life vests under your seat. In the event of a water landing, you can use them. But don't inflate them until you leave the aircraft. If the cabin loses pressure, oxygen masks will fall. 「飛行機の両側に出口がございます。そして緊急時にはフロアライトで誘導します。座席下には救命胴衣もあり、水上着陸の際には使用できます。ただし飛行機から離れるまで膨らましてはいけません。機内で気圧が低下すると、酸素マスクが落下します」と男性が案内している。

参考 b)「手荷物の取扱い」 c)「搭乗手続き」 d)「機内娯楽」

---

(80) **質問** 「観光客とタクシー運転手との間の交渉は何ですか」

正解 **d)** 「高速道路を使うかどうか」

解説 **タクシー停車所** 女性は、How much will a taxi ride cost to Asakusa? We want to go to the temple. 「浅草までのタクシー乗車料金はいくらですか。お寺に参りたいのです」と告げている。男性は To Asakusa ... maybe 4,000 yen. There is also a toll charge to use the highway. Is that OK? 「浅草までは４千円ほどです。高速道路を利用すれば有料道路通行料がかかりますがよろしいですか」と問うている。女性は How much is that? 「いくらかかりますか」と問い、男性は About 700 yen. 「約 700 円です」と返答する。女性は OK. Sure. 「了解」と返答している。

参考 a)「寺院の拝観料」

b)「目的地への道程」

c)「運送（代金）の支払い方法」

☆ destination「目的地、行き先」 transfer「運送、移動」 expressway「高速道路」

[Part A]

音声の内容

1-65 **M:** Amsterdam is perhaps Europe's smallest big city. It is a city of canals and historic buildings and almost all the major sights are accessible on foot, by bicycle, or by tram. Because it is so compact, it is very unique. About 40 percent of all the traffic in the city is bicycle traffic. There are special lanes for bicycles, too. Tourists can easily find places to rent bicycles and this can be a great way to experience the city. The cost is about 1,500 yen per day. You can even go out of the city if you have a bicycle. South of the city is the Amsterdam Forest with more than 50 kilometers of bike paths.

Amsterdam has a great amount to see and do much of it free. There are many gardens, bridges, and markets in the city that tourists can visit. The Bridge of 15 Bridges lit up at night is a quietly beautiful sight. While the Rijksmuseum costs about 2,000 yen to enter, its garden is open year-round for free.

Visitors who want to visit many of the fine museums in the city, the Rijksmuseum, the Van Gogh Museum, Rembrandt's house, or the Anne Frank House should buy an "I Amsterdam card." Both 24-hour cards and 3-day cards are available. In addition to entrance to many museums, the card gives you free public transportation, one free canal tour, and discounts on many concerts and restaurants.

Like any city, if you research a little, you can find some ideas to help you have a better trip. In summer, for example, there are free lunchtime concerts in the Concert Hall or City Hall. And the city's famous museums are sometimes open and much less crowded in the evening. Check the schedules to find the times of some of the fantastic outdoor markets, too.

第2回試験 解答と解説

Questions

(81) Why is Amsterdam convenient for sightseeing?

(82) What form of transportation is recommended?

(83) What is the entry fee for the Rijksmuseum?

(84) What free attractions does the speaker recommend?

(85) Which attraction is illuminated at night?

解答と解説

(81) 質問 「アムステルダムは観光するのになぜ便利なのですか」

正解 **d)** 「コンパクト（こじんまり）です」

解説 冒頭で、アムステルダムはヨーロッパの小さな都会 (smallest big city) であり、徒歩または自転車で市内観光ができる便利さがあると放送されている。また Because it is so compact, it is very unique 「アムステルダムはコンパクトであるため、非常にユニークです」と付け加えている。したがって d) が正解。

参考 a)「古いです」 b)「由緒ある建物があります」 c)「巨大です」

---

(82) 質問 「交通手段には何がお薦めですか」

正解 **d)** 「自転車」

解説 前述 (81) の内容に続き、About 40 percent of all the traffic in the city is bicycle traffic.「市内での交通手段の約 4 割は自転車での移動です」と放送されている。したがって d) が正解。

参考 a)「公共交通」 b)「タクシー」 c)「ボート」

---

(83) 質問 「アムステルダム国立美術館 (Rijksmuseum) の入場料はいくらですか」

正解 **c)** 「約 2,000 円」

解説 中頃で、While the Rijksmuseum costs about 2,000 yen to enter, its garden is open year-round for free.「アムステルダム国立美術館の入場料が 2,000 円であるとは言え、庭園は年中無料で開園されています」と放送されている。したがって c) が正解。

参考 a)「約 200 円」 b)「約 1,200 円」 d)「約 2,100 円」

(84) 質問 「話者が推薦する無料アトラクションは何ですか」

正解 a) 「コンサート」

解説 最後の方で、In summer, for example, there are free lunchtime concerts in the Concert Hall or City Hall.「例えば、夏にはコンサートホールあるいは市役所で無料のランチタイムコンサートがあります」と放送されている。したがって a) が正解。

参考 b)「博物館」 c)「運河観光」 d)「市役所」

(85) 質問 「夜間に照明されるアトラクションは何ですか」

正解 d) 「15 橋の橋」

解説 中頃で、The Bridge of 15 Bridges lit up at night is a quietly beautiful sight.「夜間にライトアップされる 15 橋の橋はひっそりとした美しい夜景である」と放送されている。したがって d) が正解。☆アムステルダム川に架かるマヘレの跳ね橋の美しいライトアップは有名である。

参考 a)「レンブラントの家」
　　 b)「アムステルダム国立美術館」
　　 c)「コンサートホール」

【Part B】

◀))1-66 **M:** Okinawa Prefecture, located in the southernmost part of Japan, consists of about 60 islands. The largest island is Okinawa which has many splendid seascapes and beautiful subtropical plants. Okinawa also has many places of historical interest.

Shurei-no-Mon, the Gate of Courtesy, is known as a symbol of Okinawa and as a fine example of traditional Ryukyu architecture. This is the ceremonial gate on the main approach to Shuri-jo Castle which was originally built in the early 15th century. The present gate was rebuilt in 1958 to the original design.

Okinawa Old Battle Field Quasi-National Park, located in the southern part of Okinawa, was the scene of the bloodiest fighting in the Battle of Okinawa. There are many monuments dedicated to people who died in World War II.

Himeyuri-no-To (Star Lily Tower) is dedicated to female senior high school students and teachers who died on these grounds as Japan's defeat neared.

Kompaku-no-To (Tower of Kompaku) is the memorial site at the edge of a sea cliff which is dedicated to many unknown war dead.

Mabuni-no-Oka (Mabuni Hill) is the site of the fiercest battle of the war where many soldiers and civilians died on the beautiful bluff overlooking the sea. It is now a memorial park strewn with monuments.

Questions

(86) What part of Japan is Okinawa Prefecture located in?

(87) When was Shuri-jo Castle originally built?

(88) Who is Himeyuri-no-to (Star Lily Tower) dedicated to?

(89) Who are buried in the Kompaku-no-to (Tower of Kompaku)?

(90) What is the historical site of Mabuni-no-oka (Mabuni Hill) well-known for in Okinawa?

解答と解説

(86) 質問 「沖縄県は日本のどこに位置していますか」

正解 a) 「最南端にある」

解説 冒頭で Okinawa Prefecture, located in the southernmost part of Japan「日本最南端にある沖縄県」と放送されている。したがって、a) が正解。

参考 b)「最北端にある」 c)「最東端にある」 d)「中央部にある」

(87) 質問 「最初の首里城はいつごろ建造されましたか」

正解 c) 「15 世紀」

解説 前半で、*Shuri-jo* Castle which was originally built in the early 16th century.「首里城は初めは 15 世紀初頭に建造された」と放送されている。したがって、c) が正解。

参考 a)「6 世紀」 b)「10 世紀」 d)「18 世紀」

(88) 質問 「ひめゆりの塔は誰に捧げられていますか」

正解 b) 「女子高校生とその教師」

解説 後半で、Himeyuri-no-To (Star Lily Tower) is dedicated to female senior high school students and teachers who died on these grounds as Japan's defeat neared.「ひめゆりの塔は、日本の敗北が近づいたとき当地で亡くなった女学生と教師の慰霊碑である」と放送されている。したがって、b) が正解。

参考 a)「男子高校生とその教師」
　　 c)「男子大学生とその教師」
　　 d)「女子大学生とその教師」

(89) 質問 「魂魄の塔には誰が埋葬されていますか」

正解 d) 「多数の無名戦死者」

解説 後半で、Kompaku-no-To (Tower of Kompaku) is the memorial site at the edge of a sea cliff which is dedicated to many unknown war dead.「魂魄の塔は、多くの無名戦死者に捧げられた海の断崖絶壁の縁にある追悼の地である」と放送されている。したがって、

d) が正解。

参考 a)「死亡した多数の高校生とその教師」

b)「よく知られた多数の戦死兵」

c)「死亡した多数の有名な市民」

(90) **質問** 「沖縄にある摩文仁の丘の史跡は何で知られていますか」

正解 **a)** 「激戦地」

解説 最後の方で、Mabuni-no-Oka (Mabuni Hill) is the site of the fiercest battle of the war where many soldiers and civilians died on the beautiful bluff overlooking the sea. 「摩文仁の丘は、多くの兵士や市民が海を見下ろす美しい断崖の上で命を絶った沖縄戦の激戦地である」と放送されている。したがって、a) が正解。

参考 b)「景勝地」　c)「多くの無名戦死者の地」　d)「伝統的な琉球建築の地」

1. 最初に筆記試験（試験時間は60分）、引き続きリスニング試験（試験時間は約30分）が行われます。試験監督者の指示に従ってください。

2. 問題冊子は試験監督者から開始の合図があるまで開かないでください。

3. 解答用紙（マークシート）の記入欄に、氏名・生年月日・受験番号等を記入してください。

4. 試験開始の合図後、最初に問題冊子のページを確認してください。もし乱丁や落丁がある場合は、すみやかに申し出てください。

5. 解答は全て、解答用紙の該当するマーク欄を黒鉛筆で塗りつぶしてください。
   • 黒鉛筆またはシャープペンシル以外は使用できません。
   • 解答用紙には解答以外の記入をいっさいしないでください。

6. 辞書・参考書およびそれに類するものの使用はすべて禁止されています。

7. 筆記用具が使用不能になった場合は、係員にすみやかに申し出てください。

8. 問題の内容に関する質問には、一切応じられません。

9. 不正行為があった場合、解答はすべて無効になりますので注意してください。

【筆記試験について】

1. 試験監督者が筆記試験の開始を告げてから、始めてください。

2. 各設問は1から50までの通し番号になっています。

3. 試験開始後の中途退出はできません。（リスニング試験が受けられなくなります。）

【リスニング試験について】

1. 各設問は51から90までの通し番号になっています。

2. リスニング中に問題冊子にメモをとってもかまいませんが、解答用紙に解答を転記する時間はありませんので、注意してください。

3. 放送が終了を告げたら、筆記用具を置いて、係員が解答用紙を回収するまで席を立たないでください。

全国語学ビジネス観光教育協会

筆記試験

1 観光用語の問題

[Part A] Read the following English statements from (1) to (5) and choose the most appropriate Japanese translation for each underlined part from among the four alternatives: a), b), c) and d). Blacken the letter for your answer on the answer sheet.

(1) Could you tell me how often your hotel <u>courtesy bus</u> runs to JFK International Airport?

    a) 貸切バス   b) 直行バス   c) 送迎バス   d) 循環バス

(2) Are you ready to order? Would you care for an <u>aperitif</u>?

    a) 生酒   b) 前菜   c) 食前酒   d) 食後酒

(3) My baggage is so heavy. Could you help me put it on the <u>overhead bin</u>?

    a) 貨物室   b) 貯蔵室   c) 網棚   d) 頭上荷棚

(4) PASMO is a prepaid IC card that passengers can use to pay for train or bus <u>fares</u>.

    a) 代金   b) 返金   c) 入金   d) 即金

(5) Yakushima Island is noted for its <u>primeval forests</u> of big cryptomerias called "Yaku-sugi" designated as natural monuments.

    a) 樹林   b) 山林   c) 防風林   d) 原生林

[Part B] Read the following Japanese statements from (6) to (10) and choose the most appropriate English translation for each underlined part from among the four alternatives: a), b), c) and d). Blacken the letter of your answer on the answer sheet.

(6) 滞在していたその週の間、当ホテルのおもてなしに感謝します。

We'd like to express many thanks for your _____ during the week that we stayed.

a) hospitality   b) pleasure   c) satisfaction   d) requital

(7) 私たちは短期滞在として、シンガポールで2日過ごすつもりです。

We plan to spend two days in Singapore as a _____

a) habitation   b) resident   c) short run   d) stopover

(8) 差額は改札口を通過する前に運賃精算機で支払う必要がある。

You have to pay the difference at a fare _____ machine before leaving through the ticket gates.

a) adjustment   b) box   c) collection   d) structure

(9) スイカは東京地区で幅広く使える再入金可能な前払いの乗車カードである。

SUICA is a _____ prepaid transportation card widely used in the Tokyo area.

a) exchangeable   b) changeable

c) creditable   d) rechargeable

(10) 鳴門の渦潮は瀬戸内海と紀伊水道の間で生じる。

The _____ of Naruto are created between the Inland Sea and the Kii channel.

a) low tides   b) high tides   c) tide pools   d) whirlpools

2 英語コミュニケーションの問題

[Part A] Read the following English dialogs from (11) to (15) and choose the most appropriate utterance to complete each dialog from the four alternatives: a), b), c) and d). Blacken the letter of your answer on the answer sheet.

(11) A: Good morning. We're checking out today, but are coming back tomorrow. Could you keep our luggage till we get back?

B: Sure. I'll keep your luggage in the storeroom until you get back.
_____

a) Now, put your luggage on the scale.

b) Around what time are you coming back tomorrow?

c) The break room is on the second floor next to the restroom.

d) Would you please fill in the registration form?

(12) A: I was hoping we could see a play while we're in town. But all the musicals I wanted to see are sold out and I don't think that I can understand the dramas. My English is not so good.

B: Just a moment. The tour guide said there's one really good drama playing at the Central Theatre and _____.
Shall we try to get tickets?

a) it's on an extended run

b) they have seats in the dress circle available

c) they have a high-tech multi-language subtitle system

d) the doors open for the afternoon performance at 1:00

(13) A: Could you help me? How do I get to the Fine Art Museum?

B: It's really close. _____ You can't miss it.

a) Just to straight ahead for 9 blocks until you see a bank on the corner. Turn left there.

b) Just turn right out of here, then take the first left.

c) Take the blue line for three stops and then transfer to the University bus.

d) Grab a cab going uptown. It should take no more than half an hour.

(14) A: What's the spooky thing standing in front of the restaurant?

B: That's a "tanuki" or raccoon dog. It's an example of Shigaraki pottery from Shiga Prefecture near Kyoto. It's a good-luck charm _____.

a) to help a business flourish

b) to pray for protection from fire

c) to drive away imaginary animals

d) to pray for finding a good partner

(15) A: We were hoping to have a chance to take a hot-spring bath while we're in Japan. But my husband's business schedule is full. We don't have enough time to spend a night in a resort hotel in the country.

B: Actually, there are urban hot-spring resorts in most big cities. _____ Just ask your concierge to locate one for you.

a) You can visit for a few hours any morning or evening you are free.

b) Hot-spring baths are exclusively found in country resorts. Sorry.

c) The cuisine available is really impressive, especially at this time of year.

d) That's a problem if you haven't brought your equipment.

[Part B] Read the following English conversations from (16) to (20) and choose the most appropriate utterance to complete each conversation from the four alternatives: a), b), c) and d). Blacken the letter of your answer on the answer sheet.

(16) A: I'm sorry, sir, but we're asking all passengers to please return to their seats right now. So could you please take your seat and fasten your seatbelt?

B: What? Are we landing already?

A: No, sir. _____ It shouldn't last so long.

a) The gallery is being used at the moment.

b) We're just expecting a bit of turbulence.

c) We're inspecting laptops for the next few minutes.

d) We're return all seats to their upright position.

(17) A: I'm thinking of getting a smartphone before my next trip.

B: Why?

A: Well, in addition to being able to use it for messages and making calls, it _____. And I can take pictures with it and tell my friend about my trip using Twitter.

a) has navigation software for walking and I can download a travel guide into it

b) can meet me at the airport and transport me to my hotel if I need

c) will help me avoid delays caused by poor weather conditions

d) can help the housekeeping staff tidy my room in the morning

(18) A: Is it possible to depart at 8:00 instead of 9:00 tomorrow morning? I'm a little worried about city traffic. We need to arrive at the airport no later than 11:00.

B: It should be no problem. _____

A: Well, if you think so.

a) Traffic flowing out of the city isn't heavy at all on weekends.

b) Traffic congestion is a significant problem and I agree with your suggestion.

c) The buses are fully equipped with air conditioning and rest rooms.

d) The entire trip is included in your itinerary, including this leg.

(19) A: The approach to the shrine is lined with many little shops selling various delicacies.

B: Really? _____

A: Everything is good, but I really recommend the fish-shaped sweets filled with bean paste.

a) When is the best time to visit?

b) How long will we be staying there?

c) What's for dinner this evening?

d) What do you think we should try?

(20) A: Um ... I want to go to take a bath in the large bath, but I'm not sure which one is for women and which one is for men. _____ on the wooden signs hanging out front.

B: The one on the left is for men and the one on the right is for woman tonight. But be careful. Tomorrow they will be changed. Each bath is unique and we want to give guests a chance to experience both.

A: Wow, that's interesting-confusing, but interesting.

a) I watched the demonstration

b) There's no available towel

c) I can't read the Chinese characters

d) There's a traditional craft

3 英文構成の問題

Read the following English paragraphs which contain incomplete sentences. To complete the sentence, put each set of words into the best order. When you have finished, blacken the letter on your answer sheet from among the four alternatives: a), b), c) and d) for the word in the position of the blank that has the question number from (21) to (25).

For anyone planning a trip to Japan, Kyoto is a mandatory stop on your itinerary. Having been the nation's capital for much of history, it _____ _____ (21) _____Japan's cultural traditions. Its temples, shrines, and gardens are just what visitors to Japan ___(22)___ _____ _____ _____ their trip. It is also popular of course, with domestic tourists keen to enjoy some of the history and high culture that make Kyoto so special. As the number of foreign visitors to Japan has risen over the past decade, so too has the number of foreign tourists exploring the temples and sights of Kyoto. That is having some very real effects on the tourism business in the city.

Many years ago, the average tourist to Kyoto was Japanese. Foreign tourists, while common, were a small minority of the total number of tourists. These days, however, a very large percentage of visitors ___(23)___ _____ _____ _____ are non-Japanese. Meanwhile, the number of Japanese visitors is falling. In 2018, for example, hotels in the city saw a 5.3-percent increase in overseas guests and a 4.8-percent drop in Japanese customers. Not only have percentages increased, but recent years have seen many new hotels, inns, and hostels open, greatly increasing the number of available rooms. For ___(24)___ _____ _____ _____, their trip to Kyoto is part of an introduction to Japanese culture, and so they tend to behave differently from domestic tourists, who naturally have more knowledge of the city's history, traditions, areas, and culture.

What's causing these domestic travelers to stay away from Kyoto? A big factor is the huge crowds. The crowds of tourists not only fill up Kyo-

to's most popular sights, they also fill up the buses and trains that everyone
_____ (25) _____ _____ _____. That extra congestion disrupts the quiet
elegance that many domestic visitors see as Kyoto's primary attraction.

(21) a) the   b) of   c) remains   d) heart

(22) a) to   b) on   c) see   d) expect

(23) a) to   b) city   c) the   d) flocking

(24) a) of   b) these   c) visitors   d) many

(25) a) uses   b) around   c) get   d) to

4

[Part A] Read the following information sheet and answer the questions from (26) to (30) by choosing the most appropriate answer for each question from among the four alternatives; a), b), c) and d). Blacken the letter of your answer on the answer sheet.

Skylon Tower

Celebrating
FIFTY YEARS
1965-2015

Skylon Tower

Get the best view of Niagara Falls from the Skylon Tower.

Get a great view of both the American Falls and the Canadian Falls (also known as the Horseshoe Falls) as well as the Niagara Gorge.

The Observation Deck at 160 meters from street level or 236 meters from the bottom of the falls gives you by [①] the best view of the falls. Experience a sight that will take your breath away.

Opened in 1965, it has enchanted visitors ever since. Hop aboard one of the exterior "Yellow Bug" elevators and glide smoothly to the top in just 52 seconds.

But that's not all! There are two restaurants where you can enjoy fine dining while enjoying the view from the top. At the Summit Suite Buffet have an amazing buffet-style dining. Our breakfast, lunch and dinners are superb and affordable for the whole family. At the Revolving Dining Room reach the height of full-service dining excellence with our award-winning cuisine. Enjoy your meal all the while the restaurant rotates to take in the 360 degree view in about an hour. Best of all there's no charge for the elevator if you have dinner in either restaurant.

The view at night is spectacular. The ② is especially magical when the falls are illuminated. Check out our website for details on the illumination schedule.

And there's more! Check out our Skylon Fun Center at the base of the Skylon Tower complete with an indoor arcade and the new Niagara Falls attraction 3D/4D Movie "the Legend of the Niagara Falls."

And there's even a Casino just across the street waiting for you to try your luck.

(26) Choose the most appropriate word for ①.

a) all b) far c) long d) near

(27) Choose the most appropriate word for ②.

a) atmosphere b) climate c) flavor d) phenomenon

(28) What is NOT mentioned in the advertisement?

a) Meals are available at the base of the Skylon Tower.

b) Breakfast is served at the Summit Suite Buffet.

c) Gambling is available near the Skylon Tower.

d) There is a 3D/4D Niagara Falls movie attraction at the Skylon Tower.

(29) What is FALSE about the Skylon Tower?

    a) All the people who take the elevator must pay a charge.

    b) The elevator takes less than a minute to go to the Observation Deck.

    c) The Revolving Dining Room takes about one hour to make a complete rotation.

    d) At both restaurants you can enjoy dining while enjoying the view.

(30) What is TRUE about the Skylon Tower?

    a) サミットスイートビュッフェの特徴はビュッフェです。

    b) "Yellow Bugs" はスカイロンファンセンターにあります。

    c) スカイロンタワーは 15 周年になります。

    d) タワーにある両レストランにはビュッフェがあります。

[**Part B**] Read the following information sheet and answer the questions from (31) to (35) by choosing the most appropriate answer for each question from among the four alternatives; a), b), c) and d). Blacken the letter of your answer on the answer sheet.

HokkaidoExperience.com
Let's enjoy Hokkaido

HokkaidoExperience.com is a booking service website, which lets you easily search and book outdoor adventures, arts & crafts and many more green tourism activities here in Hokkaido.

Challenge the Raging Rapids!
Rafting on Niseko's Shiribetsu-gawa River!

The guides at NAC are all well-trained professionals, _____①_____ at RAJ (Rafting Association of Japan), knowing all about rivers, life saving and first-aid.

Enjoy the activity. Enjoy the nature. Here in Niseko, Hokkaido at NAC-Niseko Adventure Centre!

Participation Fee Online:

Adults (ages 13 to 59)
   discounted price: 6,300 yen
Children (age 7 to 12)
   discounted price: 4,200 yen
Seniors (ages 60 and up):
   5,300 yen

Every season has its own taste. Enjoy the difference of each season.

School kids can join after June. Come with all your family.

Get changed at NAC CENTRE. You can enjoy tea time upstairs after the activity.

Concerning Participation

Available Time Period: Begining of April – Begining of November

Meeting Location: NAC Niseko Adventure Centre

Pick Up Service: Pick up and drop off available in the Niseko area.

② **for Participation:** Ages 13 and up *from June on: ages 7 and up

Things to Bring/Required Items:

* We recommend that those with eyeglasses wear a safety strap.
* In Spring (April-June) and Autumn (September-October) we recommend a track suit or fleece long pants and long-sleeved shirt and socks.
* In Summer (July-August) a T-shirt and shorts that can get wet or a swimsuit.

Important Notices:

* Depending on weather condition, this activity's start and ending time might change.
* If the guide decides that the weather conditions are dangerous, the tour may be cancelled.
* Please do not wear jeans or cotton pants (when wet they are heavy and dangerous).
* Please take off accessories and watches while participating in this activity.
* Please do not bring any valuables with you. Just in case they are lost or damaged we cannot accept responsibility.

\# Please refrain from drinking alcohol before the tour.

Cancellation: Cancellation penalties apply at 50% the previous day and 100% on the day.

(31) Choose the most appropriate word for 〔 ① 〕.

   a) encountered   b) registered   c) suspended   d) surrounded

(32) Choose the most appropriate word for 〔 ② 〕.

   a) Functions   b) Equipments

   c) Remarks   d) Requirements

(33) Which of the following is NOT mentioned in the advertisement of this rafting tour?

   a) Available time period.

   b) Benefits of using HokkaidoExperience.com.

   c) Participation fee.

   d) Payment method.

(34) Which of the following is TRUE about this rafting tour?

   a) You should refrain from drinking alcohol before the tour.

   b) You must take on valuables and watches while participating in this activity.

   c) You can enjoy tea time in the course of the activity in NAC Niseko Adventure Centre.

   d) You may put on a track suit or fleece long pants and long sleeved shirt and socks in August.

(35) Which of the following is FALSE about this rafting tour?

   a) 5月のツアー参加者は全員 7 歳以上でなくてはいけない。

   b) 当日のキャンセルはすべて全額に付替えられます。

   c) NAC はウェブサイトで予約すれば割引価格を提供します。

   d) NAC はニセコ区域に滞在する参加者のために無料で送迎します。

[Part C] Read the following English conversation, and answer the questions from (36) to (40) by choosing the most appropriate answer for each question from among the four alternatives; a), b), c) and d). Blacken the letter of your answer on the answer sheet.

Tourist: My Saturday meeting was cancelled and it looks like I'll have the weekend free. Can you recommend someplace for an overnight trip out of the city for my wife and me?

Hotel Concierge: Well, if you like castles, there's Matsumoto in Nagano Prefecture. Or you could go to Nikko in Tochigi Prefecture. Or there's Hakone if you would like to experience a hot-spring resort. All three of these places are easily ____(36)____ from Tokyo by express trains. It won't take you long and it's not expensive to travel there.

Tourist: My wife said she was interested in hot springs. But didn't I see something on the Internet that Hakone was closed?

Hotel Concierge: Oh, no. Hakone is still open. It's a just one area that is now closed. The Japan Meteorology Agency raised the volcano alert to level 3 in June. But it is only for the area of Owakudani.

Tourist: So is it safe?

Hotel Concierge: Oh, it should be completely safe. There was a little more steam than usual coming out of the ground in that area, so they closed an area one-kilometer around it. For tourists, the biggest problem is that the ropeway is in the ____(37)____ area, so it is closed. But if you just want to go to a hot-spring resort hotel or ryokan for the weekend, you won't have any problems.

Tourist: Are you sure?

Hotel Concierge: Japan has a lot of ____(38)____ volcanoes. The motion of the plates gives us both regular earthquakes and several volcanoes that are not sleeping. The authorities are very good at assessing the danger. There are also ____(39)____ plans ready in the case of any emergencies, such as an eruption.

Tourist: Well, if you say it's safe ... but do you think I can get a room for Saturday? It's already Thursday.

Hotel Concierge: It might be a little difficult, but I'll do my best to get you ___(40)___ .

(36) Choose the most appropriate word for ___(36)___ .

    a) accessible   b) particular

    c) adjoining   d) distant

(37) Choose the most appropriate word for ___(37)___ .

    a) isolated   b) restricted

    c) dependable   d) removable

(38) Choose the most appropriate word for ___(38)___ .

    a) extensive   b) ancient

    c) reasonable   d) active

(39) Choose the most appropriate word for ___(39)___ .

    a) evacuation   b) attention

    c) connection   d) certification

(40) Choose the most appropriate phrase for ___(40)___ .

    a) an explanation   b) a booking

    c) a destination   d) a beverage

5

[Part A] Read the following descriptions from (41) to (45) and choose the best answer to complete the sentences with blank parts from among the four alternatives: a), b), c) and d). Blacken the letter of your answer on the answer sheet.

(41) The State _____ Museum in St. Petersburg, Russia, is one of the greatest museums in the world. Once a part of Catherine II's Winter Palace, it was rebuilt as a museum in the 19th century. It houses over three million artworks, including "The Return of the Prodigal Son", one of the Rembrandt's works, and several masterpieces of Leonardo da Vinci.

    a) Hermitage   b) Louvre   c) Metropolitan   d) Prado

(42) Situated in southeast Siberia, Russia, _____ is the oldest (25 million years) and deepest (1,700m) lake in the world. It contains 20% of the world's total unfrozen freshwater reserve. Known as the "Galapagos of Russia", Baikal is home to thousands of species of plants and animals. More than 80% of the animals are endemic to the region, which is of exceptional value to evolutionary science.

    a) Lake Baikal   b) Lake Ontario

    c) Lake Leman   d) Lake Titicaca

(43) The _____ Caves in Maharashtra, India, are 30 rock-cut monuments created during the 2nd century B.C. and the 5th century A.D. The excavated caves contain masterpieces of wall paintings and sculptures of Buddhist religious art. Some paintings of people and clothing drawn on the interior walls of the Main Hall of Horyu-ji Temple in Japan carry certain similarities with murals found in the Caves in India.

    a) Ajanta   b) Bhimbetka   c) Elephanta   d) Ellora

(44) _____ is a spicy dish, originally from Hungary, usually made of beef, onions, red peppers and paprika powder. It is most often prepared as a stew. It is a popular dish as a simple home meal in Hungary. Today, it is also often served in restaurants.

a) Bouillabaisse　　b) Fondue　　　c) Goulash　　　d) Haggis

(45) When you enter a temple or mosque you will be asked to follow _____. It is a set of rules regarding what people can and can't wear. If you do not wear decent clothes for the occasion, you may not be able to enter. You may also be able to borrow clothing at the entrance if you are dressed too casually.

a) a dress code　　　　　　　b) a nature trail

c) religious regulations　　　　d) traffic rules

[Part B] Read the following descriptions from (46) to (50) and choose the best answer to complete the sentences with blank parts from among the four alternatives: a), b), c) and d). Blacken the letter of your answer on the answer sheet.

(46) _____ Catholic Church, built in 1864, is the oldest Gothic-style building in Japan. The church with beautiful stained-glass windows is dedicated to the memory of the 26 Japanese martyrs who were crucified in 1597. The church became famous worldwide as the church that discovered the "Hidden Christians" who had survived 250-year-long religious persecution. It was designated as a national treasure in 1933 and registered in 2018 as the World Heritage Site.

a) Egami Church   b) Shitsu Church

c) Urakami Cathedral   d) Oura Church

(47) _____, located in Yamaguchi Prefecture, is the most outstanding example of many limestone caves in the Akiyoshidai Plateau. It is also the largest of its kind in Asia and the third biggest limestone cave in the world. This cave has rivers, waterfalls, deep ponds and stalactites and stalagmites. It is famous for Hyakumai-zara (100 saucers) which were created through the action of limestone-rich water on a gentle slope. There are actually more than 500 saucer-like pools.

a) Akiyoshi-do   b) Gyokusen-do

c) Ryuga-do   d) Ryusen-do

(48) The _____ is an art gallery specializing in artworks from the Western traditional culture. The museum was established to house and display the private art collection of a wealthy businessman named Matsukata Kojiro. The initial Main Building was designed in 1959 by Swiss-French architect Le Corbusier and the New Building was

designed in 1979 by Maekawa Kunio. The collections largely contain works ranging from the Renaissance through the mid-20th century.

a) National Museum of Nature and Science

b) Tokyo Metropolitan Art Museum

c) National Museum of Western Art

d) Tokyo National Museum

(49) _____ is a simple and light meal served to entertain guests at a formal tea ceremony before serving the thick pasty tea (koicha). Originally the term _____ derives from the small heated stone that Zen monks held against their empty stomachs during long hours of fasting while meditating. Zen monks kept a heated [warm] stone inside the kimono bosom for helping them forget cold and hunger during Zen practice.

a) Honzen-ryori   b) Kaiseki-ryori

c) Shojin-ryori   d) Osechi-ryori

(50) _____ is the ancient method of catching fish (*ayu*) by using well-trained cormorants. They capture fish with their beaks, but have a cord tied at the base of their necks to prevent the birds from swallowing the catch. It takes place on the river at night under the light of blazing torches. Some cormorants are conducted by fishermen wearing ancient costume and ceremonial headgear on the boat.

a) Haenawa   b) Ipponzuri   c) Makiami   d) Ukai

6

Listen to the four descriptions for each picture from (51) to (55). Choose the statement that best describes what you see in the picture from among the four alternatives: a), b), c) and d). Blacken the letter of your answer on the answer sheet. The descriptions will be spoken just once.

◀)2-02 (51)

◀)2-03 (52)

(53)

(54)

(55)

第3回試験

7

Listen to the four descriptions for each illustration from (56) to (60). Choose the statement that best describes what you see in the illustration from among the four alternatives: a), b), c) and d). Blacken the letter of your answer on the answer sheet. The descriptions will be spoken just once.

2-07 (56)

2-08 (57)

Grand Hotel

Date	12/26/11		
Time	16:16		
Clerk	OPSINDY	Guest Message	
Room No.	9 0 2	Name	Ms. Watanabe

Dear Ms. Watanabe
"Please meet at 17:00 at the bus stop in front of the hotel"
From Ms. Jian

Thank you for staying with us
Telecommunication

(58)

(59)

Access to city area

 Shin-Chitose Airport

Airport Express	Fare	Time	
	¥1,040	36min	**Sapporo Station**
	¥1,740	72min	**Otaru Station**
Limousine Bus			
	¥1,000	70min	**Downtown Sapporo**

(60)

8

Listen to the first sentences from (61) to (70) and complete each dialog by choosing the best response from among the four alternatives: a), b), c) and d). Blacken the letter of your answer on the answer sheet. The sentences will be spoken twice.

2-12 (61) a) I'm sorry, sir. Please fill in this declaration form.

b) I'm sorry, sir. We'll send someone from maintenance right away.

c) I'm sorry, sir. Would you like to change your reservation?

d) I'm sorry, sir. Would you please check the thermostat?

2-13 (62) a) Certainly. Please fill in the lost property form.

b) Please use the fare adjustment machine over there.

c) You had better go to the gift shop.

d) You are allowed to bring your camera along to photograph.

2-14 (63) a) The burritos are very popular.

b) The pizza is delicious.

c) Pasta of the day.

d) Tom yum goong is spicy.

2-15 (64) a) Yes, it's included in the guest welcome package.

b) No cables are required.

c) You need a personal computer.

d) No additional fee is required.

2-16 (65) a) It's after business hours, could you try again tomorrow?

b) Unfortunately, we do not honor discount coupons here.

c) Discount coupons are an attractive offer for hotel guests.

d) Hotels.com is a popular way to find and reserve hotels online.

(66) a) Trains leave every 10 minutes from Shinjuku Station.

b) There is a loop-line bus stop in front of the station.

c) You had better take the Metro at Shibuya.

d) The bus is the only form of public transport here.

(67) a) It certainly is a popular sport these days.

b) I think you can get them on the StubHub website.

c) You can purchase team souvenirs like scarves and jerseys at Sports Mart.

d) There is a money exchange across the street.

(68) a) From the pictures, it does look very beautiful.

b) The Inland Sea has a number of islands.

c) The view from there of Mt. Ishizuchi is famous as well.

d) It's located in Aichi Prefecture.

(69) a) Yes, my father often uses the member's only lounge at Narita.

b) Yes, however I heard mileage programs are expensive to join.

c) Only low-cost carriers offer mileage programs.

d) The new airline offers a welcome drink to all passengers.

(70) a) No, it's an indoor tour.

b) It often rains in June.

c) I'll bring lunch as well.

d) The tour departure is very early.

第3回試験

9

Listen to the conversations from (71) to (80) and choose the most appropriate answer for the question following each conversation from among the four alternatives: a), b), c) and d). Blacken the letter of your answer on the answer sheet. The conversations and the questions will be spoken twice.

2-22 (71) a) Pay an additional fee for overweight luggage.

b) Use the self-check-in terminal.

c) Repack her bags.

d) Remove all metal items before proceeding.

2-23 (72) a) He doesn't like the local food.

b) Safety of his valuables.

c) A place to stay.

d) The cost.

2-24 (73) a) The clam-shell phone is cheap.

b) The customer requires a variety of features.

c) The customer is in a hurry.

d) The price was right.

2-25 (74) a) He will leave on a business trip today.

b) His co-worker is in Shanghai.

c) He is also excited to visit the theme park.

d) He was late for work.

2-26 (75) a) A walking tour.

b) Visiting the Mist House.

c) The cactus garden.

d) Grooming the gardens.

2-27 (76) a) At a train station.
　　　　 b) At a supermarket.
　　　　 c) At airport security.
　　　　 d) At customs.

2-28 (77) a) She wants to go diving.
　　　　 b) She wants to enjoy local cuisine.
　　　　 c) She wants to take it easy.
　　　　 d) She wants to go an island resort.

2-29 (78) a) Cloudy.
　　　　 b) Snow.
　　　　 c) Rain.
　　　　 d) Sunny.

2-30 (79) a) Cross the street.
　　　　 b) Go back to his hotel.
　　　　 c) Buy a ticket.
　　　　 d) Take a taxi.

2-31 (80) a) A tourist information counter clerk.
　　　　 b) A pilot.
　　　　 c) A concierge.
　　　　 d) A check-in counter clerk.

第3回試験

10

Listen to the following descriptions **[Part A]** and **[Part B]**, and answer the questions from (81) to (90). Choose the most appropriate answer for each question from among the four alternatives: a), b), c) and d). Blacken the letter of your answer on the answer sheet. The descriptions and the questions will be spoken twice.

◀)) 2-32 **[Part A]**

(81) a) About the same size as Hokkaido.
 b) About 80% the size of Hokkaido.
 c) Roughly 240 square kilometers.
 d) Almost the same size as Australia.

(82) a) Tasman is the name of the European who found this island.
 b) Tasmania is located off the east coast of Australia.
 c) The depth of the bay is about 200m.
 d) The bay is located in Northwest Park.

(83) a) Rare animals such as the Tasmanian devil.
 b) Many freshwater fish.
 c) Deep-sea fish.
 d) Curious seagulls.

(84) a) Because of it's salt water.
 b) Because of the flows of the river.
 c) Because of the weather around there.
 d) Because of the deep forest.

(85) a) The place of unique animals.
 b) The sea that time forgot.
 c) The red bay.
 d) The place of preservation.

[Part B]

(86) a) Two hours.

    b) Twelve hours.

    c) Half a day.

    d) More than a day.

(87) a) Two.

    b) Three.

    c) Four.

    d) Five.

(88) a) Two.

    b) Twenty five.

    c) Thirty.

    d) One hundred.

(89) a) They are part of Japan's capital.

    b) They are off the coast of Ecuador.

    c) They have unique plants and animals.

    d) They can only be reached by small boats.

(90) a) Making them part of Tokyo.

    b) Limiting the number of visitors to the inhabited islands.

    c) Limiting the number of visitors to the uninhabited islands.

    d) Making them accessible to many new visitors.

第3回試験

筆記試験

1　観光用語の問題

【Part A】

（1）**正解**　**c）**　「ホテルの**送迎バス**は JFK 国際空港までどのくらい運行していますか」

解説 courtesy bus 「送迎バス」。ホテルと空港・駅・繁華街などの間を無料で往復する。▶ The *courtesy bus* is parked at the rear of this airport building.「送迎バスはこの空港ビルの後部に駐車してあります」　☆ courtesy 图「優待（= hospitality）、礼儀（= etiquette）、好意（= favor）」。ホテルにおける特別な配慮（hospitality）のこと。到着時の出迎え、出発時の見送り、客室への果物または花を無料で提供する。圈 ①「儀礼上、優遇の、優待の」　▶ *courtesy* visit [call]「表敬訪問」　②「無料の、サービスの、（ホテルなどの）送迎用の」　▶ *courtesy* rates「サービス料金」

参考　☞ **Column 08** バスの種類（p.208-209）
a）「貸切バス」a chartered bus
b）「直行バス」a nonstop bus
d）「循環バス」a belt-line [circular] bus; a bus on a circular route

（2）**正解**　**c）**　「ご注文を伺います。**食前酒**はいかがですか」

解説 aperitif「食前酒、アペリチフ［アペリティフ］」（= pre-dinner aperitif）。元来、食欲を増進させるために用いられた薬草入りの酒のこと。現在では食欲増進のために食前に飲む少量の酒（= before-dinner drink）として使う。ベルモット（Vermouth）、シェリー（Sherry）、カンパリ（Campari）など。▶ *aperitif* bar「アペリチフ・バー」。レストラン利用者に対して食前に飲むカクテル類を出す酒場（drink an aperitif in the bar）。別室もしくは dining room の一角としてレストランに敷設されている場合が多い。waiting bar とも言う。

参考 a）「生酒」raw [pure] *sake*; undiluted *sake*
b）「前菜」appetizer　☆ an hors d'oeuvre また a starter とも言う。
d）「食後酒」digestif; after-dinner drinks

（3）**正解** **d)** 「手荷物は重いのです。**頭上の荷物棚**に上げてくださいますか」

解説 **overhead bin**「頭上荷棚」（= overhead compartment）。ジェット機などにある手荷物を収納する頭上の箱棚［収納庫］　▶ You may put your bag under the seat in front of you or on the *overhead bin.*「バッグはお客様の前の座席下、または頭上の荷棚に置くことができます」　☆ overhead（アクセントは over）「頭上の」（= over one's head）　▶（飛行機の機内にある）*overhead* baggage rack「荷物棚」　*overhead* shelf「頭上棚」

参考 a)「貨物室」cargo hold [compartment]
　　　 b)「貯蔵室」storeroom
　　　 c)「網棚」（電車の）overhead rack

（4）**正解** **a)** 「PASMO とは IC チップ内蔵のプリペイドカードのことで、電車やバスの**代金**の支払いに使用できる」

解説 **fares**「代金、（列車・電車・バス・船など乗物の）運賃、料金」　☆料金を意味する英単語として charge「（サービスなどの）使用料・手数料」と fee「（入場・入会などの）料金」がある。ちなみに遊園地などでの乗り物の料金には How much is one ride? と言う。fare は用いない。

参考 b)「返金」(a) refund; (a) repayment
　　　 c)「入金」receipts; receipt of money
　　　 d)「即金」ready [hard] cash

（5）**正解** **d)** 「屋久島には天然記念物に指定されている『屋久杉』と呼ばれる大きな杉の**原生林**があることで有名である」

解説 **primeval forests**「原生林（古代以来の森林）」（= a virgin forest）　▶ The world's largest *virgin* beech *forest* in Shirakami Mountain Range.「白神山地の世界最大級のブナ原生林」《青森県・秋田県》　▶ Mt. Kurohime is called the "Shinano-Fuji" because of its magnificent beauty. It is covered by *virgin forests* of birch trees and black pipes.「黒姫山はすばらしい美観のため『信濃富士』とも呼ばれている。そこはカバやクロマツの原生林で覆われている」《長野県》

参考 a)「樹林」forest
　　　 b)「山林」mountains and forests
　　　 c)「防風林」a windbreak forest

【Part B】

(6) **正解** **a)** We'd like to express many thanks for your **hospitality** during the week that we stayed.

解説 **hospitality**「(客への手厚い)もてなし」。日本のホテル・レストランでは「奉仕の心」と和訳されることがある。▶ Thank you so much for your *hospitality* on my previous trip.「先日の旅行中にはいろいろとお世話になり感謝申しあげます」*hospitality* gift ①「手土産」。食事などに招待されたときに持参する贈物。②「歓迎ギフト、参加記念品」。パーティーなどを主催するときに参加［参列］者に贈るギフト。

参考 b) pleasure「娯楽」
　　　c) satisfaction「満足」
　　　d) requital「報恩」

(7) **正解** **d)** We plan to spend two days in Singapore as a **stopover**.

解説 **stopover**「(旅行途中での)短期滞在」。途中下車、途中降機、途中寄港などの意味でもよく使用される。▶ *stopover* station「途中下車駅」make a *stopover* in Honolulu「ホノルルに途中降機する」Can we make a *stopover* on this ticket?「この切符で途中下車できますか」　☆ stop over「途中降機する（=《米》stop off, make a stopover)、途中下車［寄港］する」　▶ I *stopped over* in Milan on my way to Rome.「ローマに行く途中、ミラノに降機した」

参考 a) habitation「居住」
　　　b) resident「住居者」
　　　c) short run「急ぎの短期旅行」

(8) **正解** **a)** You have to pay the difference at a fare **adjustment** machine before leaving through the ticket gates.

解説 **adjustment**「精算」。adjustment は本来「調整、調節、修正」の意味。▶ The cabin attendant made an *adjustment* to the color on the TV monitor for me.「客室乗務員がテレビの色彩を調節してくれました」fare *adjustment*「運賃の精算」fare *adjustment* office「(駅舎の)精算所」fare *adjustment* machine「(駅舎の)精算機」　☆ adjust「精算する」　▶ *adjust* the fare「運賃を精算する」

参考 b) (fare) box「(料金)箱、(乗り物の)運賃箱」

c) (fare) collection「(料金) 徴収」

d) (fare) structure「(運賃) 体系」

---

(9) **正解** **d)** SUICA is a **rechargeable** prepaid transportation card widely used in the Tokyo area.

解説 **rechargeable** (card)「再入金可能な（カード）」。rechargeable とは「再充電することが可能な」(able to be charged) の意味。▶ *rechargeable* (battery)「再充電可能な（電池）、充電電池」 *rechargeable* electronic clock「充電式電子時計」

参考 a) exchangeable (check)「交換可能な（小切手）」

b) changeable (weather)「変わりやすい（天気）」

c) creditable (story)「信用できる（話）」

---

(10) **正解** **d)** The **whirlpools** of Naruto are created between the Inland Sea and the Kii channel.

解説 **whirlpools**「渦潮」(= whirling waves; a whirling current of the tide「潮の流れ」) ▶ The Naruto Strait is noted for the *whirlpools* of Naruto which are created between the Inland Sea and the Kii Channel.「鳴門海峡は瀬戸内海と紀伊水道の間で生じる鳴門の渦潮で有名である」《徳島県》 ☆潮の満ち引きは月や太陽の引力によって海水面の上下動が周期的に起きる現象である。鳴門海峡の海流の速度は、平常時は 13km/h から 15 km/h である。大潮の時は 20 km/h に及ぶことがある。

参考 a) low tides「干満」

b) high tides「満潮」

c) tide pools「潮だまり」(=《英》rock pools) 引き潮で岩礁などにできる水たまり。

バスの種類

bus 图「バス、乗合自動車」 ☆英国では長距離バスは **coach**（= long-distance bus）と言う。米国では長距離用の **Greyhound** がよく利用されているが coach も用いる。

【A】 air-conditioned bus　エアコン付きバス

　　　airport bus　空港バス（= airline bus）　☆空港内または市街と空港の間を運行する航空会社の直営バス

　　　airport shuttle　空港シャトル

　　　all-night bus　夜行バス

　　　amphibious bus　水陸両用バス

【B】 belt-line [loop-line] bus　循環バス（= a circular bus; a bus on a circular route）

　　　bus on a regular route　路線バス

【C】 chartered bus　貸し切りバス　　　city bus　市営バス

　　　coach　（長距離）バス　　　　　　commuter bus　通勤バス

　　　connection bus　連絡バス　☆エアポート・ターミナルと旅客ターミナルとの間を結ぶバス

　　　courtesy bus [van]　（空港周辺のホテル）送迎用バス

　　　cruise [cruising] bus　巡行［周遊］バス

　　　cyclic bus　巡回バス

【D】 direct bus　直行バス

　　　double-decker　二階建てバス（= double-deck [double-decker] bus）

　　　double mode bus　手動と自動運転の両用バス

【E】 electric(al) bus　電気バス　　　　excursion bus　小旅行バス

　　　express bus　急行バス　　　　　　expressway bus　高速（道路）バス

　　　extra bus　臨時バス

【G】 government-owned bus　国有バス

【H】 high-speed bus　（電子回路の）高速バス（= high-velocity bus）

　　　hotel airport bus　空港周辺のホテル送迎用バス

【I】 intercity bus　都市間走行バス

　　　inter-terminal bus　インターミナルバス

【K】 kneeling bus　ニーリングバス　☆老人・車椅子・ベビーカーなどが乗降しやすいように、車体が歩道側に低く傾いたリフト付きバス

【L】 late-night bus 深夜バス　　　　limited express bus 特急バス
　　 limousine (bus) 空港バス　　　　local bus 地方路線バス
　　 long-distance bus 長距離バス（= coach）
　　 low-floor bus ノンステップバス、低床バス
【M】 metropolitan bus 都（営）バス
　　 microbus マイクロバス、小型バス　☆通常は定員 11 人以上 30 人未満
　　 midnight bus 深夜バス
　　 minibus 小型バス、マイクロバス（= microbus）
　　 municipal bus 市（営）バス
【N】 nonstop bus 直行バス
【O】 one-man-operated bus ワンマンバス
　　 overloaded bus 超満員バス
　　 overnight highway bus 夜行高速バス
　　 over-the-road bus 高速道路運行バス
【P】 passenger bus 旅客バス　　　　　pickup bus 送迎用バス
　　 private bus 私営バス　　　　　　public bus 公共バス
【R】 regular [regularly-operated] bus 定期運行バス
　　 relief bus 増発バス　　　　　　route bus 路線バス
　　 rural bus 地方バス
【S】 school bus スクールバス　　　　sea bus 海上バス
　　 shoppers' bus 買い物客用バス
　　 shuttle (bus) 連絡バス、近距離往復バス、循環バス　☆ shuttle bus to and
　　　 from the airport [hotel] 空港［ホテル］までのシャトルバス
　　 sightseeing bus 観光［遊覧］バス
　　 special bus 臨時バス　　　　　　stopping bus 各駅停車バス
【T】 temporary bus 臨時バス　　　　　tour bus 観光バス（= tourist bus）
　　 town bus 都市バス　　　　　　　transfer bus 送迎バス
　　 transit bus 輸送バス　　　　　　trolley bus トロリーバス
【U】 urban bus 市内バス
【W】 water-bus 水上バス　☆ water taxi（水上タクシー）

『観光のための中級英単語と用例』（山口百々男著、三修社）より

第3回試験

解答と解説

【Part A】

(11) **正解** **b)** A：おはよう。今日チェックアウトして、明日には帰ります。戻るまで荷物を保管
してくださいますか。

B：承知しました。お戻りなるまで荷物を収納室に保管いたします。**明日は何時ご
ろにお帰りでしょうか。**

解説 ホテル　A（宿泊者）はいったんチェックアウトするが明日また帰る（get back）旨
を伝え、荷物を預かってほしいと依頼する。B（ベルボーイ）は荷物の保管を快諾する。Bは
Aの帰る時間を確認する必要がある。したがって b) が正解。

参考 a)「さて、荷物をはかりに載せてください」
　　　 c)「休憩室は2階のお手洗いの隣にあります」
　　　 d)「登録用紙にご記入ください」
　　　 ☆ get back「戻る」　storeroom「収納室」　scale「はかり」　break room「休息所」　fill in「記
　　　 入する」（= fill out）　registration (from)「登録（用紙）」

(12) **正解** **c)** A：町に滞在中演劇を見たいと思っていました。しかし見たいミュージカルはすべ
て完売しています。またドラマを理解することができないと思います。私の英
語は下手です。

B：ちょっと待ってください。ツアーガイドは、中央劇場で公演する演劇は本当に
すばらしく、ハイテクな多言語の字幕システムがあると言っていました。チケッ
トをおとりしましょうか。

解説 観光　A（観光客）は町に滞在中演劇を観賞したいと思っている。しかし英語が苦手
なので苦心する。B（友人）は中央劇場での公演情報を伝えている。Aの心配への返答として
適切なのは字幕について述べている c) となる。

参考 a)「長期公演中です」
　　　 b)「特等席が利用できます」
　　　 d)「ドアは1時になると午後の興行として開きます」
　　　 ☆ be sold out「完売する」　dress circle「（劇場にある2階の正面に半円形に突き出した）特等席」

(13) **正解** **b)** A：お尋ねしてもよろしいでしょうか。美術館へはどのようにして行きますか。

B：すごく近いですよ。**ここから外に出て右折し、最初の角を左折すればいいので
すよ。**迷うことはないでしょう。

解説 観光　A（観光客）が美術館への行き方を尋ねている。B（通行人）はすぐ近くにあると告げて、その道順を教えている。選択肢を見ると一番近いのは右折して最初の左側を行くことである。したがって b) が正解。

参考 a)「角に銀行が見えるまで9ブロックまっすぐ行き、そこを左折すればいいのですよ」

　　　 c)「ブルーラインに乗って3番目の停車所に向かい、それから大学行きバスに乗り換えなさい」

　　　 d)「住宅地区に行くタクシーを利用してください。30分以上もかからないでしょう」

　　　 ☆ transfer「乗り換える」　grab a cab「タクシーをひろう」（= get [hail] a taxi）

(14)　**正解**　**a)**　A：レストランの前に立つ不気味なものは何ですか。

　　　　　　　　 B：タヌキです。京都近郊にある滋賀県の信楽焼の陶器の見本です。タヌキは**商売繁盛**のお守りです。

解説 飲食店　A（観光客）がレストラン前の置物について尋ねる。B（ガイド）は信楽焼のタヌキだと返答する。さらにタヌキはお守りだと言っている。選択肢の to 以下で何のためのお守りかを説明するとなると正解は a) 。

参考 b)「火難除けを祈る」

　　　 c)「架空の動物を追放する」

　　　 d)「良い仲間が見つかるように祈る」

　　　 ☆ spooky (house)「気味の悪い（屋敷）、幽霊［お化け］屋敷」　a good-luck charm「お守り」　protection「保護」　imaginary (animal)「想像上の（動物）」

(15)　**正解**　**a)**　A：私たちは日本滞在中に温泉に入るチャンスがあることを希望しています。しかし主人の業務スケジュールがぎっしり詰まっています。この国でリゾートホテルに1泊して過ごす時間が十分に取れません。

　　　　　　　　 B：実際、多くの大都会には都市型の温泉場があります。**余裕がある朝方または夕方には数時間訪れることができます。**コンシェルジュに頼んでお客様にあった温泉場を見つけてください。

解説 ホテル　A（夫人）は来日中に温泉に行くことを希望するが、夫の多忙なスケジュールのため行くことができない。B（係員）は遠方に行かなくとも都会でも温泉を利用することができると言いながら、その方法を伝えている。したがって a) が正解。

参考 b)「残念ながら、温泉浴場はもっぱら田舎の行楽地にあります」

　　　 c)「特にこの時季の料理は本当に素晴らしい」

　　　 d)「備品を持って来なかった場合は問題です」

　　　 ☆ urban (problems)「都市特有の（問題）」　exclusively「もっぱら、独占的に」

【Part B】

(16) 正解 b)　A：お客様、申し訳ございませんが、すべてのご搭乗のお客様にご自分の座席に直ちにお戻りいただくようにお願いしております。ですから、着席し座席ベルトをお締めいただけるでしょうか。

　　　　B：何ですって？　もう着陸態勢に入るのですか。

　　　　A：そうではないのです、お客様。**少し乱気流が予測されます。**それほど長くは続かないと思います。

解説　機内　A（客室乗務員）が乗客に対して自分の席に戻って座席ベルトを締めるように指示している。B（乗客）は飛行機が着陸すると勘違いしている。客室乗務員は着陸ではないと否定しながら、何が起こるのを伝えている。しかしその事態も長続きはしないと言っている。その予測される何かとは、選択肢から座席ベルトに関連するものを選ぶと b) が正解。

参考　a)「画廊は目下使用中です」

　　　　c)「これから数分間ノートパソコンを点検します」

　　　　d)「全席を元の位置に戻します」

　　　　☆ land「着陸する」　turbulence「乱気流」

(17) 正解 a)　A：次に旅行する前にはスマートフォンを購入しようかと目下思案中です。

　　　　B：それまたどうしてなの？

　　　　A：そうね、メッセージや電話ができることに加え、**歩行用のナビゲーションソフトがあり、しかもその中に旅ガイドもダウンロードできるのです。**さらには写真が撮れるし、そのうえツイッターを使用して旅行について友人に知らせることができます。

解説　日常会話　A は次の旅行前にスマートフォンを買う予定である。B はその理由（Why?）を尋ねた。返答として A はスマートフォンの魅力的な機能について語っている。したがって a) が正解。

参考　b)「空港で私に会うことができ、また必要であればホテルまで私を連れて行ってくれます」

　　　　c)「悪天候の状態が原因での遅延を避けるのに役立つでしょう」

　　　　d)「朝部屋を片づけるホテルの客室係を手伝うことができます」

　　　　☆ in addition to「～に加えて」　transport「(物を)運送[郵送]する、(人を)連れて行く」　avoid「避ける」　tidy (one's room)「(部屋を)こぎれいにする」

(18) **正解** **a)** A： 明朝9時の代わりに8時に出発できますか。市内の交通状況が少々心配です。11時までには空港に着かなくてはいけないのです。

B： 問題ないですよ。週末の**市内から流れ出る交通量はまったく混雑していません**。

A： そうね、あなたがそのようなお考えであれば大丈夫でしょう。

解説 **交通機関** A（旅客）は市内の交通事情が気がかりで、11時までには空港に到着したいため明朝9時ではなく早めの8時に出発したいと告げている。B（現地ガイド）は「心配するには及ばない」と返答しているので、交通事情は混雑していないと予想される理由を述べている a) が正解。

参考 b)「交通渋滞は深刻な問題であり、あなたの提案には賛成です」

c)「バスにはエアコンとトイレが完備されています」

d)「すべての旅行は、この行程を含めあなたの旅程に含まれています」

☆ (traffic) congestion「（交通）渋滞」 significant (event)「意味深い（行事）」 agree (with)「（〜に）同意する」 leg「（旅行などの全行程中の）ひと区切り」

---

(19) **正解** **d)** A： 神社の参道にはいろいろな珍味を売る小さな仲店が多数並んでいます。

B： 本当ですか。**私たちが試食すべきものは何だと思いますか**。

A： どれもみなおいしいですが、特にお薦めするのは餡子を詰めた魚型の甘味物（鯛焼き）です。

解説 **観光** 神社参道の仲店には珍しい食べ物が売られている。どれもこれもおいしいが、A（ガイド）は特に鯛焼きを薦めている。B（観光客）の発言を推定する場合、選択肢に食べ物と関連する try（試食する）という単語がある d) が正解。

参考 a)「観光すべき最高の時季はいつですか」

b)「そこに滞在する期間はどれくらいですか」

c)「今晩のディナーは何ですか」

☆ recommend「推薦する」 bean paste「餡子」 try (food)「試食する」

---

(20) **正解** **c)** A： 大浴場へ風呂に入りに行きたいのですが、それが男性用か女性用かよくわかりません。入口前に吊られている木製の標識にある**漢字が読めません**。

B： 今晩は左側は男性用、右側は女性用です。でも要注意ですよ。明日は代わっているでしょう。どの浴槽もユニークで、お客様には両方を経験する機会を提供したいのです。

A： わお、おもしろくもあり、紛らわしくもあります。でも、やっぱりおもしろい

ですね。

解説 **銭湯** A（観光客）は大浴場に来て、その前にある男女を区分する標識を理解することができない。その理由として適切なのは c)。

参考 a)「デモ（行進）を見ました」
b)「タオルは使用できません」
d)「伝統工芸品があります」
☆ confusing (situation)「混乱した［させる］（事態）」 (traditional) crafts「（伝統的な）工芸品」

---

(21) **正解** **d)** Having been the nation's capital for much of history, it **remains the heart of** Japan's cultural traditions.

> 京都は歴史の大部分において国の首都であったため、依然として日本の文化的伝統の**中心であり続けてきた。**

解説 代名詞 (it) の次に動詞 (remains) が続く。heart「中心地」は文尾の cultural tradition「文化的伝統」と関連する。この2つの語句を結び付けるのは所属・所有を表す前置詞 (of) である。定冠詞（the）は限定語句を伴う名詞句（heart of cultural traditions）の前に付ける。

(22) **正解** **d)** Its temples, shrines, and gardens are just what visitors to Japan **expect to see on** their trip.

> 京都の神社仏閣や庭園は、来日者が旅先で**見物を期待する**ものである。

解説 関係代名詞 what が作る名詞節の主語 (visitors) ＋動詞 (expect) が結びつく。expect to (do)「(することを) 期待する、(する) つもりである」 ▶ I expect to get a chance.「チャンスを期待する」 I expect to meet her tonight.「今晩彼女に会うつもりである」 ここでは visitors expect to see (its temples, shrines and garden) となる。最後の on は、on one's trip「旅先で、旅に向う途中で」という慣用句である。

(23) **正解** **d)** These days, however, a very large percentage of visitors **flocking to the city** are non-Japanese.

> しかしながら、最近では非常に大きな割合で**都市に押し寄せる**観光客は海外からの人々である。

解説 主語 (visitors) ＋動詞 (are) ＋補語 (non-Japanese) の基本文型である。この文章の主語を説明することが問われている。flock to (the seaside) は「(海岸へ) 押し寄せる、押し掛ける、大勢の人が群がり集まる」の意味、押し掛ける先の場所は the city である。関係代名詞を用いて visitors who are flocking to the city と書き変えることができる。

(24) **正解** **d)** For **many of these visitors**, their trip to Kyoto is part of an introduction to Japanese culture, and so they tend to behave differently from domestic tourists, who naturally have more knowledge of the city's history, traditions, areas, and culture.

これら**観光客の中の大勢の人**にとって、京都への旅行は日本文化の導入の一部である。そのため彼らは、京都の歴史、伝統、地域また文化に関する知識を自然に持ち合わす国内観光客とは違った行動をとる傾向がある。

解説 many of の語法である。many students「多くの生徒」と many of students「その生徒の多く」の違いを理解すること。前者は「限定されていない多数の生徒」の意味だが、後者は「ある特定の生徒の<u>中の多数</u>の生徒」の意味である。

---

(25) **正解** **a)** The crowds of tourists not only fill up Kyoto's most popular sights, they also fill up the buses and trains that everyone **uses** **to get around**.

大勢の観光客は、京都の最も人気のある観光地を埋め尽くすだけでなく、誰もが**あちこち移動するのに使用する**バスや電車をも混雑させる。

解説 関係詞節内の主語（everyone）＋動詞（uses）が結びつく。「誰もが使用する」のだが、その目的は何かである。get around は「あちこち移動する、歩き回る」という熟語である。
▶ They *get around* a city using the taxi.「市内をタクシーであちこち移動する」（= They use the taxi to *get around*.）

【Part A】

(26)「│ ① │に該当する最も適切な単語を選びなさい」

　　正解　**b)**　(by) **far**（＋最上級）「はるかに、群を抜いて」

解説 空所の直後にある the best（最上級）に注目する。また空所前には by があり、最上級を修飾する by far であることがわかる。したがって b) が正解。

参考 a) all「すべての」　c) long「長い」　d) near「近くの」
　　　☆ (by) far「抜群の」　▶ He is *by far* the best student.「彼はずばぬけてよい学生だ」

(27)「│ ② │に該当する最も適切な単語を選びなさい」

　　正解　**a)**　**atmosphere**「雰囲気、ムード」

解説 スカイロンタワーからの眺望は壮観で、特に滝がライトアップされた時は神秘的だと述べている。空所に当てはまるものとして適当なものは a)「雰囲気」。

参考 b) climate「気候」　c) flavor「風味」　d) phenomenon「現象」

(28)「広告の中で**記載されていない**内容は次のうちどれですか」

　　正解　**a)**　「スカイロンタワーのふもとで食事をすることができる」

解説 資料には、There are two restaurants where you can enjoy fine dining while enjoying the view from the top.「**頂上から**景色を眺めながらご馳走を堪能できるレストランが2軒あります」と記載されている。食事をする場所は頂上であってふもとではない。したがって a) が正解。

参考 以下は**記載されている**内容である。
　　　b)「朝食はサミットスイートビュッフェで出される」
　　　c)「ギャンブルはスカイロンタワー近くで利用できる」
　　　d)「スカイロンタワーには 3D ／ 4D ナイアガラ滝の映画のアトラクションがある」

(29)「スカイロンタワーに関する**正しくない記述**はどれですか」

　　正解　**a)**　「エレベーターの利用者はすべて有料である」

解説 資料では、there's no charge for the elevator if you have dinner in either restaurant.「どちらかのレストランで食事をする場合エレベーターの利用は無料である」と記載されている。したがって a) が正解。

参考 以下すべて**正しい記述**である。

    b) 「エレベーターは展望デッキに行くには 1 分もかからない」

    c) 「リボルビングダイニングルームは一回りするには約 1 時間を要する」

    d) 「両レストランでは景色を見て楽しみながら食事が味わえる」

(30) 「スカイロンタワーに関する**正しい記述**はどれですか」

    正解 **a)** サミットスイートビュッフェの特徴はビュッフェです。

解説 資料では、At the Summit Suite Buffet have amazing buffet-style dining. 「サミットスイートビュッフェでは素晴らしいビュッフェスタイルの食事が出される」と記載されている。したがって a) が正解。

参考 以下すべて**正しくない記述**である。

    b) Yellow Bugs（ガラス張り高速エレベーター）はスカイロンファンセンターにあります。スカイロンファンセンターにあるのは、屋内ゲームセンターである。

    c) スカイロンタワーは 15 周年になります。50 周年である。

    d) タワーにある両レストランにはビュッフェがあります。リボルビングダイニングルームはビュッフェスタイルの提供ではない。

【Part B】

(31) 「[　①　]に該当する最も適切な単語を選びなさい」

    正解 **b)** **register(ed)**「登録する」

解説 該当箇所は、The guides at NAC are all well-trained professionals, **registered** at RAJ (Rafting Association of Japan), knowing all about rivers, life saving and first-aid. 「NAC のガイド全員は、RAJ（日本ラフティング協会）に**登録された**熟練のプロ（専門家）であり、河川、人命救助、応急［救急］処置には堪能である」となる。☆ NAC は NISEKO ADVENTURE CENTRE の略語。

参考 a) encounter(ed)「出会う」　c) suspend(ed)「中止する」　d) surround(ed)「包囲する」

(32) 「[　②　]に該当する最も適切な単語を選びなさい」

    正解 **d)** **Requirements**「要件」

解説 空所後の for Participation「参加のための」に当てはまる語を選択肢から選ぶ。Requirements for participation: Ages 13 and up *from June on: ages 7 and up 「参加要件：13 歳以上。6 月から 7 歳以上」となる。

a）Functions「機能」 b）Equipments「設備」 c）Remarks「批評」

(33) 「ラフティングツアーの広告の中で**記載されていない**内容は次のうちどれですか」

正解 **d） Payment method**「支払方法」

解説 Available Time Period「利用可能期間」、Participation Fee Online「オンライン（予約）参加費用」は明記されており、HokkaidoExperience.com を使うメリットも冒頭で「アウトドア体験、工芸体験などを探して予約するのが簡単にできる」と記載されている。しかし支払方法はどこにも掲載されていない。したがって d) が正解。☆ラフティングとは、ラフト（筏を意味するゴムボート）を利用して川下りをするレジャースポーツのこと。

参考 a）「利用可能期間」
b）「Hokkaido Experience.com. を使用する利点」
c）「参加費」

(34) 「ラフティングツアーに関する**正しい記述**はどれですか」

正解 **a）** 「ツアー前にはアルコール飲料は控えるべきである」

解説 **Important Notices** の欄の最後に、Please refrain from drinking alcohol before the tour. と明記されている。したがって a) が正解である。

参考 以下の記載は**正しくない記述**である。
b）「活動に参加している間は貴重品や時計を身に着けるべきである」身につけないようにと記載されている。
c）「NAC での活動中はお茶の時間を楽しめる」お茶を楽しめるのは活動後である。
d）「8 月にはトレパンあるいはフリースの長ズボン、長袖シャツとソックスを着用するかもしれない」8 月ではなく春（4〜6 月）と秋（9、10 月）の格好の説明。

(35) 「ラフティングツアーに関する**正しくない記述**はどれですか」

正解 **a）** 5 月のツアー参加者は全員 7 歳以上でなくてはいけない。

解説 (32) の Requirements for Participation で前述したように、「6 月から 7 歳以上」と記載されている。したがって a) が正解。

参考 以下すべて**正しい記述**である。
b）「当日のキャンセルはすべて全額に付替えられます」
c）「NAC はウェブサイトで予約すれば割引価格を提供します」
d）「NAC はニセコ区域に滞在する参加者のために無料で送迎します」

【Part C】

(36)「　(36)　に該当する最も適切な単語を選びなさい」

　正解　**a)　accessible**「行きやすい」

解説 ホテル・コンシェルジュは、松本、日光、箱根の3か所を薦めている。東京からは急行電車があり、長時間かからない「行きやすい」場所である。したがって a) が正解。　☆ accessible「行きやすい」　▶ The shopping district is easily *accessible* from our hotel by car.「ショッピング地区はホテルから車で行きやすいところにある」

参考 b) particular「特別な」
　　　c) adjoining「接続する」
　　　d) distant「遠い」

---

(37)「　(37)　に該当する最も適切な単語を選びなさい」

　正解　**b)　restricted** (area)「制限された（領域）」

解説 ホテル・コンシェルジュは、大涌谷が封鎖されていることを説明している。(It's a just one area that is now closed ... it is only for the area of Owakudani.) ロープウェーがあるのはその大涌谷で、closed と似た意味の単語を選ぶ。したがって b) が正解

参考 a) isolated「孤立した、隔離された」
　　　c) dependable「信頼できる、頼りになる」
　　　d) removable「移動できる、除去できる」

---

(38)「　(38)　に該当する最も適切な単語を選びなさい」

　正解　**d)　active** (volcano)「活発な（火山）、活（火山）」

解説 ホテル・コンシェルジュは、空所後に The motion of the plates gives us ... several volcanoes that are not sleeping. と補足している。休火山の反対の意味となるよう単語を選ぶ。したがって d) が正解。

参考 a) extensive (fields)「広大な（畑）」
　　　b) ancient (relics)「古代の（遺跡）」
　　　c) reasonable (price)「手頃な（値段）」

---

(39)「　(39)　に該当する最も適切な語句を選びなさい」

　正解　**a)　evacuation** (plan)「避難（計画）」

解説 ホテル・コンシェルジュは、箱根が安全かどうか心配する観光客に向けて、噴火など

の緊急事態が起きた場合の対策がなされていると説明している。緊急時の対策として考えられるのは避難計画である。したがって a) が正解。

b) attention「注意」

c) connection「結合」

d) certification「証明」

(40)「 ___(40)___ に該当する最も適切な単語を選びなさい」

正解 **b)** **a booking**「予約」(= reservation)

解説 ホテル・コンシェルジュが、宿泊予約がとれるか心配する客に対して伝えている言葉なので、予約に関する選択肢を選ぶ。したがって a) が正解。

参考 a) an explanation「説明」

c) a destination「目的地」

d) a beverage「飲み物」

5　海外観光と国内観光の問題

【Part A】

(41)　正解　a）　Hermitage「エルミタージュ（美術館）」

和訳　ロシアのサンクトペテルブルクにある国立**エルミタージュ美術館**は、世界最大の美術館の１つである。かつてはカタリーナ［エカチェリーナ］２世の冬宮殿の一部であり、19世紀に美術館として再建された。美術館には、レンブラントの作品『放蕩息子の帰還』またレオナルド・ダ・ヴィンチの傑作など300万点以上が所蔵されている。

解説　解法のカギは、「ロシアの美術館」そして「カタリーナ２世の冬宮殿」である。☆1990年にユネスコ世界遺産に登録された。

参考　世界における代表的な美術館。
- b) Louvre「ルーヴル（美術館）」。フランスのパリにある美術館。名画『モナ・リザ』をはじめ、紀元前から中世まで芸術作品を多数所蔵する。
- c) Metropolitan「メトロポリタン（美術館）」。アメリカのニューヨークにある世界最大級の美術館。日本の名画、浮世絵、焼物、鎧兜なども多数所蔵されている。
- d) Prado「プラド（美術館）」。スペインのマドリードにある美術館。ゴヤの「黒い絵」シリーズをはじめ油彩画や彫刻などを多数所蔵している。

---

(42)　正解　a）　Lake Baikal「バイカル湖」

和訳　ロシア南東部シベリアにある**バイカル湖**は、世界最古（2,500万年）また最大水深（1,700m）の湖である。世界中の凍っていない淡水量の20％がここにある。バイカル湖は「ロシアのガラパゴス諸島」として知られ、数千種の動植物が生息する。80％以上の動物はこの地域の固有種であり、生物進化の科学にとって絶大な価値を有している。

解説　解法のカギは、「ロシアの湖」そして「ロシアのガラパゴス諸島」と称されるほど固有種の動植物が多数見られる生物進化の博物館でもあるという点である。☆1996年にユネスコ世界遺産に登録された。

参考　下記は世界有数の湖沼である。
- b) Lake Ontario「オンタリオ湖」。北アメリカ大陸にある五大湖のうち最小の湖。氷河によって削られて形成されたとされる淡水湖。
- c) Lake Leman「レマン湖」。スイスとフランスにまたがる三日月型の湖。約15,000年前の氷期の後、ローヌ地方の氷河によって形成されたとされる淡水湖。
- d) Lake Titicaca「チチカカ湖」。南アメリカ大陸のペルー南部（60％）とボリビア西部（40％）にまたがる淡水湖。汽船などが航行可能な湖として世界最高所にあると言われる。

---

(43) 正解 a) Ajanta「アジャンター（石窟群）」

和訳 インドのマハーラーシュトラにある**アジャンター**石窟群は、紀元前2世紀から紀元後5世紀にかけて石を切り抜いて築かれた30のモニュメントである。発掘された石窟から仏教芸術の壁画や彫刻の傑作が発見された。日本の法隆寺金堂の内陣の壁に描かれた人物と衣装の絵画は、インドの石窟群に見られる壁画と類似性がある。

解説 解法のカギは、「法隆寺金堂に描かれた仏教絵画（壁画）との類似性」である。岡倉天心はアジャンター石窟群を訪れ、即座に法隆寺金堂の壁画との類似を見出している。☆ 1983年に世界遺産に登録された。

参考 インドのユネスコ世界遺産。
- b) Bhimbetka「ビームベートカー（岩陰遺跡）」。インドに残る旧石器時代の岩陰遺跡。
- c) Elephanta「エレファンタ（石窟群）」。インド西部に残る石窟寺院群。
- d) Ellora「エローラ（石窟群）」。インド・アウランガーバード郊外に残る石窟寺院群。

(44) 正解 c) Goulash「グーラッシュ」

和訳 **グーラッシュ**は、ハンガリー起源のスパイシーな（辛い）料理であり、牛肉、タマネギ、赤トウガラシ、そしてパプリカパウダーなどで作られる。シチューとして料理されることが非常に多い。ハンガリーでは簡単な家庭料理として人気が高い。現在ではレストランでもよく出される。

解説 解法のカギは、「ハンガリーの最も代表的な家庭料理」である。日本の味噌汁のようなものだとも言われる。また日本のハヤシライスのもとになったという説もある。

参考 ヨーロッパの代表的な郷土料理。
- a) Bouillabaisse「ブイヤベース」。南フランスの寄せ鍋料理。魚貝類を香味野菜で煮込む海鮮料理で、マルセイユの名物。
- b) Fondue「フォンデュ」。スイス地方の鍋料理。白ワインで煮溶かしたチーズを、フォークで刺したパン切れにからませて食べるチーズフォンデュなどがある。
- d) Haggis「ハギス」。スコットランドの伝統料理。羊の内蔵を羊の胃袋に詰め茹で煮込んだ郷土料理。

(45) 正解 a) a dress code「服装規定」

和訳 寺院やモスクに入るとき**服装規定**を厳守するように注意されるだろう。着てもよい服、着てはいけない服に関する規定である。その場に相応しい服装を着ていない場合は入ることができないかもしれない。ラフな普段着であれば、入り口で衣服を借りることができる場合もある。

解説 解法のカギは、「着てもよい服、着てはいけない服に関する規定」である。

参考 b) a nature trail「自然遊歩道」

c) religious regulations「宗規」

d) traffic rules「交通規定」

【Part B】

(46) 正解 d) Oura Church「大浦天主堂」

和訳 **大浦天主堂**は、1864 年に建てられたカトリック教会であり、日本最古のゴシック様式の建物である。美しいステンドグラス窓のあるこの教会は、1597 年に磔刑にされた二十六聖人の殉教者を記念して建てられた。教会は 250 年間にわたる長い迫害を生き抜いてきた「潜伏キリシタン」が発見された教会として世界的に知られている。1933 年に国宝に指定され、2018 年世界遺産に登録された。

解説 解法のカギは、「日本最古のゴシック様式の教会」、「潜伏キリシタンが発見された教会」である。正式名は「日本二十六聖殉教者聖堂」。日本初の小バジリカ（basilica）（ローマ教皇から特権を受けたカトリック聖堂）に指定される。

参考 長崎県にある由緒あるカトリック教会群。

a) Egami Church「江上天主堂」。長崎県五島市にある教会。国指定の重要文化財、県指定の有形文化財、ユネスコ指定の世界遺産。

b) Shitsu Church「出津教会堂」。長崎県長崎市にある教会。国指定の重要文化財、県指定の有形文化財、ユネスコ指定の世界遺産。

c) Urakami Cathedral「カトリック浦上教会」（旧称：浦上天主堂）。長崎県長崎市にある教会。1945 年原爆投下で破壊され、1959 年再建される。被爆マリア像は国連本部に原爆の悲惨さと戦争の不条理を世界に示している。

(47) 正解 a) Akiyoshi-do「秋芳洞」

和訳 山口県にある**秋芳洞**は、秋吉台にある数多くの鐘乳洞の中でも最も顕著なものである。この秋芳洞は、この種のものではアジア最大、また世界第 3 位の大きさの鐘乳洞でもある。ここには川、滝、深い池、それに鍾乳石や石筍などがある。特に有名なのは百枚皿で、石灰石の豊富な水の作用によってゆるやかな傾斜地にできたものである。実際には 500 枚以上の皿状の小池が連なっている。

解説 解法のカギは、「山口県・秋吉台の日本最大規模の鍾乳洞」、特に世界的に有名な石灰華段の「百枚皿」である。1955 年には秋吉台国定公園に、1964 年には特別天然記念物に指定された。

参考 日本三鍾乳洞（秋芳洞・龍河洞・龍泉洞）

b）Gyokusen-do「玉泉洞」。沖縄県にある鍾乳洞。おきなわワールド文化王国・玉泉洞にあり、全長 5,000 m で国内最大級と言われる玉泉洞は、同時に国内最多数の鍾乳石がある。国指定の天然記念物。

c）Ryuga-do「龍河洞」。高知県にある鍾乳洞。弥生時代の穴居痕跡があるため、国の天然記念物また史跡に指定さている。特に石灰華で包まれた弥生式土器は希少である。

d）Ryusen-do「龍泉洞」。岩手県にある鍾乳洞。世界有数の透明度のある青い地底湖（第 3 地底湖は水深 98 m）が 8 か所ある。国の天然記念物。

---

(48) **正解** **c）** **National Museum of Western Art**「国立西洋美術館」

和訳 国立西洋美術館は西洋伝統文化の美術作品を専門とする美術館である。美術館は富豪で実業家の松方幸次郎の私有財産である美術コレクションを収蔵・展示するために設立された。最初の本館は 1959 年スイス出身のフランスの建築家ル・コルビュジエによる設計、新館は 1979 年前川國男による設計である。コレクションはルネサンス期から 20 世紀半ばまで広く収集されている。

解説 解法のカギは「松方幸次郎のコレクション」、「ル・コルビュジエと前川國男の設計」である。☆ 2016 年 7 月『ル・コルビュジエの建築作品・近代建築運動への顕著な貢献』（The Architectural Work of Le Corbusier, an Outstanding Contribution to the Modern Movement）という正式名称でユネスコ世界文化遺産に登録された。

参考 上野に点在する博物館・美術館。

a）National Museum of Nature and Science「国立科学博物館」。1877 年国立で唯一の総合科学博物館が創設された。2007 年には日本館がオープンし、科学博物館における日本最大の常設展示場となった。博物館の目標は地球上の生命の進化研究である。博物館は日本館（国指定の重要文化財）と地球館の 2 棟の展示館から成る。

b）Tokyo Metropolitan Art Museum「東京都美術館」。1926 年日本最初の東京府美術館として開館した。1943 年には現在名に改称された。1975 年には日本の建築家前川國男によって設計された新館が完成。

d）Tokyo National Museum「東京国立博物館」。日本と東洋の由緒ある美術品と考古遺物を保管・展示する目的で、1872 年に創設された日本最古の博物館。博物館には縄文時代から 20 世紀までの日本の歴史に及ぶ芸術品 11 万点以上が収蔵されている。本館、東洋館、表慶館、法隆寺宝物館、平成館がある。

---

(49) **正解** **b）** **Kaiseki-ryori**「懐石料理」

和訳 懐石料理とは正式な茶道の席で、濃茶を出す前に客に出される質素な料理である。元来「懐石」という言葉は、禅宗の僧侶が瞑想しながら長時間断食をした際に胸に当てていた、小さな温められた石という由来がある。禅僧が座禅中、寒さや飢えをしのぐ［腹を温める］ために温石を着物の懐に入れていた。

解説 解法のカギは「着物の懐にいれていた石」である。☆懐石料理には3つの原則がある。① 旬の食材を使う。② 食材の風味や香りを活かす。③ おもてなしの心を大切にする。

参考 代表的な日本料理。

- a) Honzen-ryori「本膳料理」。基本は一汁三菜である。汁物を1つ、三菜（①なます、②煮物、③焼き物）の3つである。ご飯と香の物は含まない。
- c) Shojin-ryori「精進料理」。肉や魚はなく野菜や大豆の加工品（豆腐・味噌・醤油など）を使用する。主として寺の宿坊で使用する。
- d) Osechi-ryori「御節料理」。新年のために準備される伝統料理。御節料理は元旦または正月三が日に食する日本の伝統料理。御節料理は1年の無病息災などを願って作られる。また主婦が3日間休めるように、食材が3日間保存できるように作られている。 ☞ **Column 09** 御節料理

---

(50) 正解 d) Ukai「鵜飼」（cormorant fishing/fishing with cormorants）

和訳 鵜飼はよく訓練された鵜を操りながら魚（鮎）を捕る古風な漁法。鵜は嘴で鮎を捕るが、捕獲したものを飲みこまないように首元にひもを結んでいる。かがり火のもとで夜の川で行う。昔ながらの格好と正式な頭飾りをつけて船に乗り行われることもある。

解説 解法のカギは「鮎をとる昔からの鵜を使った漁法」である。☆鵜飼は『古事記』にも載っているほどの日本古来の漁法である。用具一式は国の重要有形民族文化財に指定されている。

参考 日本古来の漁業法。

- a) Haenawa「延縄（漁業）」。一本の幹縄に、釣り針を先端に付けた枝縄、浮子を付けた浮標縄を間隔を置いて結び付けた漁具。
- b) Ipponzuri「一本釣り」。一本の釣り糸で魚（イカやカツオなど）を釣る漁法。
- c) Makiami「巻き網」。魚の群れを探し、網で囲い込んで捕る漁法。

御節料理

Osechi-ryori (variety of) special New Year's dishes; (a variety of) traditional dishes prepared for the New Year's.

Osechi-ryori is a traditional Japanese dishes served on the New Year holidays [during the first three days of the New Year]. A variety of ingredients are artistically arranged in a set of three-tiered [three-layered] lacquer boxes.

正月の３が日に食する料理。多種多様な食材が３段重ねの漆塗りの重箱に芸術的に盛られている。

【関連語】正式には５段であるが、最近では「３段の重箱」（山の幸、海の幸、里の幸の３要素）に盛り付けられている。

一の重（on the first tier）口取り [hors d'oeuvres]：

数の子（herring roe）、黒豆（black beans）、田作り（young, dried sardines）、紅白の蒲鉾（boiled fish paste colored red and white）、紅白なます [刻み大根と人参]（red and white pickles; pickles [grated radish and carrots] colored red and white）、昆布巻き（rolled *kombu* [kelp]）、栗きんとん（sweet potatoes mixed with chestnuts）、ごぼう（burdock）、いくら（salmon row）、酢の物（vinegared food）など。

二の重（on the second tier）焼き物 [grilled fish and meat]：

甘鯛(broiled sea bream)、伊達巻(*date* roll)、かち栗(dried chestnuts)、鮭(salmon)、伊勢エビ（lobster, prawn）、鶏（chicken）など。

三の重（on the third tier）煮物 [boiled vegetables]：

大根（*daikon*, Japanese radish）、人参（carrot）、蓮根（lotus root）、里芋（taro potato）、竹の子(bamboo shoots)、ゆり根（lily bulb）など。

★食材には縁起（food bringing good lucks; food charged with good wishes）を担ぐものが多い。

『和英：日本の文化・観光・歴史辞典 [改訂版]』（山口百々男著、三修社）より

リスニング試験

6 「写真」による状況把握

音声の内容

2-02 (51) a) The hotel asks for guest's cooperation for their eco-program.
   b) Guests should hang this card outside the door if they need bed-making.
   c) The hotel offers new linen every other morning.
   d) The hotel encourages guests not to bring towels in the room.

2-03 (52) a) A man is loading boxes of goods into the truck.
   b) A street vendor is now putting items on the stall.
   c) Souvenirs are piled everywhere on the shelves.
   d) The back of the truck is converted into a stall to sell souvenirs.

2-04 (53) a) There is debris piled up in the construction site.
   b) Tourists must avoid obstacles to move around.
   c) A lot of stone pillars remain here and there in the historic site.
   d) The open-air museum is flat and very spacious.

2-05 (54) a) The two-storied old style building is surrounded by stone walls.
   b) Tourists with umbrellas are walking along the well-arranged sand garden.
   c) The garden is set out neatly in a grid.
   d) Tourists are gathering under the large umbrella to see the monument.

(55) a) There are skyscrapers in the center of the city.

b) Thatched houses are exhibited inside the museum.

c) These houses were built with the floors elevated above the ground.

d) There are a few stray farm houses in a peaceful rural area.

解答と解説

(51) **正解** **a)** 「ホテルはエコプログラムに関する宿泊客の協力を求めている」

解説 カードには「寝具の交換を希望しない場合にはこのカードをドアの外に吊るしてください。エコプログラムを支援していただき感謝します」と記載されている。☞ **Column 10 ホテル客室の種類（p.231）**

参考 b)「ベッドメイキングが必要な場合、宿泊客はドアの外にこのカードをかけるべきだ」

c)「ホテルは隔朝に新しいリンネルを備える」

d)「ホテルはタオルを部屋に持ち込まないよう宿泊客に働きかけている」

☆ cooperation「協力」 encourage「励ます、助長する」

---

(52) **正解** **d)** 「トラックの後部は土産物を販売する屋台に改造されている」

解説 1人の男性が移動販売車 (moving stall; mobile selling [sales] vehicle) に似たトラックで商売している。米国では mobile catering vehicles と言う。日本でも人気のあるキッチンカー（和製英語）は food car [truck] と呼んでいる。

参考 a)「男性は商品の箱をトラックに積んでいる」

b)「露店商人は今屋台に商品を置いている」

c)「土産物が棚のあらゆるところに積み上げられている」

☆ load「（物を）積む」 vendor「行商人」 stall「屋台」 pile「積み上げる」 convert「改造 [改装] する、転換する」

---

(53) **正解** **c)** 「多数の石柱が史跡のあちこちに残存する」

解説 由緒ある観光地の史跡がある。選択肢に記す a) debris「瓦礫（がれき）」、b) obstacles「障害物」、また d) open-air museum「野外博物館」は見あたらない。

参考 a)「瓦礫が建設現場に積み上げられている」

b)「観光客はあちこち移動するために障害物を避けなくてはいけない」

d)「野外博物館は平坦で広々としている」

☆ debris「瓦礫」 avoid (obstacles)「(障害物を) 避ける」 (stone) pillars「(石) 柱」

---

(54) 正解 b)「傘をさしている観光客はきちんと整備された砂庭を散策している」

解説 日本の世界文化遺産、銀閣寺である。向月台と銀沙灘と呼ばれる砂盛りの横を傘をさす多数の観光客が巡回している。

参考 a)「2階建の古風な建物は石垣で囲まれている」

c)「庭園は碁盤目状にきちんと整備されている」

d)「観光客は記念碑を見るために大きな傘の下に集合している」

☆ stone walls「石垣」 in a grid「碁盤目状に」 gather「集まる」

---

(55) 正解 c)「これらの家は高床式で建設されている」

解説 奈良の正倉院の高床式倉庫のような建物である。日本には、登呂遺跡《静岡県》や吉野ケ里遺跡《佐賀県》など多数ある。

参考 a)「都心には超高層ビルがある」

b)「茅葺き家は博物館の中に展示されている」

d)「のどかな農村地域には農家がわずかながら散在する」

☆ skyscraper「高層ビル」 thatched house「茅葺き家屋」 (houses built with) the floors elevated above the ground「高床 (式住居)」

ホテル客室の種類

a hotel room, 《英》a guest room

1. single(-bedded) room　シングルベッドがある部屋。☆ SWB（single with bath）浴室付シングルルーム。

2. twin(-bedded) room　シングルベッドが2つある部屋。☆ TWB（twin with bath）浴室付きツインルーム。

3. double(-bedded) room　2人用ベッドがある部屋。☆ DWB（double with bath）浴室付きダブルルーム。

4. triple(-bedded) room　3人用の客室にツインベッドとエキストラベッドがある部屋。

5. suite room　寝室、浴室、居間、応接室などが続きになっている豪華なダブルベッド（あるいはツインベッド）の客室。junior suite room、semi suite、bachelor suite または presidential [deluxe] suite room（最高スイート）などの呼称がある。

6. studio room　スタジオルーム。スタジオベッド（ソファー兼用の補助ベッド）を備えた客室。通常は、シングルベッドともう1つソファーベッドがある部屋。

7. condominium　コンドミニアム。台所、浴室、居間と寝室が1～2室あり、6人まで宿泊が可能な客室。

8. penthouse　最上階にある最高級の特別客室。

9. connecting room　コネクティングルーム。隣接した2つの客室を連結して内側からのドアを利用して往来できる続きの複数の客室。中間のドアは二重構造になっており、各部屋の内部からロックできる。廊下を経由せずに往来できるため家族客や団体客などに利用されることが多い。

10. adjoining room　アドジョイニングルーム。相互に隣り合った部屋。または廊下をはさんで向かいあった客室。独立し2室以上の続き部屋。例えば、社長と秘書といったように各部屋はプライバシーを保ちながら、近隣にあるという便利さがある。connecting room と異なり連結ドアはない。

11. blocking room　ブロッキングルーム。航空会社の乗務員のために長期占有契約をした客室。あるいは特定 VIP または国際会議などのために事前に一括予約してある特別客室。blocked room とも言う。

『観光のための中級英単語と用例』（山口百々男著、三修社）より

7 「イラスト描写」による状況把握

音声の内容

■)) 2-07 (56) a) Alcatraz is a minor attraction in San Francisco.

b) You can get a ticket for the Alcatraz tour online by yourself.

c) You can make reservations at 415-981-7265.

d) Only online reservations are available for this Alcatraz tour.

■)) 2-08 (57) a) The hotel provides guests with information about the city sightseeing tour.

b) The message says Ms. Jian may be late for the meeting time.

c) The hotel got a phone call and message for Ms.Watanabe.

d) Opsindy left the message for Ms. Jian.

■)) 2-09 (58) a) The Nile River meets the Mediterranean Sea at Cairo.

b) Luxor is located north of Cairo.

c) The Nile River runs through Egypt from east to west.

d) Aswan is located at the north end of Lake Nasser.

■)) 2-10 (59) a) It takes 63 minutes and costs 1,040 yen to get to Sapporo Station from Shin-Chitose Airport by train.

b) Buses are cheaper and faster than trains for getting to downtown Sapporo.

c) Otaru Station is accessible within one hour by train.

d) To get to downtown Sapporo, the train is faster than limousine, but the fare is not so different.

(60) a) The Seven Gods of Good Fortune are believed to arrive on a ship full of treasures.

b) According to the legend, seven goddesses come to save people on New Year's Day.

c) The woodblock print depicts some lively townspeople in the Edo period.

d) Seven merchants in traditional clothes are packed in a small boat going on a treasure hunt.

解答と解説

(56) 正解 **b)** 「アルカトラズ観光のチケットは自分でオンラインを通して入手できる」

解説 アルカトラズは、米国カリフォルニア州サンフラシスコ湾に浮かぶ断崖の小島。1933年には連邦収容所になったが63年に閉鎖された。

参考 a)「アルカトラズはサンフランシスコにあるマイナーな観光地である」
c)「415-981-7265 で予約できる」
d)「アルカトラズ観光はオンラインのみで予約できる」

(57) 正解 **c)** 「ホテルは渡辺氏への電話と伝言を受けた」

解説 グランドホテルは、「ホテル前のバス停で17時に集合してください」というジャン氏からの伝言を受け、渡辺氏に伝えている。

参考 a)「ホテルは宿泊客に市内観光ツアーに関する情報を提供する」
b)「伝言によるとジャン氏は会議の時間に遅れるとのこと」
d)「オプシンディはジャン氏への伝言を残した」
☆ provide (人) with (物)「(人に物を) 提供 [供給] する」

(58) 正解 **d)** 「アスワンはナセル湖の北端に位置している」

解説 アスワンはエジプト南部、ナイル川中流の東部にある都市。イラストではナセル湖（ナイル川中流の人造湖）とルクソール（ナイル川中流東岸にある観光都市）の中間に位置する。

参考 a)「ナイル川はカイロで地中海と合流する」
b)「ルクソールはカイロの北部にある」
c)「ナイル川は東から西へエジプトを流れる」

(59) **正解** **d)** 「札幌の都心へ行くには、列車はリムジンより早いが、運賃はさほど違わ
ない」

解説 千歳空港から札幌に行くための運賃（fare）に関して、バスは 1,000 円だが、列車は
1,040 円である。またバスは 70 分かかるのに対して列車は 36 分で到着する。

参考 a)「列車で新千歳空港から札幌へ行くには 63 分と 1,040 円を要する」
b)「札幌の都心に行くためにはバスは列車より安価で早い」
c)「小樽駅は列車で 1 時間以内で行ける」

(60) **正解** **a)** 「七福神は宝（を満載した）船に乗って来ると信じられている」

解説 七福神は、庶民の身近にあって暮らしに幸運をもたらすとして日本で信仰されている
七柱の福の神である。☞ **Column 11 七福神**（p.235-236）

参考 b)「伝説によれば、7 人の女神は正月に人々を救済するために来る」
c)「木版画には江戸時代における陽気な町民が描かれている」
d)「伝統的な衣装を着る 7 人の商人は宝探しに行く小舟にあふれている」
☆ legend「伝説」　woodblock print「木版画」

七福神

The Seven Lucky Deities [Gods]; the Seven Deities of Good Luck

The Seven Gods that bring good luck including Japanese Shintoism, Chinese Taoism, Chinese Buddhism and Hinduism. On New Year's Eve, a treasure boat [ship] bearing the Seven Lucky Gods is believed to come to Japan and bring good luck for the coming year.

福徳（good fortune）の神として信仰される七神、神道（恵比寿）、道教（福禄寿・寿老人）、中国の仏教（布袋）そしてヒンドゥー教（大黒天・毘沙門天・弁財天）などの神や聖人からなる（神仏習合）。大晦日には七福神と宝物を載せた船が来日し、来る年の幸運をもたらすと言われる。

① **弁財天** The Goddess of Eloquence, Music and Wisdom. She is a talented beauty and plays a *biwa* lute [four [five]-stringed musical instrument] 弁舌・音楽・知恵の女神。琵琶を弾く才媛美女。☆「弁天」とも言う。インド・ヒンドゥー教の女神（female deity of India）

② **毘沙門天** The God of War and Warriors. He is fierce looking with glaring eyes. He is clad in armor, holding a spear in his left hand and a small pagoda in his right hand. He subjugates evildoers and protects people from evils by the power of his spear and pagoda. 戦争と軍人の神。怒りの形相で、甲冑をまとい、左手には槍、右手には小宝塔を持つ。剣と宝塔の威力で悪人を制覇し、人を悪から守護する。☆元来、インドのヒンドゥー教の「クヴァーラ神」、後に仏教の「多聞天」、現在の「毘沙門天」となる。

③ **大黒天** The God of Wealth and Harvest. He is a smiling old man wearing a hood. He is usually seated on two bales of rice as he brings good luck to farmers. He carries a huge sack full of treasures on his left shoulder and holds a magical gavel that brings good luck in his right hand. He is popularly known as Okuninushi no Mikoto of Japanese myth. 福富と豊作の神。頭巾をかぶり微笑む老人。豊作をもたらす神でもあるので通常は２つの米俵の上に座っている。左肩に大きいな袋（bag）を担ぎ、右手に打ち出の小槌（lucky mallet symbolic of good luck）を持つ。通称日本神話に登場する大国主命。☆別称「大黒」、「大黒様」。インドのヒンドゥー教のシヴァ神と日本古来の大国主命の習合。

④ **恵比須** The God of Fishery and Commerce. He carries a fishing rod on his right shoulder and holds a red seabream under his left arm. He is represented as a portly, big smiling figure with pointed hat and long robe. 漁業と商業の神。

右肩には釣竿（fishing pole）、左腕の下には鯛を持っている。風折烏帽子と長い衣をまとい、小太りで、微笑む姿をしている。☆商売繁盛と五穀豊穣の神として日本の土着信仰の対象である。

5 **福禄寿** The God of Wealth and Longevity. He is an old man with a long bald head and a long full beard. He has a crooked cane with a rolled-up scroll tied to it on his left hand. He is usually accompanied by a crane, symbolic of longevity.　富福と長寿の神。長い頭は禿げ、ひげが長い老人。左手には巻物を付けた曲がった杖（staff）を持つ。通常は長寿の象徴である鶴を伴う。☆中国・道教で理想とされる幸福・俸禄・長寿の三徳を備える。

6 **布袋** The God of Happiness and Contentment. He has a fat potbelly and a smiling face with puffed–out cheeks. He carries a big sack filled with treasures on his back. He has a flat fan in his hand.　幸福と満悦の神。太鼓腹とふっくらとした頬をした笑顔を浮かべる。大きな宝袋（treasure bag）を背負っている。手には扇を持っている。☆中国・唐の末期の明宗に実在した仏教の僧。

7 **寿老人** The God of Longevity. He is an old man with a long head and a white beard. He holds a flat fan in one hand and carries a holy cane with a rolled scroll attachéd to the top. He is usually accompanied by a stag, symbolic of longevity.　長寿の神。頭が長く白いひげをたらし、手にはうちわと上に巻物をつけた杖（staff）を持つ。通常は長寿の象徴である鹿をつれている。☆中国・道教の神である南極星の化身の老子。

『和英：日本の文化・観光・歴史辞典［改訂版］』（山口百々男著、三修社）より

8 「対話」に関する内容把握

「音声の内容」

2-12 **(61)** Hello, the safe in my room doesn't seem to be functioning properly.

2-13 **(62)** I've lost my camera. Can you help me?

2-14 **(63)** This is our first time to a Mexican restaurant. What do you recommend?

2-15 **(64)** I'd like to use the wireless internet connection in my room. Do I require a password?

2-16 **(65)** Hi, I got this discount coupon from my hotel. Can I use it here?

2-17 **(66)** Excuse me, could you tell me which bus goes to the outlet mall?

2-18 **(67)** I would like to purchase tickets to see the soccer game at the National Stadium.

2-19 **(68)** The travel guide says the Izu Peninsula is a popular hot spring and scuba diving resort area.

2-20 **(69)** Airline mileage plans offer members a number of benefits.

2-21 **(70)** Did you check the weather forecast for tomorrow's Tsukiji tour?

「解答と解説」

(61) 問い 「すみません、部屋の金庫は適正に機能しないようです」

正解 **b)** 「申し訳ございません。補修管理部から誰かをすぐに送ります」

解説 ホテル 宿泊客が部屋に備わっている金庫 (safe) が故障しているのに気づきフロントに知らせる。当然ながら補修できる人 (someone from maintenance) を行かせることになる。したがって b) が正解。

参考 a) 「申し訳ございません。この申告用紙にご記入ください」

c) 「申し訳ございません。お客様の予約を変更されたいのですか」

d) 「申し訳ございません。温度自動調節器をチェックしてくださいますか」

☆ fill in 「記入する」(= fill out) declaration form 「申告書」

(62) 問い 「カメラをなくしました。どうすればよいのでしょうか」

正解 a) 「承知しました。紛失物届書にご記入ください」

解説 警察 カメラを紛失したので戸惑っている。係員はその対処を尋ねられているので、紛失物届書（lost property form）への記入を勧めるのが自然である。したがって a) が正解。

参考 b)「あちらの運賃精算機をご利用ください」

c)「土産物店に行くほうがよいでしょう」

d)「カメラを携帯して写真を撮ることができます」

☆ lost property form「遺失物届書」 fare adjustment machine「運賃精算機」

---

(63) 問い 「メキシコ・レストランへは初めてです。お薦めは何ですか」

正解 a) 「ブリトーはとても好評です」

解説 レストラン 客は初めてメキシコ料理を経験するのでお薦めは何かを尋ねている。選択肢の料理を見ると、b) pizza や c) pasta はイタリア料理、また d) Tom yum goong はタイ料理の海老スープでメキシコ料理ではない。残るのはブリトー（小麦粉で作られたトルティーヤ［トウモロコシの粉を水で溶き、薄焼きにしたもの］に炒めたひき肉や野菜などの具材を乗せて巻いたメキシコ料理）だけである。したがって a) が正解。

参考 b)「ピザはおいしいです」 c)「本日お薦めのパスタです」 d)「トムヤムクンは辛い」

☆ recommend「薦める」 (pasta) of the day「日替わり（のパスタ）」 ▶「日替わり弁当」boxed lunch with today's [daily] special menu

---

(64) 問い 「部屋でワイヤレスでインターネットに接続したいのです。パスワードは必要ですか」

正解 a) 「はい、来客用のウェルカムパックに含まれています」

解説 ホテル 宿泊客は部屋でネット接続する場合、パスワードが要るかどうかを尋ねている。職員は要か不要かに関する返答が問われる。選択肢を見ると、b) cable、c) P.C.、d) additional fee はパスワードとは無縁である。海外のホテルの部屋でよく見かける、来客用に必要品一式が入っている包み（the guest welcome package）にはインターネット接続の案内があるはずである。したがって a) が正解。

参考 b)「ケーブルは不要です」 c)「パソコンは必要です」 d)「追加料金は請求されない」

☆ require「請求［要求］する」 additional fee「追加料金」

(65) **問い**　「私が泊まるホテルからこの割引券を貰いました。ここで使えますか」

　　　正解　**b)**　「残念ですが、ここでは割引券は受け付けません」

解説　**観光**　旅行者はホテルから割引クーポンを入手した。当地で使用できるかどうかを確認している。返答は使えるか使えないかである。選択肢には Unfortunately, we do not ... の文を見かける。したがって b) が正解。

参考 a)「営業時間外です。明日再度あたってみてくださいますか」
　　　 c)「割引券はホテル宿泊客にとって魅力的な提供だ」
　　　 d)「ホテルズドットコム（ホテル等の宿泊施設のオンライン予約サービス）はオンラインでホテルを見つけて予約する人気の高い方法である」
　　　 ☆ honor「（有効と見なして）受け取る、引き受ける」

(66) **問い**　「すみませんが、どのバスがアウトレットモールに行くのでしょうか」

　　　正解　**b)**　「駅前に循環バス停があります」

解説　**観光**　旅行者はアウトレットモールに行くバスの所在地を尋ねている。選択肢を見ると、a) や c) は電車（train）についてで、d) はアウトレットモールに行くバスの話題ではない。モールに行く循環バス停（loop-line [belt-line] bus）の所在地を提示している b) が正解。

参考 a)「電車は新宿駅から 10 分おきに出ています」
　　　 c)「渋谷でメトロ（地下鉄）を利用するほうがよいでしょう」
　　　 d)「ここでの交通機関はバスしかありません」
　　　 ☆ loop-line bus stop「循環バス停」

(67) **問い**　「国立競技場でサッカーの試合を見るためにチケットを買いたいのです」

　　　正解　**b)**　「スタブハブのウェブサイトで入手できると思います」

解説　**日常会話**　サッカーの試合を観戦するためチケットを買いたいと話している。どこで買えるかを知りたいと思われる。StubHub は米国のオンラインチケット販売ウェブサイト事業会社のことである。したがって b) が正解。

参考 a)「それ（サッカー）は確かに最近人気のあるスポーツです」
　　　 c)「スポーツマートでスカーフやジャージのようなチームの土産物を購入できます」
　　　 d)「道の向こう側に両替所があります」
　　　 ☆ money exchange「両替所」

(68) **問い**　「旅行ガイドの記事によれば、伊豆半島は温泉とスキューバー・ダイビングの
　　　　　　　人気があるリゾート地ですね」

　　　正解　**a)**　「写真から見れば、そこは非常に綺麗な景観です」

解説 日常会話　伊豆半島は静岡県の東端部に位置し、駿河湾と相模灘を隔てている半島で
ある。選択肢を見ると消去法で解答できる。b)「瀬戸内海」（本州西部、四国・九州に囲まれ
た日本最大の内海）、c)「石鎚山（愛媛県）」、c)「愛知県」ではない。したがって a) が正解。

参考　b)「（瀬戸）内海には多数島々が散在します」
　　　　c)「石鎚山からの眺望も有名です」
　　　　d)「そこは愛知県に位置します」
　　　　☆ peninsula「半島」

(69) **問い**　「航空会社のマイレージプランは会員に多くの特典を提供しています」

　　　正解　**a)**　「はい、私の父は成田空港でメンバー専用ラウンジをよく使用します」

解説 空港　マイレージプランは Frequent Flyer Program [FFP] とも言う。搭乗距離に応
じて無料航空券、アップグレード（upgrade）などの特典を提供する航空会社のサービスの
ことで、会員カードが発行される。a) が正解。

参考　b)「そうですが、マイレージプランは加入するには高いと聞きました」
　　　　c)「LCC（格安航空会社）のみがマイレージプログラムを提供します」
　　　　d)「新しい航空会社は乗客全員にウェルカムドリンクを提供します」
　　　　☆ welcome drink（和製英語）は、宿泊者に対するサービスで、到着時に無料で飲める飲料を指す。
　　　　　ちなみに果物の場合は welcome fruits と言う。機内で最初に出される飲み物のことを指す場合
　　　　　もある。

(70) **問い**　「明日の築地ツアーの天気予報をチェックしましたか」

　　　正解　**a)**　「いいえ、それは室内ツアーです」

解説 観光　明日の天気予報を調べたかどうか問われているので、返答は Yes あるいは No
である。したがって a) が正解。

参考　b)「6 月にはよく雨が降ります」
　　　　c)「私はランチを持参します」
　　　　d)「ツアーの出発は非常に早いです」
　　　　☆ (weather) forecast「（天気）予報」

音声の内容

2-22 **(71)** M: Good afternoon, ma'am. May I have your passport?

F: Here you are. I checked in online. Here is my smartphone with the confirmation information.

M: Thank you. Would you please put your luggage on the scale?

F: Certainly.

M: Ma'am, although your bags are under the weight limit, one of them weighs more than the 23kg per bag limit.

Question What will the woman most likely do next?

2-23 **(72)** M: Hello I'm looking for a place for a couple of nights. Do you have any vacancy?

F: First, welcome to Go Backpackers youth hostel! And, yes, we do have a couple of beds in a shared room. Would you like to take it?

M: Well, how many people are sharing the room? Do you have a private locker or something to keep my valuables?

F: All our rooms have six beds per room. We do offer a private locker and a safe is available free of charge.

Question What does the man seem concerned about?

2-24 **(73)** F: Welcome to Digital Phones.

M: Hi, I'm going to be here for a week or so and I need a mobile phone.

F: We have a variety of phones to choose from like our simple clam-shell phones through full service smartphones. What feature do you need?

M: I need to surf the internet, connect to my business e-mail account, make phone calls, and if it has an alarm, that would be great.

F: It sounds like one of our smartphones would be perfect for you. How about this Virgin Mobile smartphone? It's five pounds per day plus airtime.

M: That will do.

Question Why did the service staff suggest the smartphone?

2-25 (74) F: Shall we wake up the kids and get ready to go to the theme park?

M: Sure, just give me a couple minutes to finish writing this work e-mail. I need to send this to Paul in Shanghai.

F: Okay. We really appreciate you bringing us on this business trip! It'll be the first time for the kids to go to Tokyo Disneyland.

M: Yes. I'm glad we could all come together. I think I've been looking forward to this as much as they have!

Question Why is the man pleased?

2-26 (75) F: I'm very much looking forward to visiting the Singapore Botanic Gardens today.

M: Indeed, the idea of spending a whole day there is really exciting!

F: The brochure says that there are over 1,000 species of orchids and three hectares of natural and groomed gardens!

M: I can't wait to see the Tan Hoon Siang Mist House too!

Question What is the man looking forward to?

2-27 (76) F: I'm sorry but you can't take that bottle on the flight.

M: What am I supposed to do with it?

F: There is a trash can over there if you want to dispose of it now. You can also drink it here, if you want. The rest of your belongings have been checked and they are over there.

M: Well, I'm not thirsty and I only have a few minutes before my flight begins boarding. I guess I'll throw it away.

Question Where are these people?

2-28 (77) F: My husband and I are looking for a nice resort for Christmas— someplace warm.

M: We have some Caribbean cruises you might be interested in. They're perfect if you want to enjoy the weather, eat well, and take it easy.

F: Actually, I was hoping to do some diving.

M: Well, then an island resort is probably a better choice.

Question Why did the man suggest an island resort?

(78) **F:** I wonder if it is going to rain tomorrow.

M: The weather forecast said we can expect showers all day and possibly thunderstorms in the afternoon.

F: Well, then I think I'll plan on spending the day in the gallery tomorrow and leave the canal tour until the day after.

M: Good idea.

Question What is the weather forecast for tomorrow?

(79) **M:** Does the bus to the airport stop here? I need to get to the airport by 5:00 and they told me at my hotel that I could catch the airport bus at this stop.

F: No, it doesn't. You'll need to cross the street. The airport bus stop is on the other side, about 100 meters up the street. Over there. But one just left. I don't think you'll be able to get to the airport by 5:00 if you wait for the next one.

M: Oh, well. I guess I'll have to take a taxi. I was hoping to save some money with the bus.

Question What will the man do next?

(80) **M:** Here you are. Here's your passport, and your boarding pass. I've circled the gate number here. Please be sure to be at the gate at least 30 minutes before boarding time.

F: Is it a long way to the gate?

M: Umm, yes, it is. You're right at the end of the terminal.

Question Who is the passenger speaking with?

解答と解説

(71) **質問**　「女性は次に何をすると予測されますか」

　　　正解　**c）**　「彼女のバッグを詰め直す」

解説　**空港**　男性は、まず May I have your passport?「旅券を拝見できますか」、次に Would you please put your luggage on the scale?「荷物をはかりに載せてください」と伝える。女性は Certainly.「承知しました」と返答する。その後、男性は although your bags are under the weight limit, one of them weighs more than the 23kg per bag limit.「荷物は重量制限内ですが、そのうち1つのバッグの重量が一個あたりの重量制限の23kg以上です」と伝えている。予測される行動は、選択肢の中から判断すると、「荷造りのやり直し」である。

参考　a）「重量超過の荷物に関する追加料金を支払う」

　　　b）「セルフチェックインターミナルを使用する」

　　　d）「移動する前に金属製品をすべて取り除く」

　　　☆ overweight (luggage)「重量超過の（手荷物）」　procced「移動する、進む」

---

(72) **質問**　「男性が懸念しているのは何ですか」

　　　正解　**b）**　「自分の貴重品の安全性」

解説　**ホテル**　男性は I'm looking for a place for a couple of nights. Do you have any vacancy?「2泊できる場所を探しています。空き部屋がありますか」と尋ねている。女性は

we do have a couple of beds in a shared room. 「相部屋に2台ベッドがあります」と返答する。男性は Well, how many people are sharing the room? Do you have a private locker or something to keep my valuables? 「部屋を共有するのは何人ですか、そして個人用ロッカーあるいは貴重品を保管できるようなものがありますか」と尋ねている。女性は All our rooms have six beds per room. We do offer a private locker and a safe is available free of charge. 「当ホテルは全室1部屋につき6台のベッドがあります。個人用ロッカーがあり、金庫も無料で利用できます」と伝えている。

参考 a) 「彼は地元料理は好きではない」 c) 「滞在場所」 d) 「費用」
☆ valuables 「貴重品」

(73) **質問** 「接客担当職員がスマートフォンを提案するのはなぜですか」

正解 **b)** 「顧客はいろいろな機能の特徴を求めている」

解説 携帯電話販売店 男性は I need a mobile phone. 「携帯電話を求めています」と言う。女性は We have a variety of phones ... What feature do you need? 「多種多様な電話機があります……どのような機能が必要ですか」と尋ねる。男性は I need to surf the internet, connect to my business e-mail account, make phone calls, and if it has an alarm, that would be great. 「インターネットを閲覧すること、ビジネス電子メール・アカウントに接続すること、電話ができること、さらにアラームがあれば最高です」と返答する。女性は It sounds like one of our smartphones would be perfect for you. How about this Virgin Mobile smartphone? It's five pounds per day plus airtime. 「お客様にとって当店のスマホの1つがうってつけです。バージンモバイルのスマホはいかがでしょうか。通信時間（の料金）を加えて1日につき5ポンドです」と言っている。男性は That will do. 「それで結構です」と返答している。

参考 a) 「貝殻型（二つ折り形式）の携帯電話は安価である」
c) 「顧客は急いでいる」
d) 「値段は正当だった」
☆ in a hurry 「急いで」

(74) **質問** 「男性はなぜ喜んでいるのですか」

正解 **c)** 「彼もテーマパークに行くのを楽しみにしている」

解説 観光 女性は、Shall we wake up the kids and get ready to go to the theme park? 「子供たちを起こしてテーマパークに行く準備をしましょうか」と言っている。さらに It'll be the first time for the kids to go to Tokyo Disneyland.「子供たちは東京ディズニーランドに行くのは初めてだね」と付言している。男性は、I think I've been looking forward to this as much as they have!「僕も子供たちと同じように楽しみにしているよ」と言っている。したがって c) が正解。

参考 a)「今日彼は出張に出発する」

b)「彼の仕事仲間は上海にいる」

d)「彼は仕事に遅れた」

☆ on a business trip「出張で」

---

(75) 質問「男性が楽しみにしているのは何ですか」

正解 b)「ミストハウスを訪れること」

解説 観光 女性は I'm very much looking forward to visiting the Singapore Botanic Gardens today.「シンガポール植物園（世界遺産）に行くことを非常に楽しみにしています」と言っている。男性は I can't wait to see the Tan Hoon Siang Mist House too!「僕もタン・フーン・シアン・ミストハウスを見るのが待ちきれないよ」と言っている。

参考 a)「徒歩旅行」 c)「サボテン庭園」 d)「庭園を手入れすること」

☆ cactus「サボテン（仙人掌）」。サボテン科の常緑多年草。復 cactuses、cacti ▶ *Cactus* Park「サボテン公園」《静岡県・伊東温泉》 *Cactus* Garden「サボテン園」《宮崎県・日南海岸》

---

(76) 質問「この人たちはどこにいるのですか」

正解 c)「空港保安検査所」

解説 空港 女性は I'm sorry but you can't take that bottle on the flight.「申し訳ないのですが機内にはあの（液体入りの）ボトルを持ち込めません」と言っている。さらに There is a trash can over there if you want to dispose of it now. You can also drink it here, if you want.「今お捨てになりたいならばあちらにゴミ箱があります。お望みならばここでお飲みになることもできます」と告げる。男性は I guess I'll throw it away.「それを捨てようと思います」と返答する。☆ security check「検問、保安検査」（= security control, security inspection）。会話は空港などで出国前にハイジャック防止のため手荷物、携帯品または身体の検査をしている場面である。

参考 a)「駅舎」 b)「スーパーマーケット」 d)「税関」

(77) 質問「男性が島リゾートを提案するのはなぜですか」

正解 a)「彼女はダイビングをしに行きたい」

解説 旅行代理店　女性はMy husband and I are looking for a nice resort for Christmas —someplace warm.「主人ともどもクリスマスを迎えるにあたりどこか暖かい素敵なリゾートを探しています」と言っている。男性は We have some Caribbean cruises you might be interested in.「興味がもてそうなカリブ海のクルーズがあります」と告げている。女性は Actually, I was hoping to do some diving.「実は少しダイビングをしたかったのです」と言うと、男性は Well, then an island resort is probably a better choice.「それでは、島リゾートのほうを選ぶほうがよさそうですね」と返答している。

参考 b)「彼女は地元料理を楽しみたい」
　　　 c)「彼女はのんびりしたい」
　　　 d)「彼女は島リゾートに行きたい」

(78) **質問**　「明日の天気予報はどうでしょうか」

　　　正解　c)　「雨」

解説 日常会話　女性は I wonder if it is going to rain tomorrow.「明日は雨が降るのかしら」と言っている。男性は The weather forecast said we can expect showers all day and possibly thunderstorms in the afternoon.「天気予報によれば、終日雨で、午後は雷雨かもしれない」と返答している。

参考 a)「曇り」　b)「雪」　d)「晴れ」

(79) **質問**　「男性の次の行動は何ですか」

　　　正解　d)　「タクシーに乗ること」

解説 日常会話　男性は、Does the bus to the airport stop here? I need to get to the airport by 5:00 and they told me at my hotel that I could catch the airport bus at this stop.「空港行きのバスはここに停車しますか。5時までには空港に着きたいのですが、ホテル従業員はこの停留所で空港行きのバスに乗れると言っています」と言う。女性は No, it doesn't.「いいえ、停車しません」と返答している。女性は You'll need to cross the street. The airport bus stop is on the other side, about 100 meters up the street. Over there.「道路を渡る必要があります。空港行きのバス停は反対側で、約100メートル先にあります。あそこです。」と告げる。さらに But one just left. I don't think you'll be able to get to the airport by 5:00 if you wait for the next one.「すでにバスは出ました。次のバスを待てば5時までに空港に行くことはできないと思います」と言っている。男性は Oh, well. I guess I'll have to take a taxi.「それじゃ、タクシーに乗らなくてはいけないということですね」と返

答している。

a) 「道路を渡ること」

b) 「ホテルに戻ること」

c) 「チケットを買うこと」

(80) 質問 「乗客は誰と話していますか」

正解 **d)** 「搭乗手続き係員」

解説 **空港** 男性は、乗客に旅券と搭乗券を手渡し（Here's your passport, and your boarding pass.）、Please be sure to be at the gate at least 30 minutes before boarding time.「搭乗時間の少なくとも 30 分前には必ずゲートに来てください」と告げる。女性は Is it a long way to the gate?「ゲートまでは遠いですか」と尋ねる。男性は yes, it is. You're right at the end of the terminal.「はい、遠いです。あなたはターミナルの端にいます」と言っている。

参考 a) 「観光案内所職員」 b) 「パイロット」 c) 「コンシェルジュ」

[Part A]

音声の内容

02-32 F: Tasmania is an island roughly 80% the size of Hokkaido in Japan, located 240km off the southeast corner of Australia. The island, discovered by a European named Tasman, is the smallest state in Australia. Many unique and rare animals, such as the Tasmanian devil, attract many tourists from all over the world.

Recently, a very rare bay was discovered on this island. The bay is located in Southwest National Park. People can reach this site only by ship. This quiet bay is called "the sea that time forgot," because many deep-sea fish that usually swim in 200 to 1,000m seas are living at the bottom of the bay, though it's only 10 to 20m deep. The most mysterious thing is the color and quality of the water. The color is red and the surface part is fresh water.

The reason for this curious phenomenon is that the river flows include red color dirt which washes out over the surface of the bay. The red surface shuts out the sun light, so the bottom is very comfortable for the deep-sea creatures. If you want to go there, it's impossible without the permission of the government because the place is strictly preserved.

Questions

(81) How big is Tasmania?

(82) Which statement is correct?

(83) What kind of creatures are living in the unique bay?

(84) Why is the bay red?

(85) How is the bay known by locals?

(81) **質問**　「タスマニア島の大きさはどのくらいですか」

　　　正解　**b)**　「北海道の約80％の大きさ」

解説　冒頭で Tasmania is an island **roughly 80% the size of Hokkaido** in Japan「タスマニアは日本の**北海道の約80％の大きさの島**」と放送されている。したがって正解は b)。

参考　a)「北海道とほぼ同じ大きさ」
　　　　c)「約240平方キロメートル」
　　　　d)「オーストラリアとほぼ同じ」

(82) **質問**　「正しい記述はどれですか」

　　　正解　**a)**　「タスマンはこの島を発見した欧州人の名前である」

解説　前半では、The island, **discovered by a European named Tasman**「タスマンという名前の欧州人に発見された島」と放送されている。したがって正解は a)。

参考　b)「タスマニアはオーストラリアの東海岸沖にある」
　　　　c)「湾の深さは約200メートルである」
　　　　d)「湾はノースウェスト公園にある」

(83) **質問**　「このユニークな湾にはどのような種類の生き物が生息していますか」

　　　正解　**c)**　「深海魚」

解説　中頃では、many **deep-sea fish** that usually swim in 200 to 1,000m seas are living at the bottom of the bay「通常200から1,000メートルの海で泳ぐ多くの**深海魚**が湾の底に生息している」と放送されている。したがって正解は c)。

参考　a)「タスマニアデヴィル（夜行性で肉食性の有袋類）のような珍しい動物」
　　　　b)「多くの淡水魚」
　　　　d)「奇妙なカモメ」

(84) **質問**　「その湾が赤いのはなぜですか」

　　　正解　**b)**　「川の流れのため」

解説　後半で **the river flows** include red color dirt which washes out over the surface of the bay.「**川の流れ**が赤い色の土を含んでいて、その湾の表面をおおっている」と放送されている。したがって正解は b)。

(85) 質問 「地元の人々にはその湾はどのように知られていますか」

正解 **b)** 「時を忘れ去った海」

解説 中頃で、This quiet bay is called **"the sea that time forgot"**「その静かな湾は『**時を忘れた海**』と呼ばれています」と放送されている。したがって正解は b)。

参考 a)「ユニークな動物のいる場所」

c)「赤い湾」

d)「保護された場所」

[Part B]

▶2-33 **M:** Tokyo is generally recognized as a vast city. But did you know that a group of subtropical islands blessed with nature in the southern sea, called the Ogasawara Islands, is also a part of the capital of Japan?

Located in the Pacific Ocean around 1,000 kilometers south of central Tokyo, the Ogasawara Islands were designated as a national park in 1972, and were registered as a UNESCO World Natural Heritage Site in 2011. At that time, they were Japan's fourth site to be registered as a World Natural Heritage Site.

The Ogasawara Islands chain consists of about 30 islands, none of which are inhabited except the Chichi-jima and the Haha-jima islands. Chichi-jima Island can be reached in about 25 and a half hours by ferry from Tokyo Bay.

The island chain has never been connected with a continent and it is rich in unique animal and plant species. In some ways, it is similar to the Galapagos Islands, which are located far off the coast of Ecuador. In fact, the Ogasawara Islands are sometimes called the "Galapagos of the Orient."

The recent UNESCO designation of the islands has brought some problems, however. More and more tourists are now visiting. Some people worry that this trend could also lead to the destruction of the natural environment. In order to protect the islands, some regulations have been made. For example, only 100 tourists are now allowed to visit Minami-jima, the most popular spot in the Ogasawara Islands chain, and they are permitted to stay only for two hours. Hopefully, this wonderful chain of islands can be enjoyed by many people but also protected for future generations.

(86) How long does it take to get to Chichi-jima Island by ferry from Tokyo Bay?

(87) How many sites in Japan were registered as a UNESCO World Natural Heritage Site before the Ogasawara Islands?

(88) How many islands in the chain have people living on them?

(89) What is so special about the nature of the Ogasawara Islands?

(90) What idea is being tried to protect parts of the Ogasawara islands?

解答と解説

(86) 質問 「東京湾から父島までフェリーで行くとどのくらいかかりますか」

正解 **d)** 「1 日以上」

解説 中頃で、Chichi-jima Island can be reached in **about 25 and a half hours** by ferry from Tokyo Bay. 「東京湾から父島までフェリーで行く場合 **25 時間半**で着きます」と放送されている。したがって d) が正解。

参考 a)「2 時間」 b)「12 時間」 c)「半日」

(87) 質問 「小笠原諸島の前にユネスコ世界自然遺産として登録された日本での世界遺産は何件ありますか」

正解 **b)** 「3 件」

解説 前半では、the Ogasawara Islands ... were registered as a UNESCO World Natural Heritage Site in 2011. At that time, they were Japan's fourth site to be registered as a World Natural Heritage Site. 「2011 年小笠原諸島はユネスコ世界自然遺産に登録されました。当時、ユネスコ世界自然遺産として日本で 4 番目に登録された場所でした」と放送されている。したがって b) が正解。☆ 屋久島（1993 年）、白神山地（1993 年）、知床（2005 年）。小笠原諸島（2011 年）。

参考 a)「2 件」 c)「4 件」 d)「5 件」

(88) 質問 「小笠原諸島に住民が暮らす島はいくつありますか」

正解 **a)** 「2島」

解説 中頃では、The Ogasawara Islands chain consists of about 30 islands, none of which are inhabited except the **Chichi-jima** and the **Haha-jima** islands. 「小笠原諸島は大小30余の島々から成り立ち、そのうち**父島**と**母島**を除く島は無人です」と放送されている。したがって a) が正解。

参考 b)「25島」　c)「30島」　d)「100島」

---

(89) 質問 「小笠原諸島の自然界に関する特色は何ですか」

正解 **c)** 「ユニークな動植物が見られること」

解説 中頃では、The island chain has never been connected with a continent and it is rich in **unique animal and plant species**. 「諸島は、これまでどの大陸ともつながったことがなく、そのおかげで**ユニークな固有の動植物**に恵まれています」と放送されている。したがって c) が正解。

参考 a)「日本の首都の一部である」
　　　b)「エクアドル領の沿岸沖にある」
　　　d)「小型船でのみ到着できる」

---

(90) 質問 「小笠原諸島の要所を保護するためどのような試案が講じられていますか」

正解 **c)** 「無人島への来訪者の人数制限をすること」

解説 最後の方で、In order to protect the islands, some regulations have been made. For example, only 100 tourists are now allowed to visit Minami-jima, the most popular spot in the Ogasawara Islands chain, and they are permitted to stay only for two hours. 「諸島を保護するため、規定が定められました。例えば、小笠原諸島で最も人気のある南島に行くには、100名のみが許可され、しかも2時間のみの滞在が許されています」と放送されている。したがって c) が正解。

参考 a)「東京の一部にすること」
　　　b)「有人島への来訪者の人数制限をすること」
　　　d)「初めての来訪者が行きやすいようにすること」

観光英語検定試験

１級の概要

観光英検 1 級の試験

 1級試験では、国際舞台で活躍する観光業・旅行業・エアライン業・ホテル・レストラン業などの各種業界、また通訳ガイドや国際添乗員などを目指している人を対象に、「筆記試験」と「面接試験」を実施することにより、実践的な「観光ビジネス英語」の運用能力を測定する試験である。

(1) 「筆記試験」

 海外・国内における観光事情に関する内容について規定時間内で「英文和訳」・「和文英訳」を行う。筆記試験では「語学」と「知識」の両面を受信型英語で実施し、筆記による「正しいコミュニケーション」能力を測定する。

(2) 「面接試験」

 原則として、ネイティブスピーカーによる英語のインタビュー試験を面接にて行う。「面接試験」では「語学」と「知識」の両面を発信型英語で実施し、口頭による「正しいコミュニケーション」が円滑に行われるかを審査する。

 特に国内で活躍する「通訳ガイド」と海外で活躍する「国際添乗員」に目標を設定し、そのいずれかの業務面における英語が適切に運用されるかを審査する。

試験会場における試験実施

● 試験会場は、東京と大阪の2会場である。
● 試験時間は、午前9時～午後5時までに、順次実施する。☆受験票にて集合時間・試験開始時間等を案内する。
● 試験実施の順路は次の通りである。
　①「待機室」集合（注意事項の説明5分）➡ 移動 ➡ ②「筆記試験室」➡ 移動 ➡ ③「面接試験室」➡ 試験終了

(1) 試験会場に入る前

 受験票（受験番号・集合時間・試験時間・持ち物等記載）及び試験会場案内が試験日の1週間前までに受験者宛に送付される。試験日当日は、受験票と身分証明書を受付に提示し、係員の指示に従って試験室に入る。

(2) 試験会場にて

 受験者は、試験会場にて「筆記試験」（10分程度）を受験する。

筆記試験が終わると、受験者は 1 人ずつ試験官（1 人）のもとで**「面接試験」**（10 分程度）を受験する。

(3) 試験所要時間

　試験所要時間は全体を通じて約 20 分程度である。

試験内容

【第 1 部】筆記試験の形式と内容

試験会場には、試験監督者がいる。
受験者は、試験監督の指示に従って「観光事情」に関する試験用紙が置かれた机に向かって着席し、筆記試験を受ける。

(1) 筆記試験の形式

　筆記試験には「英文和訳」と「和文英訳」の試験がある。
　各試験には 2 問の課題（海外観光・国内観光）がある。
　配点は各 10 点とする。

(2) 筆記試験の内容

❶ 英語による観光事情に関する「英文和訳」

出題例 1 「ヨセミテ国立公園」

◆ 次の英文を日本語に訳しなさい。　　　　　　　　　　　　（10 点）

So startled and inspired were our forefathers by this picturesque range of geography that they took the novel step, in 1872, of declaring in an act of Congress that Yellowstone be set aside as the world's first national park, for the benefit and enjoyment of the people.

_____

_____

_____

_____

◆ 次の英文を日本語に訳しなさい。 (10点)

The Island of Itsukushima, in the Seto inland Sea, has been a holy place as an object of veneration since ancient times. The first shrine buildings here were probably erected in the 6th century. The present shrine dates back to the 12th century and the harmoniously arranged buildings reveal great artistic and technical skill. General Taira no Kiyomori erected and dedicated the shrine to the glory of the Taira clan in 1168, towards the end of the Heian Era.

_____

_____

_____

_____

_____

❷ 日本語による観光事情に関する「和文英訳」

◆ 次の日本文を英語に訳しなさい。 (10点)

バンコクの典型的なアジア風のたたずまいは、チャオプラヤー川沿いに熱帯地方固有の古い町並みが残ってはいるが、今では乱立する高層ビルの陰にほとんど隠れている。

_____

_____

_____

_____

_____

◆ 次の日本文を英語に訳しなさい。　　　　　　　　　　　　　　（10 点）

中尊寺は、天台宗の東北大本山である。その寺院には昔のままの建造物である金色堂と経蔵が往時の姿をしのばせる。藤原家三代のミイラが納められ、阿弥陀三体の下に埋葬されている。御堂は金箔の装飾と黒漆塗りが施されている。

_____

_____

_____

_____

_____

【第 2 部】 面接試験の形式と内容

試験会場には、1 名のネイティブスピーカーの試験官がいる。

受験者は試験官と 1 対 1 で「海外観光事情」また「国内観光事情」に関する英問英答を行う。

(1) 面接試験の形式

受験者は試験官の英語での質問に英語で答える。下記の試験内容に応じて、配点は各設問10 点または 20 点とする。

(2) 面接試験の内容

面接内容は「海外観光事情」と「国内観光事情」に関する記事である。

《A》指定された記事内容に関する英問英答。各設問には 5 題の質問が設定されている。

[1] 英語で書かれた海外観光事情に関する記事内容について、試験官から英語で質問される。受験者は記事内容を見ながら英語で答える。　　　　　　　　（10 点）

HAWAII'S BIG ISLAND ISN'T JUST BIG, IT'S STILL GROWING

Famous for the active Kilauea volcano, Hawaii's Big Island is home to a list of fascinating diversities. Eleven different climate zones generate everything from lush rain forests to arid deserts, black sand beaches to snow-capped mountaintops. The Big Island is Hawaii's biggest playground.

T r a v e l   T i p s

Getting to Hawaii's Big Island

Hawaii's Big Island has two main airports, Kona International Airport (KOA) and Hilo International Airport (ITO). There are direct flights from the mainland U.S. to Kona, but most flights arrive from Honolulu International Airport (HNL) on Oahu.

Staying on Hawaii's Big Island

In Kona and on the Kohala Coast you'll find many hotels, luxury resorts, and condominiums. In Hilo, you'll also find hotels of every size as well as small, charming inns. The area around Volcanoes National Park also has bed and breakfasts, lodges, and rentals.　If you're staying in Kona, and you plan to visit Volcanoes National Park, consider staying in Hilo or in the Volcanoes National Park area for a night because a one-day round trip may not give you enough time to explore the park.

Anytime of year is a good time to visit Hawaii's Big Island. The average temperature here is between 75°-85° F. Summer, between April and November, is warmer and drier while winter, between December and March, is a bit cooler. The Kona side of the island is sunnier and drier, while the Hilo side is wetter and more tropical. Trade winds keep things comfortable year-round.

Traveling on Hawaii's Big Island

Hawaii's Big Island lives up to its name, so you should consider renting a car to really get the most out of your visit. Many visitors also enjoy taking bus tours to conveniently explore the Island. Other options include shuttles and taxis. The Hele-On Bus provides bus service between Kona and Hilo.

質問事項：5題

Q1: How can international tourists get to Hawaii's Big Island?

Q2: Where are the affordable accommodations?

Q3: What is the temperature on the Island?

Q4: Where on the island is it dry?

Q5: What is the recommended transportation for traveling on the island?

[2] 日本語で書かれた国内観光事情に関する記事内容について、試験官から英語で質問される。受験者は記事内容を見ながら英語で答える。　　　　（10点）

出題例2　「世界遺産・姫路城」

400年の時を越え、日本の宝から世界の宝へ

国宝姫路城は平成5年12月、奈良の法隆寺とともに、日本で初の世界文化遺産となりました。

シラサギが羽を広げたような優美な姿から「白鷺城」の愛称で親しまれる姫路城。白漆喰総塗籠造りの鮮やかな白の城壁や5層7階の大天守と東、西、乾の小天守が渡櫓で連結された連立式天守が特徴です。今、私たちが目にしている姫路城の大天守は、慶長14年（1609年）に建築されたもの。400年以上が経過した現在でも、その美しい姿を残しています。

姫路城ご利用案内

姫路城の入城料金や開城時間などをご案内します。

姫路城の入城料金一覧

大人（18歳以上）1000円
小人（小学生・中学生・高校生）300円
30人以上（大人）800円
30人以上（小人）240円

> 小学校就学前は無料です。
> 18歳で高校生の場合は、小人料金が適用されます。
> 小学校・中学校・高校の教育旅行については、生徒15人につき引率教師1人は無料となります。

開城時間

午前9時00分から午後4時00分まで（閉門は午後5時00分）

休城日

12月29日・30日

アクセス

姫路駅北口から神姫バス乗車「大手門前」下車徒歩5分 JR姫路駅、山陽姫路駅から徒歩20分。駐車場については下記をご覧ください

Q1: When was the castle tower of Himeji Castle built?

Q2: Why is it called Shirasagi Castle?

Q3: How much is the admission fee for one adult and one elementary school student?

Q4: What time is the opening time today?

Q5: How can I get to Himeji Castle from the north exit of Himeji Station?

《B》特定の課題（与えらえた題目）に関する英語による説明。受験者は試験官から特定の課題に関する設問が与えられ、英語で即答する。受験者が特定の課題について説明し終えると、試験官はその内容に関して質問をすることがある。

[3] 英語で提示された海外観光に関する課題について、受験者は試験官に英語で説明する。 (20 点)

出題例 3 「ルーブル美術館」

"Please tell me about Louvre Museum in brief?"

質疑応答：1 ～ 3 題

Q1: How do you get there from here?

Q2: The Louvre exhibition may be held in Japan as well. Have you ever been there?

Q3: What are the specialties of Paris?

[4] 英語で提示された国内観光に関する課題について、受験者は試験官に英語で説明する。 (20 点)

出題例 4 「有馬温泉」

"Please tell me about Arima Onsen in brief?"

質疑応答：1〜3題

> Q1: What kind of souvenirs do you have?
>
> Q2: How do you go from here?
>
> Q3: Is there a hot spring in your area?

評価基準と配点

筆記試験と面接試験における各 10 点の配分は下記のとおりである。

(1) 筆記試験：「読む」・「書く」の両面における評価基準。

　　[1] 単語と連語　　　　4 点

　　[2] 文法と語法　　　　3 点

　　[3] 構成と字数制限　　3 点

(2) 面接試験：「聞く」・「話す」の両面における評価基準

　　合否判定に当っては、試験会場（東京・大阪）の試験官ごとに評価基準が異なることがないように、以下の評価項目ごとに合格基準を設けている。

　　[1] 発音と発声　　　　3 点

　　[2] 単語と語法　　　　3 点

　　[3] 観光事情の知識　　4 点

合否の判定

全試験の点数配分は 100 点である。合否の判定は、筆記・面接それぞれが概ね 7 割の点数を合格基準として行う。

解答欄 (見本：縮小サイズ)

問	a	b	c	d
1	ⓐ	ⓑ	ⓒ	ⓓ
2	ⓐ	ⓑ	ⓒ	ⓓ
3	ⓐ	ⓑ	ⓒ	ⓓ
4	ⓐ	ⓑ	ⓒ	ⓓ
5	ⓐ	ⓑ	ⓒ	ⓓ
6	ⓐ	ⓑ	ⓒ	ⓓ
7	ⓐ	ⓑ	ⓒ	ⓓ
8	ⓐ	ⓑ	ⓒ	ⓓ
9	ⓐ	ⓑ	ⓒ	ⓓ
10	ⓐ	ⓑ	ⓒ	ⓓ
11	ⓐ	ⓑ	ⓒ	ⓓ
12	ⓐ	ⓑ	ⓒ	ⓓ
13	ⓐ	ⓑ	ⓒ	ⓓ
14	ⓐ	ⓑ	ⓒ	ⓓ
15	ⓐ	ⓑ	ⓒ	ⓓ
16	ⓐ	ⓑ	ⓒ	ⓓ
17	ⓐ	ⓑ	ⓒ	ⓓ
18	ⓐ	ⓑ	ⓒ	ⓓ
19	ⓐ	ⓑ	ⓒ	ⓓ
20	ⓐ	ⓑ	ⓒ	ⓓ
21	ⓐ	ⓑ	ⓒ	ⓓ
22	ⓐ	ⓑ	ⓒ	ⓓ
23	ⓐ	ⓑ	ⓒ	ⓓ
24	ⓐ	ⓑ	ⓒ	ⓓ
25	ⓐ	ⓑ	ⓒ	ⓓ
26	ⓐ	ⓑ	ⓒ	ⓓ
27	ⓐ	ⓑ	ⓒ	ⓓ
28	ⓐ	ⓑ	ⓒ	ⓓ
29	ⓐ	ⓑ	ⓒ	ⓓ
30	ⓐ	ⓑ	ⓒ	ⓓ
31	ⓐ	ⓑ	ⓒ	ⓓ
32	ⓐ	ⓑ	ⓒ	ⓓ
33	ⓐ	ⓑ	ⓒ	ⓓ
34	ⓐ	ⓑ	ⓒ	ⓓ
35	ⓐ	ⓑ	ⓒ	ⓓ
36	ⓐ	ⓑ	ⓒ	ⓓ
37	ⓐ	ⓑ	ⓒ	ⓓ
38	ⓐ	ⓑ	ⓒ	ⓓ
39	ⓐ	ⓑ	ⓒ	ⓓ
40	ⓐ	ⓑ	ⓒ	ⓓ
41	ⓐ	ⓑ	ⓒ	ⓓ
42	ⓐ	ⓑ	ⓒ	ⓓ
43	ⓐ	ⓑ	ⓒ	ⓓ
44	ⓐ	ⓑ	ⓒ	ⓓ
45	ⓐ	ⓑ	ⓒ	ⓓ
46	ⓐ	ⓑ	ⓒ	ⓓ
47	ⓐ	ⓑ	ⓒ	ⓓ
48	ⓐ	ⓑ	ⓒ	ⓓ
49	ⓐ	ⓑ	ⓒ	ⓓ
50	ⓐ	ⓑ	ⓒ	ⓓ

問	a	b	c	d
51	ⓐ	ⓑ	ⓒ	ⓓ
52	ⓐ	ⓑ	ⓒ	ⓓ
53	ⓐ	ⓑ	ⓒ	ⓓ
54	ⓐ	ⓑ	ⓒ	ⓓ
55	ⓐ	ⓑ	ⓒ	ⓓ
56	ⓐ	ⓑ	ⓒ	ⓓ
57	ⓐ	ⓑ	ⓒ	ⓓ
58	ⓐ	ⓑ	ⓒ	ⓓ
59	ⓐ	ⓑ	ⓒ	ⓓ
60	ⓐ	ⓑ	ⓒ	ⓓ
61	ⓐ	ⓑ	ⓒ	ⓓ
62	ⓐ	ⓑ	ⓒ	ⓓ
63	ⓐ	ⓑ	ⓒ	ⓓ
64	ⓐ	ⓑ	ⓒ	ⓓ
65	ⓐ	ⓑ	ⓒ	ⓓ
66	ⓐ	ⓑ	ⓒ	ⓓ
67	ⓐ	ⓑ	ⓒ	ⓓ
68	ⓐ	ⓑ	ⓒ	ⓓ
69	ⓐ	ⓑ	ⓒ	ⓓ
70	ⓐ	ⓑ	ⓒ	ⓓ
71	ⓐ	ⓑ	ⓒ	ⓓ
72	ⓐ	ⓑ	ⓒ	ⓓ
73	ⓐ	ⓑ	ⓒ	ⓓ
74	ⓐ	ⓑ	ⓒ	ⓓ
75	ⓐ	ⓑ	ⓒ	ⓓ
76	ⓐ	ⓑ	ⓒ	ⓓ
77	ⓐ	ⓑ	ⓒ	ⓓ
78	ⓐ	ⓑ	ⓒ	ⓓ
79	ⓐ	ⓑ	ⓒ	ⓓ
80	ⓐ	ⓑ	ⓒ	ⓓ
81	ⓐ	ⓑ	ⓒ	ⓓ
82	ⓐ	ⓑ	ⓒ	ⓓ
83	ⓐ	ⓑ	ⓒ	ⓓ
84	ⓐ	ⓑ	ⓒ	ⓓ
85	ⓐ	ⓑ	ⓒ	ⓓ
86	ⓐ	ⓑ	ⓒ	ⓓ
87	ⓐ	ⓑ	ⓒ	ⓓ
88	ⓐ	ⓑ	ⓒ	ⓓ
89	ⓐ	ⓑ	ⓒ	ⓓ
90	ⓐ	ⓑ	ⓒ	ⓓ

解 答 欄 （見本：縮小サイズ）

筆記

	a	b	c	d
1	ⓐ	ⓑ	ⓒ	ⓓ
2	ⓐ	ⓑ	ⓒ	ⓓ
3	ⓐ	ⓑ	ⓒ	ⓓ
4	ⓐ	ⓑ	ⓒ	ⓓ
5	ⓐ	ⓑ	ⓒ	ⓓ
6	ⓐ	ⓑ	ⓒ	ⓓ
7	ⓐ	ⓑ	ⓒ	ⓓ
8	ⓐ	ⓑ	ⓒ	ⓓ
9	ⓐ	ⓑ	ⓒ	ⓓ
10	ⓐ	ⓑ	ⓒ	ⓓ
11	ⓐ	ⓑ	ⓒ	ⓓ
12	ⓐ	ⓑ	ⓒ	ⓓ
13	ⓐ	ⓑ	ⓒ	ⓓ
14	ⓐ	ⓑ	ⓒ	ⓓ
15	ⓐ	ⓑ	ⓒ	ⓓ
16	ⓐ	ⓑ	ⓒ	ⓓ
17	ⓐ	ⓑ	ⓒ	ⓓ
18	ⓐ	ⓑ	ⓒ	ⓓ
19	ⓐ	ⓑ	ⓒ	ⓓ
20	ⓐ	ⓑ	ⓒ	ⓓ
21	ⓐ	ⓑ	ⓒ	ⓓ
22	ⓐ	ⓑ	ⓒ	ⓓ
23	ⓐ	ⓑ	ⓒ	ⓓ
24	ⓐ	ⓑ	ⓒ	ⓓ
25	ⓐ	ⓑ	ⓒ	ⓓ
26	ⓐ	ⓑ	ⓒ	ⓓ
27	ⓐ	ⓑ	ⓒ	ⓓ
28	ⓐ	ⓑ	ⓒ	ⓓ
29	ⓐ	ⓑ	ⓒ	ⓓ
30	ⓐ	ⓑ	ⓒ	ⓓ
31	ⓐ	ⓑ	ⓒ	ⓓ
32	ⓐ	ⓑ	ⓒ	ⓓ
33	ⓐ	ⓑ	ⓒ	ⓓ
34	ⓐ	ⓑ	ⓒ	ⓓ
35	ⓐ	ⓑ	ⓒ	ⓓ
36	ⓐ	ⓑ	ⓒ	ⓓ
37	ⓐ	ⓑ	ⓒ	ⓓ
38	ⓐ	ⓑ	ⓒ	ⓓ
39	ⓐ	ⓑ	ⓒ	ⓓ
40	ⓐ	ⓑ	ⓒ	ⓓ
41	ⓐ	ⓑ	ⓒ	ⓓ
42	ⓐ	ⓑ	ⓒ	ⓓ
43	ⓐ	ⓑ	ⓒ	ⓓ
44	ⓐ	ⓑ	ⓒ	ⓓ
45	ⓐ	ⓑ	ⓒ	ⓓ
46	ⓐ	ⓑ	ⓒ	ⓓ
47	ⓐ	ⓑ	ⓒ	ⓓ
48	ⓐ	ⓑ	ⓒ	ⓓ
49	ⓐ	ⓑ	ⓒ	ⓓ
50	ⓐ	ⓑ	ⓒ	ⓓ

リスニング

	a	b	c	d
51	ⓐ	ⓑ	ⓒ	ⓓ
52	ⓐ	ⓑ	ⓒ	ⓓ
53	ⓐ	ⓑ	ⓒ	ⓓ
54	ⓐ	ⓑ	ⓒ	ⓓ
55	ⓐ	ⓑ	ⓒ	ⓓ
56	ⓐ	ⓑ	ⓒ	ⓓ
57	ⓐ	ⓑ	ⓒ	ⓓ
58	ⓐ	ⓑ	ⓒ	ⓓ
59	ⓐ	ⓑ	ⓒ	ⓓ
60	ⓐ	ⓑ	ⓒ	ⓓ
61	ⓐ	ⓑ	ⓒ	ⓓ
62	ⓐ	ⓑ	ⓒ	ⓓ
63	ⓐ	ⓑ	ⓒ	ⓓ
64	ⓐ	ⓑ	ⓒ	ⓓ
65	ⓐ	ⓑ	ⓒ	ⓓ
66	ⓐ	ⓑ	ⓒ	ⓓ
67	ⓐ	ⓑ	ⓒ	ⓓ
68	ⓐ	ⓑ	ⓒ	ⓓ
69	ⓐ	ⓑ	ⓒ	ⓓ
70	ⓐ	ⓑ	ⓒ	ⓓ
71	ⓐ	ⓑ	ⓒ	ⓓ
72	ⓐ	ⓑ	ⓒ	ⓓ
73	ⓐ	ⓑ	ⓒ	ⓓ
74	ⓐ	ⓑ	ⓒ	ⓓ
75	ⓐ	ⓑ	ⓒ	ⓓ
76	ⓐ	ⓑ	ⓒ	ⓓ
77	ⓐ	ⓑ	ⓒ	ⓓ
78	ⓐ	ⓑ	ⓒ	ⓓ
79	ⓐ	ⓑ	ⓒ	ⓓ
80	ⓐ	ⓑ	ⓒ	ⓓ
81	ⓐ	ⓑ	ⓒ	ⓓ
82	ⓐ	ⓑ	ⓒ	ⓓ
83	ⓐ	ⓑ	ⓒ	ⓓ
84	ⓐ	ⓑ	ⓒ	ⓓ
85	ⓐ	ⓑ	ⓒ	ⓓ
86	ⓐ	ⓑ	ⓒ	ⓓ
87	ⓐ	ⓑ	ⓒ	ⓓ
88	ⓐ	ⓑ	ⓒ	ⓓ
89	ⓐ	ⓑ	ⓒ	ⓓ
90	ⓐ	ⓑ	ⓒ	ⓓ

解答欄 （見本：縮小サイズ）

筆記

1	ⓐ	ⓑ	ⓒ	ⓓ
2	ⓐ	ⓑ	ⓒ	ⓓ
3	ⓐ	ⓑ	ⓒ	ⓓ
4	ⓐ	ⓑ	ⓒ	ⓓ
5	ⓐ	ⓑ	ⓒ	ⓓ
6	ⓐ	ⓑ	ⓒ	ⓓ
7	ⓐ	ⓑ	ⓒ	ⓓ
8	ⓐ	ⓑ	ⓒ	ⓓ
9	ⓐ	ⓑ	ⓒ	ⓓ
10	ⓐ	ⓑ	ⓒ	ⓓ
11	ⓐ	ⓑ	ⓒ	ⓓ
12	ⓐ	ⓑ	ⓒ	ⓓ
13	ⓐ	ⓑ	ⓒ	ⓓ
14	ⓐ	ⓑ	ⓒ	ⓓ
15	ⓐ	ⓑ	ⓒ	ⓓ
16	ⓐ	ⓑ	ⓒ	ⓓ
17	ⓐ	ⓑ	ⓒ	ⓓ
18	ⓐ	ⓑ	ⓒ	ⓓ
19	ⓐ	ⓑ	ⓒ	ⓓ
20	ⓐ	ⓑ	ⓒ	ⓓ
21	ⓐ	ⓑ	ⓒ	ⓓ
22	ⓐ	ⓑ	ⓒ	ⓓ
23	ⓐ	ⓑ	ⓒ	ⓓ
24	ⓐ	ⓑ	ⓒ	ⓓ
25	ⓐ	ⓑ	ⓒ	ⓓ
26	ⓐ	ⓑ	ⓒ	ⓓ
27	ⓐ	ⓑ	ⓒ	ⓓ
28	ⓐ	ⓑ	ⓒ	ⓓ
29	ⓐ	ⓑ	ⓒ	ⓓ
30	ⓐ	ⓑ	ⓒ	ⓓ
31	ⓐ	ⓑ	ⓒ	ⓓ
32	ⓐ	ⓑ	ⓒ	ⓓ
33	ⓐ	ⓑ	ⓒ	ⓓ
34	ⓐ	ⓑ	ⓒ	ⓓ
35	ⓐ	ⓑ	ⓒ	ⓓ
36	ⓐ	ⓑ	ⓒ	ⓓ
37	ⓐ	ⓑ	ⓒ	ⓓ
38	ⓐ	ⓑ	ⓒ	ⓓ
39	ⓐ	ⓑ	ⓒ	ⓓ
40	ⓐ	ⓑ	ⓒ	ⓓ
41	ⓐ	ⓑ	ⓒ	ⓓ
42	ⓐ	ⓑ	ⓒ	ⓓ
43	ⓐ	ⓑ	ⓒ	ⓓ
44	ⓐ	ⓑ	ⓒ	ⓓ
45	ⓐ	ⓑ	ⓒ	ⓓ
46	ⓐ	ⓑ	ⓒ	ⓓ
47	ⓐ	ⓑ	ⓒ	ⓓ
48	ⓐ	ⓑ	ⓒ	ⓓ
49	ⓐ	ⓑ	ⓒ	ⓓ
50	ⓐ	ⓑ	ⓒ	ⓓ

リスニング

51	ⓐ	ⓑ	ⓒ	ⓓ
52	ⓐ	ⓑ	ⓒ	ⓓ
53	ⓐ	ⓑ	ⓒ	ⓓ
54	ⓐ	ⓑ	ⓒ	ⓓ
55	ⓐ	ⓑ	ⓒ	ⓓ
56	ⓐ	ⓑ	ⓒ	ⓓ
57	ⓐ	ⓑ	ⓒ	ⓓ
58	ⓐ	ⓑ	ⓒ	ⓓ
59	ⓐ	ⓑ	ⓒ	ⓓ
60	ⓐ	ⓑ	ⓒ	ⓓ
61	ⓐ	ⓑ	ⓒ	ⓓ
62	ⓐ	ⓑ	ⓒ	ⓓ
63	ⓐ	ⓑ	ⓒ	ⓓ
64	ⓐ	ⓑ	ⓒ	ⓓ
65	ⓐ	ⓑ	ⓒ	ⓓ
66	ⓐ	ⓑ	ⓒ	ⓓ
67	ⓐ	ⓑ	ⓒ	ⓓ
68	ⓐ	ⓑ	ⓒ	ⓓ
69	ⓐ	ⓑ	ⓒ	ⓓ
70	ⓐ	ⓑ	ⓒ	ⓓ
71	ⓐ	ⓑ	ⓒ	ⓓ
72	ⓐ	ⓑ	ⓒ	ⓓ
73	ⓐ	ⓑ	ⓒ	ⓓ
74	ⓐ	ⓑ	ⓒ	ⓓ
75	ⓐ	ⓑ	ⓒ	ⓓ
76	ⓐ	ⓑ	ⓒ	ⓓ
77	ⓐ	ⓑ	ⓒ	ⓓ
78	ⓐ	ⓑ	ⓒ	ⓓ
79	ⓐ	ⓑ	ⓒ	ⓓ
80	ⓐ	ⓑ	ⓒ	ⓓ
81	ⓐ	ⓑ	ⓒ	ⓓ
82	ⓐ	ⓑ	ⓒ	ⓓ
83	ⓐ	ⓑ	ⓒ	ⓓ
84	ⓐ	ⓑ	ⓒ	ⓓ
85	ⓐ	ⓑ	ⓒ	ⓓ
86	ⓐ	ⓑ	ⓒ	ⓓ
87	ⓐ	ⓑ	ⓒ	ⓓ
88	ⓐ	ⓑ	ⓒ	ⓓ
89	ⓐ	ⓑ	ⓒ	ⓓ
90	ⓐ	ⓑ	ⓒ	ⓓ

【監修者（解説執筆）】

山口百々男 （やまぐち　ももお）

サレジアン・カレッジ（哲学科・神学科）。ラテン語・イタリア語に精通。ハーバード大学留学（英語）。東京大学研修（教育）。大阪星光学院中学・高等学校およびサレジオ学院高等学校の元教頭。旧通訳ガイド養成所（現・文際学園日本外国語専門学校および大阪外語専門学校）の初代校長兼元理事（創業に参画）。全国専門学校日本語教育協会（元理事）。英検１級２次面接元試験官。全国語学ビジネス観光教育協会（元理事）付属観光英検センター顧問。著書に『和英：日本の文化・観光・歴史辞典［改訂版］』、『英語で伝える日本の文化・観光・世界遺産』、『英語で伝える江戸の文化・東京の観光』、『観光のための初級英単語と用例』、『観光のための中級英単語と用例』（以上、三修社）など多数。

● **音声ダウンロード・ストリーミング**

CD と同内容の音声をご利用いただけます。

1. PC・スマートフォンで本書の音声ページにアクセスします。

   https://www.sanshusha.co.jp/np/onsei/isbn/9784384060058/

2. シリアルコード「06005」を入力。

3. 音声ダウンロード・ストリーミングをご利用いただけます。

かんこうえいけん　きゅう　せいせん か こ もんだい
観光英検 2 級の精選過去問題

2021 年 9 月 30 日　第 1 刷発行

編　者―全国語学ビジネス観光教育協会 観光英検センター

監修者―山口百々男

発行者―前田俊秀

発行所―株式会社 三修社

　　　　〒 150-0001 東京都渋谷区神宮前 2-2-22

　　　　TEL 03-3405-4511　FAX 03-3405-4522

　　　　振替 00190-9-72758

　　　　https://www.sanshusha.co.jp

　　　　編集担当　伊藤宏実・三井るリ子

印刷製本―日経印刷株式会社

カバーデザイン　　　峯岸孝之（COMIX BRAND）

本文デザイン・DTP　藤原志麻

音声 CD 制作　　　　高速録音株式会社

観光英検の受験対策にお薦め

観光のための
初級英単語と用例

観光英検３級 ～２級対応

観光のための
中級英単語と用例

観光英検２級 ～１級対応

山口百々男 著／藤田玲子 校閲／ Steven Bates 校閲

A5 判／並製／ 224 ページ
定価各 1,980 円（本体 1,800 円＋税）
初級　ISBN978-4-384-05724-9　　中級　ISBN978-4-384-05723-2

「観光・旅行」に関連した英単語を学ぶための用語・用例集。観光英語検定試験
の３級～２級に対応した初級編、２級～１級に対応した中級編、それぞれに必要
な語彙を収録しました。
◇ 観光業・旅行業を目指す方に
◇ 団体あるいは個人で海外旅行される方に
◇ 海外からの旅行者を案内したい方に
◇ 観光英検、全国通訳案内士試験の受験対策

三修社
https://www.sanshusha.co.jp

英語で伝える日本の文化・観光・世界遺産

山口百々男 著　牧野眞一 校閲　デリック・ブリス 校閲

A5 判／並製／ 308 ページ　ISBN978-4-384-05800-0
定価 2,200 円（本体 2,000 円 + 税）

海外から日本を訪れる人々に「英語で日本を正しく紹介する」ための必読書。第 1 部では、日本各地の観光名所を解説。地域別に各章、対訳付きのガイドと観光客のサンプルダイアローグ、日本語による知識面の解説、Q&A 形式の英語での解説例を用意。第 2 部では、日本のユネスコ世界遺産（文化遺産と自然遺産）について、ひとつひとつ Q&A 形式で解説。

英語で伝える江戸の文化・東京の観光

山口百々男 著

A5 判／並製／ 340 ページ　ISBN978-4-384-05865-9
定価 2,200 円（本体 2,000 円 + 税）

皇居から東京スカイツリーまで、江戸文化の残る東京の歴史的資産・観光名所を 150 項目取り上げ、英語によるガイド方法を紹介。歴史的・文化的な背景を盛り込んだ記述は、全国通訳案内士試験の対策にも役立つように配慮。

改訂版　和英：日本の文化・観光・歴史辞典

山口百々男 編著

B6 判／並製／ 516 ページ　ISBN978-4-384-05183-4
定価 3,300 円（本体 3,000 円 + 税）

日本の文化や歴史、観光名所などを英語で紹介するための和英辞典。見出し語数 5400 語。「日本の祭」紹介、歴史年表の付録つき。

https://www.sanshusha.co.jp